Warren E. Bitters, CFA is a Portfolio Manager with Santa Barbara Bank & Trust where he is responsible for managing the investment portfolios of trust accounts, managed agencies, and qualified retirement plans. In addition, Mr. Bitters participates in setting overall bank investment policy, including asset allocation policy.

Mr. Bitters also teaches English as a Second language for Santa Barbara City College Adult Education and has taught a training course for immigrants preparing to take the United States Citizenship history and government exam.

Mr. Bitters lives in Santa Barbara, California, USA with his wife Vira and three daughters, Lilliana, Cecilia, and Jessica.

ASSET ALLOCATION AND PORTFOLIO OPTIMIZATION

WARREN E. BITTERS

VISION BOOKS
(Incorporating Orient Paperbacks)
New Delhi • Mumbai • Hyderabad

www.visionbooksindia.com

ISBN 81-7094-571-2

This Indian Sub-continent edition published in agreement with
The Glenlake Publishing Company Ltd., USA
by
Vision Books Pvt. Ltd.
(Incorporating Orient Paperbacks & CARING imprints)
24 Feroze Gandhi Road, Lajpat Nagar III
New Delhi-110024, India.

Phone: (+91-11) 2983 6470
Fax: (+91-11) 2983 6490
E-mail: visionbk@vsnl.com

Printed at
Rashtra Rachna Printers
C-88, Ganesh Nagar, Pandav Nagar Complex
Delhi-110092, India.

Contents

Acknowledgments

It never fails that a project of this type turns into a much bigger job than anybody ever imagined. This one was no exception. For anybody considering undertaking such a project while raising two small children and expecting another, I would highly recommend that you reconsider. Seriously though, I would like to thank my spouse Vira and daughters Liliana and Cecilia for all their support. I am optimistic that my daughters will soon realize that their daddy is *not* attached surgically to his computer. I am hopeful that the newborn will not enter this world to a daddy who spends all his time feverishly pecking away at his computer. I promise the whole family that next year we will go camping, plant a garden, see some movies, ride our bicycles, and enjoy some more time together, just like a normal family does.

I would like to thank Tom Nugent. Without Tom's encouragement and comments over the years, the ideas in this book would never have found their way onto paper.

I would like to thank Glenlake Publishing for giving me the opportunity to undertake this project. I have especially appreciated Barbara Craig's patience, encouragement, and sense of humor.

Lastly, I would like to thank the imaginative thinkers of the past whose research has served as the building blocks for my research. Through my research and the process of putting these words on paper, I have learned more and reaped more benefits than I could have imagined I would. It is my hope that this book will add something to our current body of knowledge and that a few intellectually curious readers will take some of the ideas contained herein to the next level. I welcome comments, responses, and opinions, and I look forward to your questions, discussions, and arguments. I do not believe that anything contained in this book is *the answer.* Through the process of discussing the merits and possible flaws in the ideas contained herein we will all learn more and ultimately we will improve the ideas. One of my strongest beliefs is that what we currently know in the investment field is only a small fraction of what we will know fifty years from now, perhaps only ten per cent. Even in just the last few years, we have made tremendous strides in the general field of investment management as well as the specific field of asset allocation. I look forward to enjoying the next fifty years, in both the roles of student and teacher.

Warren E. Bitters, CFA
Santa Barbara, CA

CHAPTER 1

Introduction

I have set about to write this book on asset allocation based on the notion of advancing critical thinking. The term "critical" is "characterized by careful and exact evaluation and judgment." Going beyond the dictionary definition, I hope to provide material that pushes the current level of research in a given field (in this case, asset allocation) to new heights. My purpose is not to present material that summarizes in a nice neat package the composite body of research in this area. Rather, to look at some of the most important research done in the areas of investment management and asset allocation, in particular, and make a careful and exact evaluation and judgment of their work. In many cases, this will lead to looking at these works in a whole new way and developing new interpretations.

Critical can also mean "inclined to judge severely and adversely." It is not my intention in cases where interpretations may differ from those of the original authors to imply they were wrong or that the ideas presented here are necessarily better. The gains to the investment profession from the works of the authors mentioned in this book are immeasurable and their contributions should not be minimized in any way. The intention in this work is to look at these author's works from different angles to get a different perspective. With all due respect, I do not look upon the work of any of them as *the answer* any more than I look at this work as *the answer.* All are simply steppingstones in the quest for more knowledge and a better understanding of investment management.

For the reader looking for a more straightforward review of asset allocation, Gibson's *Asset Allocation: Balancing Financial Risk* is an excellent choice. Gibson's book deftly takes the reader from point A to point Z. This book does not go from point A to point Z. Many of the more elementary asset allocation concepts are not covered here. Instead, dissected are many of the niche subjects within the study of asset allocation to gain new insights.

The New Science of Asset Allocation has six chapters and an extensive bibliography. The first is this introduction. Chapter Two covers the topic of dollar cost averaging in detail. Although long considered an appropriate investment strategy, I show that dollar cost averaging is suboptimal both empirically and theoretically to lump sum investing. Chapter Three explores the conclusion by Brinson, Hood, and Beebower that asset allocation policy explains 93.6% of investment return. What does that mean? Findings show that asset allocation policy may not be as important as Brinson, Hood, and Beebower concluded. Provided are a number of models that look at the importance of asset allocation in new ways. Chapter Four continues the discussion of the Brinson, Hood, and Beebower study by expanding upon their general framework for investment return attribution. Specifically, the framework presented here introduces the concepts of passive asset allocation policy *versus* active asset allocation policy. In addition, Chapter Four blends recent research on the importance of style analysis into the Brinson, Hood, and Beebower framework. Chapter Five reviews some of the literature on the ability of certain predictive variables to determine future asset class returns. Out of that, a method of using the resulting estimated asset class returns in a tactical asset allocation program is suggested, including a discussion on some of the pitfalls of such a system. Lastly, Chapter Six addresses the issue of portfolio optimization. Portfolio optimization has been a hot topic among researchers in the last decade. The optimization issue is approached from three separate directions. The first examines the concept of optimization to maximize the likelihood of achieving an investor's specific upside target. The second looks at Markowitz optimization from the point of view that the inputs are likely to be erroneous. Traditional Markowitz theory provides a way to measure the expected return and variance of all available portfolios. Added to the Markowitz model is the concept that the inputs to the model are themselves subject to error. Hence, the portfolio must be optimized relative to return, risk, and errors in the estimated inputs. I refer to this kind of optimization as "three dimensional portfolio optimization." Finally, I look at a way to combine Markowitz theory with results published in the area of human behavioral psychology. The assumption that humans are not necessarily rational expected utility maximizes but rather, somewhat less rational, exhibiting slightly different but, nevertheless, predictable behavior is made. Examined are some of the characteristics that this kind of model would have.

Perhaps the most important part of the book, the bibliography, comes last. Compiled is a listing of chapter references and a listing of references covering a wide variety of concepts related to asset allocation. The motivated reader will find tremendous value in locating and studying these outstanding resources.

CHAPTER 2

Dollar Cost Averaging

The asset allocation decision can be one of the most complex and important decisions that the investor makes. Less obvious in importance are the decisions to invest in the first place and the timing of the initial investments. To use an analogy, deciding to invest is like deciding to go for a swim. Generally, swimming is a pleasurable experience but the initial prospect of jumping into the water can be uncomfortable. The water will eventually feel fine, once we get used to its temperature, but at first it can feel very cold. Anybody who has ever stood poolside understands this dilemma. Two choices face us: walk to the end of the diving board and jump or head for the stairs and tiptoe in. Similarly, in investing, we have two choices: invest all at once or invest gradually over time.

Dollar cost averaging is a technique that purports to help the investor avoid putting all of his money at risk at the wrong time. Simply put, dollar cost averaging means investing the same fixed amount of money in a risky investment at regular intervals of time, regardless of whether prices go up or down. For example, an investor with $120,000 to invest might decide to invest the $120,000 all at once, or he might decide to invest $10,000 in twelve regular monthly intervals. Investment professionals and academics have long touted the benefits of dollar cost averaging. Stories from very reputable sources extolling the almost magical ability of dollar cost averaging to enhance return and reduce risk are abundant.

According to its proponents, one important advantage of dollar cost averaging is that it turns the natural volatility exhibited by risky investments into an advantage. Since the investor is investing equal dollar amounts at each investment point, he will always buy more shares when prices are low and fewer shares when prices are high. Thus, the dollar cost averager does not regard a decline in price as a negative but instead, as an opportunity to buy more shares when prices are low and temporarily more attractive. Presumably, when the share price rebounds to a normal level, the investor enjoys a double benefit. First, the price rebound itself provides an above-average investment return. Second, since he buys more shares when prices are low, the above-average investment return applies to more shares. In addition, the strategy automatically treats an increase in price, which could be a result of a temporary market overvaluation, cautiously. During times of higher prices, fewer shares are purchased. If the investment subsequently experiences below-average, or even negative, returns as it corrects to a normal price level, it will affect fewer shares. On the surface, this sounds like a win-win situation.

Another benefit of dollar cost averaging is that it forces a disciplined approach to investing. Many investors find investing in a declining market an uncomfortable experience, although history has shown that, for long-term investors, down markets are the best time to be buying. A systematic and consistent plan, throughout all types of market environments, prevents emotion from getting in the way of rational decision making.

The most important characteristic of dollar cost averaging is that the average cost per share is always lower than the average of the share prices over the investment time frame. Again, this is a direct result of the fact that the investor purchases more shares when prices are low and fewer shares when prices are high. This is a simple and indisputable mathematical fact. Thus, dollar cost averaging works best when investing in volatile securities. More volatility leads to a greater fluctuation in share prices over the investment time frame which leads to a greater difference between the average cost per share and the average of the share prices. This is the value-added from a dollar cost averaging strategy. It certainly seems reasonable, from a mathematical perspective, that if the average cost per share is lower than the average of the share prices that dollar cost averaging must add to investment return. Furthermore, from an intuitive perspective, it seems plausible that by investing gradually into an investment, rather than all at once, we can reduce the seriousness of a subsequent decline in the value of the investment. Thus, claims that dollar cost averaging increases return while reducing risk seem to have a sound foundation.

In this chapter, we challenge the notion that dollar cost averaging adds to investment return and reduces risk. We will show that dollar cost averaging is inferior to investing all at once in just about every way, both empirically and theoretically. Once we have revealed the flaws in dollar cost averaging theory, we will review two examples, written by well-meaning investment professionals from reputable firms, that are designed to perpetuate the dollar cost averaging myth. Both examples completely fall apart when analyzed at even the most elementary level. Next, we will take a brief look at some of the past research on dollar cost averaging to gain an understanding of why it gained a foothold in the investment community. Finally, we will introduce a psychological framework as a supplement to the standard Markowitz mean-variance framework that helps to explain the continuing use of the dollar cost averaging strategy. For purposes of brevity, we will use the abbreviations DCA for dollar cost averaging and LSI for the alternative strategy, lump sum investing.

Before continuing, it is important to distinguish the difference between DCA as an alternative strategy to LSI, as opposed to a consequence of a regular saving program. Obviously, for the individual investor who is making regular investments into a risky investment as part of an ongoing saving program, the alternative choice of investing all at once does not exist because he has not earned the source of cash for the investment yet. In this case, the benefits of DCA described above are simply an attractive byproduct of the saving plan. The discussion that follows will address the issue of the investor who has a lump sum to invest and must contemplate investing all at once or gradually over time.

A Typical Dollar Cost Averaging Example

Chart 2–1 is a typical illustration of the concept of DCA. In this case, the investor makes equal investments of $10,000 in twelve successive months. The hypothetical investment gyrates wildly in price. It begins at $25, falls to $10, rallies to $40, then ends up at $25, the same as the starting price. At a price of $25, the investor buys 400 shares. When the price decreases to $10, he buys 1,000 shares. With a similar increase in price to $40, he buys 250 shares. The important observation to be made is that a particular dollar decrease in price has a greater effect on the number of shares that are purchased than the same dollar increase in price does. This is why the average cost per share is always less than the average of the share prices.

Table 2–1 illustrates the DCA concept in more detail. Over the course of the year, the investor makes twelve investments of $12,000, totaling $120,000. The average share price is $25. If the average cost per share had been $25, he would have purchased only 4,800 shares. Under DCA, the average cost per share is always lower than the average share price. This means that the investor will always purchase more shares than he would have if he had paid the average share price. In this case, he pur-

CHART 2–1 Dollar Cost Averaging: A Typical Example

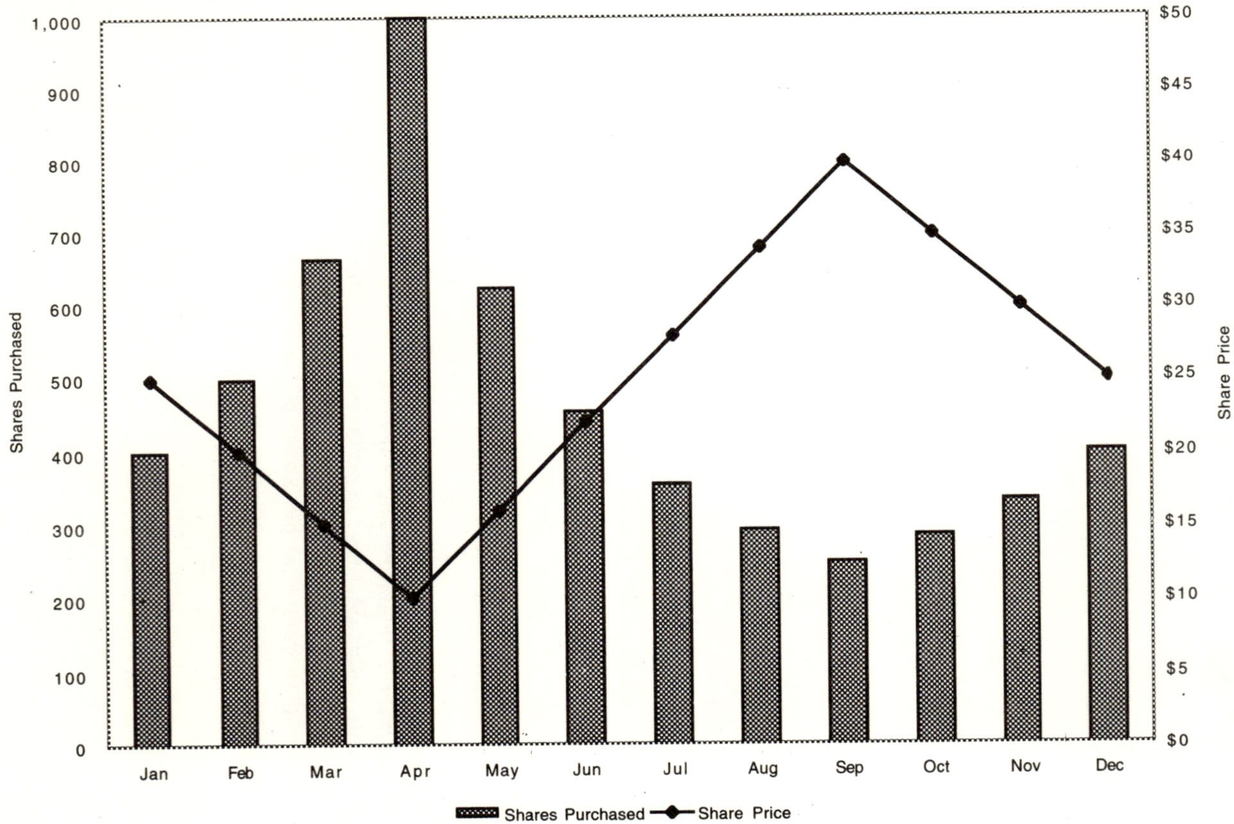

TABLE 2–1 DCA versus LSI: A Typical Example

Month	Invest-ment	Share Price	Shares Purchased	Cumulative Shares Purchased	Value of DCA Portfolio	Value of LSI Portfolio
Jan	10,000	25.00	400.0	400.0	120,000	120,000
Feb	10,000	20.00	500.0	900.0	118,000	96,000
Mar	10,000	15.00	666.7	1,566.7	113,500	72,000
Apr	10,000	10.00	1,000.0	2,566.7	105,667	48,000
May	10,000	16.00	625.0	3,191.7	121,067	76,800
Jun	10,000	22.00	454.5	3,646.2	140,217	105,600
Jul	10,000	28.00	357.1	4,003.4	162,094	134,400
Aug	10,000	34.00	294.1	4,297.5	186,114	163,200
Sep	10,000	40.00	250.0	4,547.5	211,899	192,000
Oct	10,000	35.00	285.7	4,833.2	189,162	168,000
Nov	10,000	30.00	333.3	5,166.5	164,996	144,000
Dec	10,000	25.00	400.0	5,566.5	139,163	120,000
Total	120,000		5,566.5			

Avg. Share Price	25.00	Arithmetic Mean	147,656	120,000
Avg. Cost Per Share	21.56	Standard Deviation	34,702	42,933
Final DCA Portfolio Value	139,163	DCA Investment Return		16.0%
Final LSI Portfolio Value	120,000	LSI Investment Return		0.0%

chased 5,566.5 shares at an average cost per share of $21.56. In other words, DCA allowed for the purchase of 766.5 additional shares. The LSI investor, if he had invested all $120,000 in January at a share price of $25, would have finished the year with exactly $120,000, a 0.0% return. The DCA investor, by taking advantage of the volatility of the investment, finished the year with a portfolio value of $139,163, a 16.0% return, even though the value of the investment did not increase at all. Almost every introductory textbook on investing gives an example similar to this to extol the virtues of DCA.

If we look closer, the DCA strategy appears even more attractive. Table 2–1 and Chart 2–2 detail the values of the DCA and LSI portfolios at each intermediate step throughout the year. We calculate DCA Portfolio Value by multiplying the cumulative shares purchased by the current share price and adding the uninvested portion of the portfolio. We calculate LSI Portfolio Value by multiplying the current share price by the number of shares purchased initially. It is immediately apparent that the value of the DCA portfolio is superior to the LSI portfolio at every step along the way. Furthermore, the 60% decline in the value of the risky investment that occurred between January and April decimated the value

CHART 2-2 Portfolio Value: A Typical Example

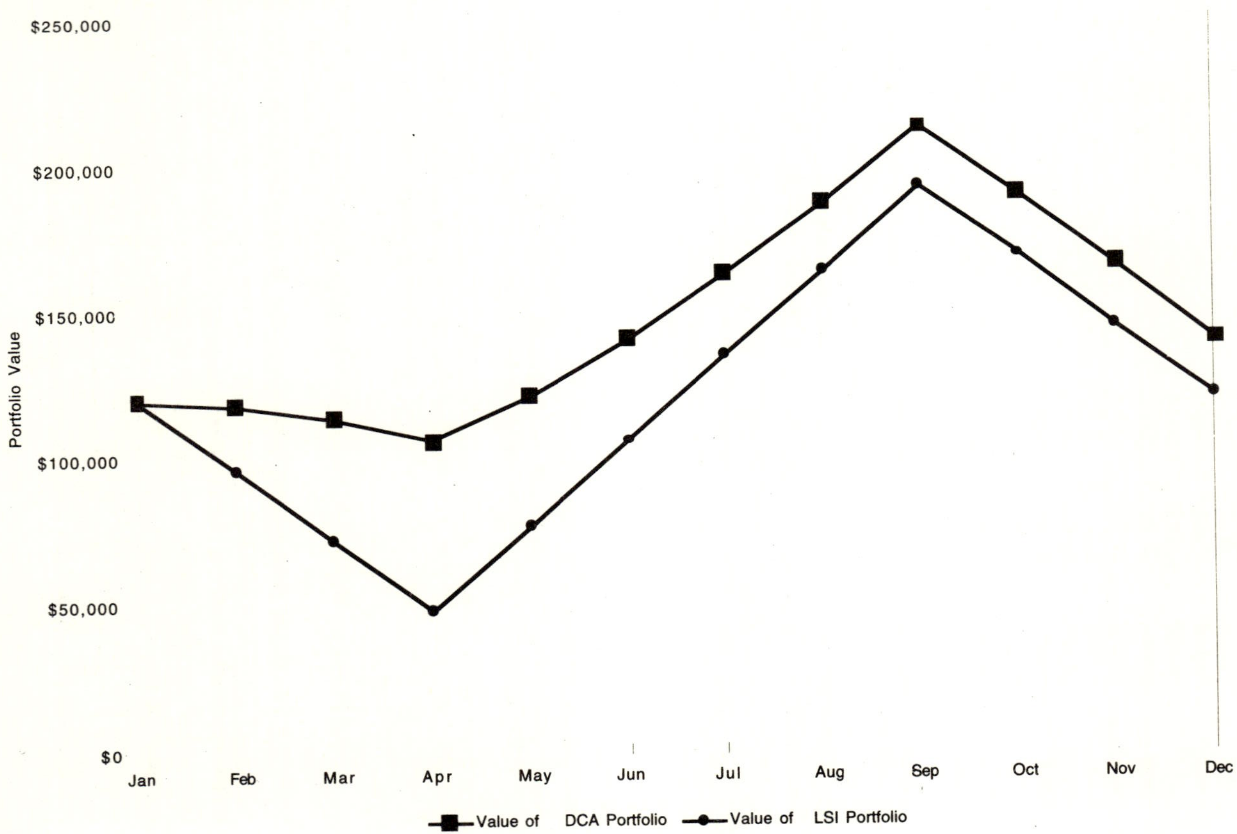

of the LSI portfolio while only moderately affecting the DCA portfolio. This is because only 25% of the DCA portfolio had been invested in the risky investment prior to the market bottom in April. The other 75% was safely sheltered in the risk-free investment. Table 2–1 indicates that the average value of the DCA portfolio over the investment horizon was $147,656 versus $120,000 for LSI. In addition, if we define risk as the standard deviation of the values of the two portfolios, DCA is significantly less risky as well. Its standard deviation is $34,702 versus $42,933 for LSI. Considering this evidence alone, the implication is that DCA added significantly to investment return, while reducing risk.

One important caveat that we normally associate with DCA is that it cannot prevent the occurrence of a loss during a period of prolonged market declines. The investor will have a loss on his investment whenever the current share price is below the average cost per share. The forgotten caveat is that the investment may do well, in which case the investor would have been better off investing all at once, rather than dollar cost averaging. Looking back to the first example, our hypothetical investment had a 0.0% return, with a ridiculously high 104.7% annualized standard deviation. While any risky investment can produce a zero return, or even a negative return, we would expect that the rational investor would not consider such a risky investment unless it provided a risk premium sufficient to warrant investment. In other words, the expected return would have to be higher than the risk-free rate for anyone to consider it. Yet, little of the discussion of DCA considers this fact.

A More Realistic Dollar Cost Averaging Example

Chart 2–3 is similar to Chart 2–1 except that in this case, the share price begins at $25, then fluctuates in value between $19 and $36, before finishing at $30. As before, the investor purchases more shares when prices are low and fewer shares when prices are high. The main difference in this example is that the ending value is 20% higher than the beginning value, which better reflects our expectation that the risky investment would increase in value. In addition, the volatility is lower than in the first example.

Table 2–2 shows that the average share price is $27.50, but the average cost per share is only $26.33. Again, dollar cost averaging allows for the purchase of additional shares. If the investor had invested $120,000 at $27.50 per share, he would have purchased only 4,363.6 shares, resulting in a final portfolio value of $130,909. Under DCA, he purchases a total of 4,557.4 shares, resulting in a final portfolio value of $136,723, a 13.9% return. However, in this case, if the investor had simply invested all $120,000 in January when the share price was $25.00, he would have purchased 4,800 shares and the final portfolio value would have been

CHART 2–3 Dollar Cost Averaging: A Realistic Example

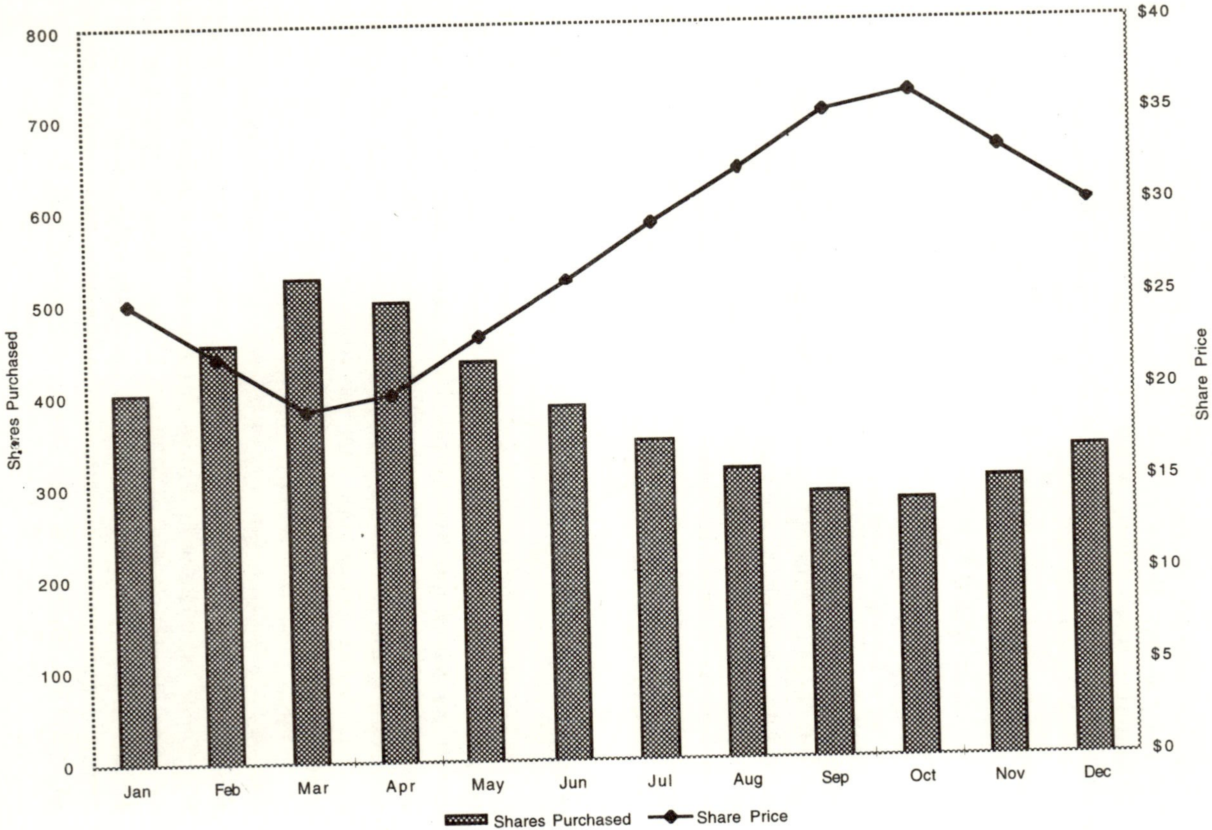

TABLE 2–2 DCA versus LSI: A Realistic Example

Month	Investment	Share Price	Shares Purchased	Cumulative Shares Purchased	Value of DCA Portfolio	Value of LSI Portfolio
Jan	10,000	25.00	400.0	400.0	120,000	120,000
Feb	10,000	22.00	454.5	854.5	118,800	105,600
Mar	10,000	19.00	526.3	1,380.9	116,236	91,200
Apr	10,000	20.00	500.0	1,880.9	117,617	96,000
May	10,000	23.00	434.8	2,315.6	123,260	110,400
Jun	10,000	26.00	384.6	2,700.3	130,207	124,800
Jul	10,000	29.00	344.8	3,045.1	138,308	139,200
Aug	10,000	32.00	312.5	3,357.6	147,443	153,600
Sep	10,000	35.00	285.7	3,643.3	157,516	168,000
Oct	10,000	36.00	277.8	3,921.1	161,159	172,800
Nov	10,000	33.00	303.0	4,224.1	149,396	158,400
Dec	10,000	30.00	333.3	4,557.4	136,723	144,000
Total	120,000		4,557.4			

Avg. Share Price	27.50	Arithmetic Mean	134,722	132,000
Avg. Cost Per Share	26.33	Standard Deviation	16,149	28,026
Final DCA Portfolio Value	136,723	DCA Investment Return		13.9%
Final LSI Portfolio Value	144,000	LSI Investment Return		20.0%

$144,000. A closer look at Table 2–2 and Chart 2–4 reveals that during the period of initial price declines, the DCA portfolio was superior to LSI, as we would expect. As the share price increased, the LSI portfolio overtook DCA. An important distinction is that the return on the DCA portfolio is a function of the current share price and the average cost per share, while the return on the LSI portfolio is a function of the current share price and the original share price. When the average cost per share under DCA is lower than the original share price paid under LSI, the DCA strategy will outperform LSI. Otherwise, LSI will outperform. Ironically, the current share price does not impact which strategy outperforms.

Testing Dollar Cost Averaging Using Actual Returns

If the data in Chart 2–3 represent "normal" price movement for the risky investment then it is reasonable to believe that perhaps it is normal for LSI to outperform DCA. We have no proof yet, but at least we can begin to consider this a possibility. To test the relative merits of DCA and LSI we will look at the historical results that would have been achieved in the past under each strategy. Table 2–3 illustrates our model. The investor has

CHART 2–4 Portfolio Value: Realistic Example

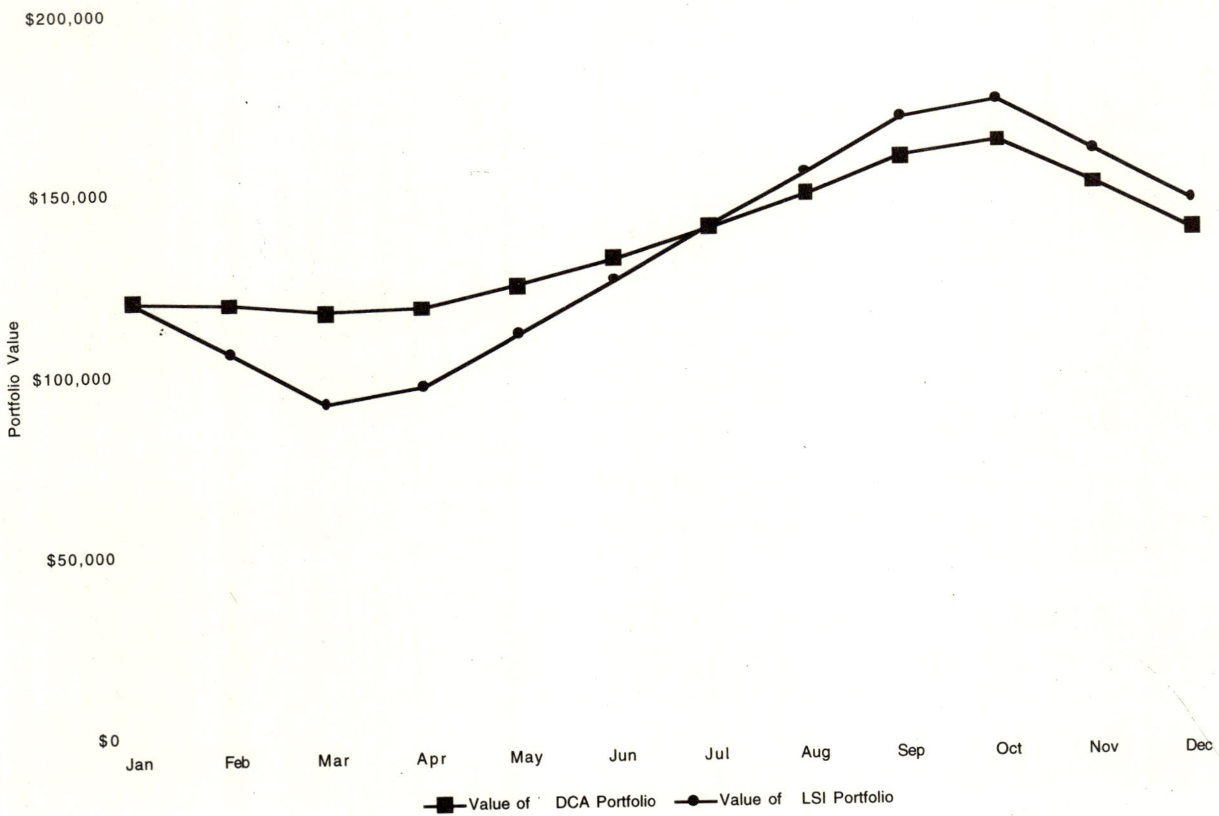

TABLE 2–3 DCA versus LSI: 1995

			DCA					LSI	
Date	Stock Return	Bills Return	Amount Invested in Stocks	Amount Invested in Bills	Month-end Value of Stocks	Month-end Value of Bills	Month-end Total Portfolio	Amount Invested in Stocks	Month-end Value of Stocks
Jan-95	2.60%	0.42%	10,000	110,000	10,260	110,462	120,722	120,000	123,120
Feb-95	3.88%	0.40%	20,260	100,462	21,046	100,864	121,910	123,120	127,897
Mar-95	2.96%	0.46%	31,046	90,864	31,965	91,282	123,247	127,897	131,683
Apr-95	2.91%	0.44%	41,965	81,282	43,186	81,639	124,826	131,683	135,515
May-95	3.95%	0.54%	53,186	71,639	55,287	72,026	127,313	135,515	140,868
Jun-95	2.35%	0.47%	65,287	62,026	66,821	62,318	129,139	140,868	144,178
Jul-95	3.33%	0.45%	76,821	52,318	79,379	52,553	131,933	144,178	148,979
Aug-95	0.27%	0.47%	89,379	42,553	89,621	42,753	132,374	148,979	149,381
Sep-95	4.19%	0.43%	99,621	32,753	103,795	32,894	136,689	149,381	155,640
Oct-95	-0.35%	0.47%	113,795	22,894	113,397	23,002	136,398	155,640	155,096
Nov-95	4.40%	0.42%	123,397	13,002	128,826	13,056	141,882	155,096	161,920
Dec-95	1.85%	0.49%	138,826	3,056	141,394	3,071	144,466	161,920	164,915

$120,000 to invest and has two choices: invest $10,000 at the beginning of each of the next twelve months or invest all $120,000 at once. We assume that the risky investment is the Standard & Poor's 500 stock index and the risk-free investment used for the uninvested portion of the DCA portfolio is U.S. Treasury Bills. For our purposes, we will use the monthly return series as tabulated by Ibbotson Associates.

With DCA, we must track what is essentially two separate portfolios, the stock portfolio and the bill portfolio, each of which have their own returns. At each month-end, we transfer $10,000 from the bill portfolio to the stock portfolio. By the end of the year, stocks comprise the entire portfolio except for the interest earned on the bills during the year. With LSI, we invest all $120,000 in the stock index at the beginning of the year and the final portfolio value simply reflects the return on the stock market for the year. The example shown in Table 2–3 illustrates the case where the investor begins investing on January 1, 1995. Since 1995 was a particularly good year in the U.S. stock market, we would expect LSI to easily outperform DCA in this case. The results in the table confirm this prediction. DCA produced a final portfolio value of only $144,466, a 20.39% return, compared with $164,915 for LSI. However, this is just one sample. A long-term historical look at the results for DCA and LSI would be more helpful. Using the Ibbotson Associates data allows us to analyze 829 different starting points, beginning with January 1, 1926, to see how frequently and by what margin one strategy outperforms the other.

A Long Run Analysis

Table 2–4 indicates the number of times each strategy produced superior returns and the average margin for each strategy when it was more successful, separated by decade. Out of 829 samples, LSI produced a higher investment return than DCA 543 times to 286, nearly a two to one ratio. The dominance of LSI is consistent over time. Only in the 30's did LSI fail to beat DCA in this category. The average margin measures the average amount by which one strategy outperforms the other, counting only those cases where it outperforms. The average margin for LSI was substantially greater than the average margin for DCA, 10.71% versus 7.96%. Again, the dominance of LSI is consistent over time, with only the decade of the 60's showing a higher average margin for DCA. The Net LSI Advantage column indicates the overall advantage of LSI, using all observations. We calculate Net LSI Advantage as follows:

$$\frac{(\text{LSI \# of Times Better} \bullet \text{LSI Average Margin}) - (\text{DCA \# of Times Better} \bullet \text{DCA Average Margin})}{\text{Total Number of Observations}}$$

TABLE 2–4 DCA versus LSI: 1926–1995

	DCA		***LSI***		
Decade	**# of Times Better**	**Avg. Margin**	**# of Times Better**	**Avg. Margin**	**Net LSI Advantage**
20's	11	7.25%	37	15.02%	9.92%
30's	63	13.77%	57	20.98%	2.74%
40's	37	5.84%	83	10.66%	5.57%
50's	26	3.93%	94	11.50%	8.16%
60's	39	7.38%	81	6.59%	2.05%
70's	56	6.88%	64	7.69%	0.89%
80's	40	7.35%	80	10.06%	4.26%
90's	14	3.22%	47	5.71%	3.66%
Total	286	7.96%	543	10.71%	4.27%

This is equivalent to the difference between the arithmetic means of all the observations.

The most important observation to be made from Table 2–4 is that LSI has outperformed DCA, on average, by 4.27% and has produced higher returns than DCA in every decade. In terms of investment return, this is a clear victory for LSI. Simply put, LSI is superior to DCA more often, and when it is better, it is better by more. To use an analogy, this is similar to what would happen if you stepped into the ring with a professional boxer. He would not only hit you more often than you could hit him but he would also hit you harder than you could hit him.

Most investors feel particularly uncomfortable investing all at once when the market is at a high level. At such a time, the desire to invest gradually is especially strong. Table 2–5 is similar to Table 2–4, except that it includes only those cases where the Ibbotson Associates S&P 500 cumu-

TABLE 2–5 DCA versus LSI: 1926–1995 Market Highs

	DCA		***LSI***		
Decade	**# of Times Better**	**Avg. Margin**	**# of Times Better**	**Avg. Margin**	**Net LSI Advantage**
20's	9	6.01%	27	15.47%	10.10%
30's	0		0		
40's	4	9.64%	15	12.82%	8.09%
50's	14	5.32%	63	11.58%	8.51%
60's	21	6.29%	40	4.32%	0.67%
70's	19	3.95%	15	3.25%	-0.77%
80's	24	6.38%	41	8.26%	2.85%
90's	10	3.71%	27	3.32%	1.42%
Total	101	5.59%	228	8.73%	4.33%

lative wealth index is within 98% of its all-time high. Ibbotson Associates developed the cumulative wealth index to tabulate the growth of a dollar over time. It includes both capital appreciation and reinvestment of dividends. Intuitively, we might expect that the results would be different in this case. After all, we would expect that the likelihood of a decline in the market is highest when the market is already at its high. Furthermore, we might expect that additional upside potential is lowest when the market is at a high. All of this taken together would lead one to expect that DCA would fare better against LSI at market highs. However, the results shown in Table 2–5 do not support this notion. LSI outperforms in more than two out of three cases and the average margin for LSI is significantly higher than for DCA, 8.73% versus 5.59%. There is some statistical bias in these data because they emphasize some time periods more than others. For example, the bull markets of the 50's and 80's produced ongoing all-time market highs so there are more observations from those decades. The 30's, which followed the U.S. stock market collapse of 1929, produced no observations because it was not until the 40's that the U.S. stock market recovered from the crash and reached market highs again. The 70's, which produced only 34 total observations, did show a clear advantage for DCA. DCA outperformed LSI 19 times to 15 and the average margin for DCA was 3.95% versus 3.25% for LSI. Also, the average margin for DCA was higher than the average margin for LSI in the 60's and 90's. Nevertheless, the Net LSI Advantage at market highs is 4.33% versus 4.27% for all observations. In other words, DCA does not appear to offer any better performance at market highs than it does at any other time.

Up to now, we have assumed that DCA versus LSI was a fair comparison. In reality, it is a comparison between one strategy that invests in a changing mix of a risky investment and a risk-free investment with another strategy that invests in the risky investment for the entire investment period. Chart 2–5 illustrates this idea in more detail, based on the model used in Table 2–3. Under DCA, the portfolio holds 8.3% in stocks and 91.7% in bills in the first month. In each subsequent month, we invest another 8.3% of the portfolio in stocks until the twelfth month. Over this time frame, the average percentage of the portfolio invested in stocks is 54.2%. For bills, the average is 45.8%. The formula for the percentage invested in the risky investment is $\frac{(n+1)}{2n}$, where n is the number of periods in the investment horizon. In our example, n = 12, so the percentage invested in the risky investment is $13/24$, or 54.2%. The percentage invested in the risk-free investment is $11/24$, or 45.8%. If the expected return on the risky investment is higher than the expected return of the risk-free investment, and why else would we consider investing in it, we

CHART 2–5 Changing Asset Allocation Under DCA

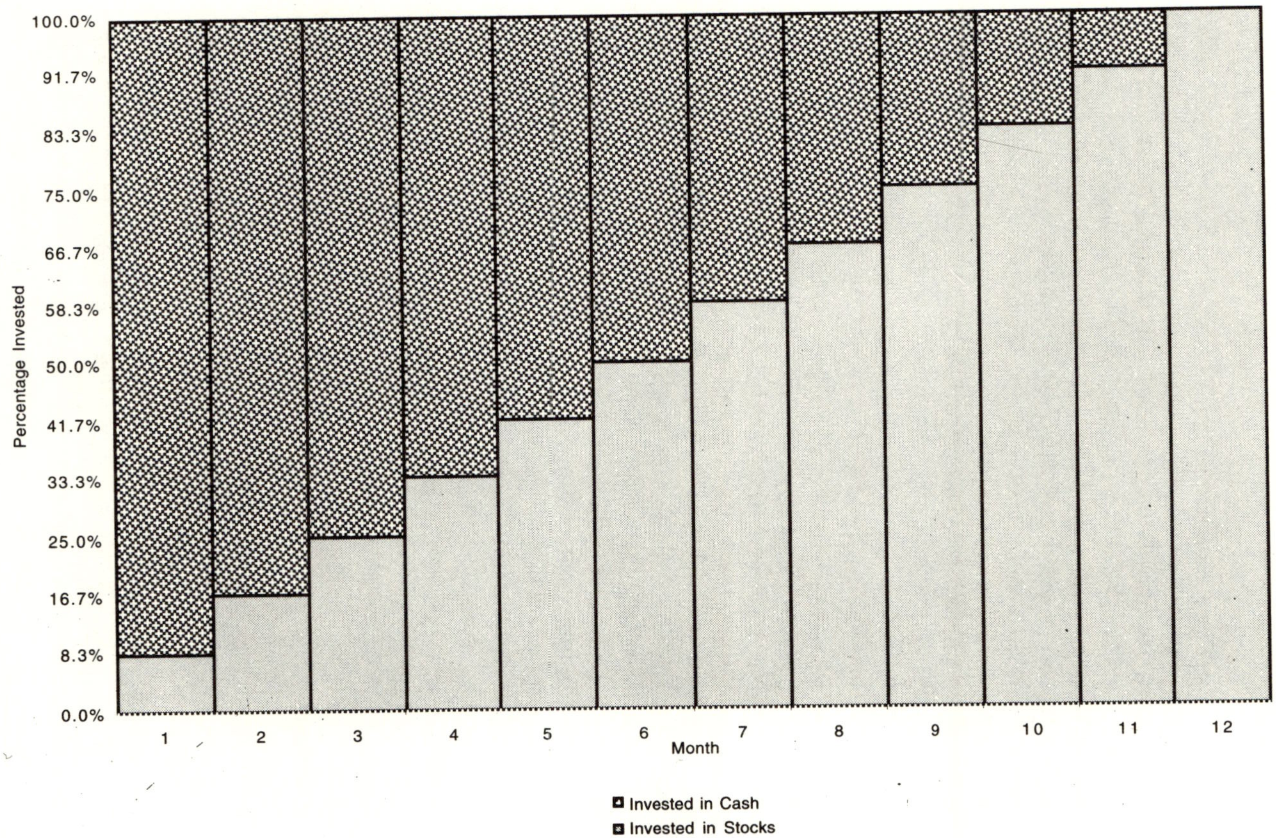

would expect that a 54.2% investment in the risky investment should return less than a 100% investment in the same investment. We would also expect it to be much less risky as well.

Modified LSI

Table 2–6 presents our earlier model in a somewhat different light. This table provides the arithmetic means and standard deviations of the returns from DCA and LSI, separated by decade. As we have already seen, the LSI returns were superior to the DCA returns in every decade. Over 829 observations, LSI had an arithmetic mean of 12.78% versus 8.51% for DCA, a difference of 4.27%. The difference between the arithmetic means is the same as what we previously called Net LSI Advantage. Perhaps the biggest surprise from Table 2–6 is the huge difference in the standard deviations of returns under DCA and LSI. In every decade, the LSI standard deviation is nearly twice the DCA standard deviation. Overall, the standard deviation of returns under DCA is 12.77%, while under LSI it is 22.24%. If we define the standard deviation of investment returns as risk, we conclude that DCA is less risky than LSI. This is entirely in line with what we would expect, considering that we are comparing an average 54.2% investment in a risky investment with a 100% investment in the same risky investment. Furthermore, this result is in line with the standard deviations observed in Table 2–2, which depicts "normal" price movement of the risky investment.

So far, we have seen that DCA leads to significantly lower returns than LSI. We have also seen that DCA exposes the investor to less risk. It is not easy to tell whether the risk reduction effect is greater or less than the return reduction effect. We would hope, if DCA is to stand up as a reasonable investment strategy, that DCA offers a true risk reduction effect.

TABLE 2–6 DCA versus LSI: Arithmetic Mean and Standard Deviation

	DCA		***LSI***	
Decade	**Arithmetic Mean**	**Standard Deviation**	**Arithmetic Mean**	**Standard Deviation**
20's	12.34%	15.19%	22.26%	25.25%
30's	3.50%	22.27%	6.24%	40.17%
40's	7.34%	10.67%	12.91%	18.76%
50's	10.38%	8.97%	18.54%	16.54%
60's	6.36%	8.11%	8.41%	13.62%
70's	8.19%	10.02%	9.08%	15.83%
80's	12.94%	10.40%	17.20%	17.49%
90's	10.15%	5.86%	13.81%	9.30%
Total	8.51%	12.77%	12.78%	22.24%

Since we have determined that under DCA the investor is 54.2% invested in the risky investment and 45.8% invested in the risk-free investment, we can even the playing field by comparing DCA to a modified LSI strategy. In the modified LSI strategy we will initially invest 54.2% of the portfolio in the S&P 500 index and the other 45.8% in Treasury Bills. Earlier, we examined the results of a DCA strategy that invested $10,000 every month for twelve months with an LSI strategy that invested $120,000 up front. Now, we will compare the DCA strategy with a modified LSI strategy that invests $65,000 in stocks and the remaining $55,000 in cash. This represents $^{13}/_{24}$ and $^{11}/_{24}$ of the initial $120,000, respectively. In making this comparison, the investment returns should more closely match so we can compare the risk characteristics of the two strategies.

Rebalanced versus Non-Rebalanced

One obstacle that we face in measuring the modified LSI portfolio return is how we treat portfolio drift. Portfolio drift occurs when the returns on stocks and bills differ so that the asset mix gradually changes over time. One solution is to rebalance the portfolio at the end of every month to the original asset mix. Table 2–7 illustrates how rebalancing works. The modified LSI portfolio on the left is not rebalanced, while the modified LSI portfolio on the right is. On January 1, 1995, we invested $65,000 in stocks and $55,000 in bills. The January return on stocks was 2.60%, while the return on bills was 0.42%. Since the return on stocks was higher, the proportion of the portfolio invested in stocks drifted higher than the original 54.2%. At month-end, the stock portfolio was worth $66,690, or 54.7% of the total portfolio value of $121,921. In the non-rebalanced portfolio, we leave the $66,690 in stocks and the $55,231 in bills. In the rebalanced portfolio, we transfer $649 from stocks to bills at month-end, bringing the value of the stock portfolio at the beginning of February to $66,041 and the value of the bill portfolio to $55,880. We continue this process for twelve months. Without rebalancing, portfolio drift can be quite significant, especially in a year such as 1995 when the S&P 500 index produced a 37.5% return. By the end of the year, the modified LSI portfolio without rebalancing held $89,329 in stocks out of a total portfolio of $147,408. During the year, the stock position drifted from 54.2% to 60.6%. By year-end 1995, the modified LSI strategy without rebalancing produced an ending portfolio of $147,408, an investment return of 22.84%, while modified LSI with rebalancing resulted in a final portfolio value of $146,305, a 21.92% return. These results compare favorably with the results over the same time period for DCA, as indicated in Table 2–3. For purposes of comparing DCA with modified LSI we will consider both the non-rebalancing and the rebalancing modified LSI strategies.

TABLE 2–7 Modified LSI: 1995

			Modified LSI (Without Rebalancing)					*Modified LSI (With Rebalancing)*				
Date	**Stock Return**	**Bills Return**	**Amount Invested in Stocks**	**Amount Invested in Bills**	**Month-end Value of Stocks**	**Month-end Value of Bills**	**Month-end Total Portfolio**	**Amount Invested in Stocks**	**Amount Invested in Bills**	**Month-end Value of Stocks**	**Month-end Value of Bills**	**Month-end Total Portfolio**
Jan-95	2.60%	0.42%	65,000	55,000	66,690	55,231	121,921	65,000	55,000	66,690	55,231	121,921
Feb-95	3.88%	0.40%	66,690	55,231	69,278	55,452	124,729	66,041	55,880	68,603	56,104	124,707
Mar-95	2.96%	0.46%	69,278	55,452	71,328	55,707	127,035	67,550	57,157	69,549	57,420	126,969
Apr-95	2.91%	0.44%	71,328	55,707	73,404	55,952	129,356	68,775	58,194	70,776	58,450	129,227
May-95	3.95%	0.54%	73,404	55,952	76,303	56,254	132,558	69,998	59,229	72,763	59,549	132,311
Jun-95	2.35%	0.47%	76,303	56,254	78,096	56,519	134,615	71,669	60,643	73,353	60,928	134,281
Jul-95	3.33%	0.45%	78,096	56,519	80,697	56,773	137,470	72,735	61,545	75,157	61,822	136,980
Aug-95	0.27%	0.47%	80,697	56,773	80,915	57,040	137,955	74,197	62,782	74,398	63,077	137,475
Sep-95	4.19%	0.43%	80,915	57,040	84,305	57,285	141,590	74,466	63,009	77,586	63,280	140,866
Oct-95	-0.35%	0.47%	84,305	57,285	84,010	57,554	141,565	76,303	64,564	76,035	64,867	140,903
Nov-95	4.40%	0.42%	84,010	57,554	87,707	57,796	145,503	76,322	64,580	79,680	64,852	144,532
Dec-95	1.85%	0.49%	87,707	57,796	89,329	58,079	147,408	78,288	66,244	79,736	66,568	146,305

Historical Perspective

Table 2–8 summarizes the results of DCA and the two modified LSI strategies over the seventy year period from 1926 through 1995. Within individual decades, the arithmetic means differ by up to 1.37%, but in aggregate the arithmetic means of investment returns are similar for all three investment strategies. Modified LSI without rebalancing produced slightly better returns than DCA. Modified LSI with rebalancing produced the same returns as DCA. The big difference lies in the riskiness of the three strategies. In aggregate and in each decade, DCA is riskier than either of the modified LSI strategies, as measured by standard deviation. Based on this empirical evidence, DCA clearly is suboptimal within a Markowitz mean-variance framework. In short, we have shown that DCA produces lower returns than LSI and when we modify the LSI strategy to equalize investment returns, DCA is riskier.

Theoretical Reasons Why LSI Outperforms DCA

We have shown that DCA comes up short against LSI empirically. We will now focus on some of the theoretical reasons why this should be so. We begin by defining r_r as the single-period expected return of the risky investment and r_f as the single-period expected return of the risk-free investment. Next, we define n as the number of periods in the investment horizon. In all the previous examples, the single-period has been one month and n has been 12. The equations that follow generalize for any length single-period or value for n. For purposes of this discussion, we assume that r_r and r_f do not change during the investment horizon.

TABLE 2–8 DCA versus Modified LSI: Arithmetic Mean and Standard Deviation

	DCA		*Modified LSI*			
			Without Rebalancing		*With Rebalancing*	
Decade	**Arithmetic Mean**	**Standard Deviation**	**Arithmetic Mean**	**Standard Deviation**	**Arithmetic Mean**	**Standard Deviation**
20's	12.34%	15.19%	13.71%	13.65%	13.29%	13.02%
30's	3.50%	22.27%	3.57%	21.64%	3.45%	21.20%
40's	7.34%	10.67%	7.21%	10.20%	6.97%	9.60%
50's	10.38%	8.97%	10.94%	8.70%	10.57%	8.12%
60's	6.36%	8.11%	6.41%	7.06%	6.36%	6.96%
70's	8.19%	10.02%	7.91%	8.58%	7.92%	8.73%
80's	12.94%	10.40%	13.34%	9.26%	13.30%	8.94%
90's	10.15%	5.86%	9.57%	5.34%	9.57%	5.15%
Total	8.51%	12.77%	8.65%	12.09%	8.51%	11.76%

Our first goal is to identify the expected investment return for each investment strategy over the investment horizon. The simplest case is LSI, because it only involves the risky investment. Under LSI, we make the entire investment up front and it compounds at the expected single-period rate of return for the entire investment horizon. Therefore,

$$E(r_{LSI}) = (1+r_r)^n.$$

DCA is a little more complicated. Each single investment under DCA is a miniature LSI investment. In the first month, or whatever single-period is being used, we invest $^1/_n$ of the total amount in the risky investment. The expected return of this investment is the same as under LSI, $(1+r_r)^n$. The contribution to portfolio return is simply the weighted expected return from this investment, $^1/_n(1+r_r)^n$. The second investment sits in the risk-free investment for one month before being invested in the risky investment for n-1 months. Its expected return is $(1+r_f)(1+r_r)^{n-1}$. This process continues in a similar fashion for each investment. The overall expected return of the DCA strategy is:

$$E(r_{DCA}) = 1/n \sum_{1=n}^{n} (1+r_f)^{(i-1)}(1+r_r)^{(n-i+1)}.$$

We can identify the expected return of the two modified LSI strategies as well. The easier case is modified LSI without rebalancing. We can look at this as two separate LSI portfolios, the first invested in the risky investment and the second invested in the risk-free investment. Once we have made the initial investments, the portfolio remains unchanged. Borrowing from the LSI formula, the contribution to total portfolio return from the portion invested in the risky investment is $\frac{n+1}{2n}(1+r_r)^n$. Likewise, the contribution to total portfolio return from the portion invested in the risk-free investment is $\frac{n-1}{2n}(1+r_f)^n$. Combining the two, the formula for the expected return of modified LSI without rebalancing is:

$$E(r_{w/o\ reb}) = \frac{n+1}{2n}(1+r_r)^n + \frac{n-1}{2n}(1+r_f)^n.$$

The modified LSI strategy with rebalancing is only subtly different from modified LSI without rebalancing. In the first period, the expected return of the portfolio is simply the weighted expected return of the risky investment and the risk-free investment. This works out to $\frac{n+1}{2n}(1+r_r) +$

$\frac{n-1}{2n}(1+r_f)$. In each subsequent period, since we are rebalancing, the expected return for the portfolio is exactly the same. Thus, for the entire investment period, the expected return of modified LSI with rebalancing is:

$$E(r_{w/\ reb}) = \left[\frac{n+1}{2n}(1+r_r) + \frac{n-1}{2n}(1+r_f)\right]^n .$$

The table below summarizes the results for the four strategies.

LSI $E(r_{LSI}) = (1+r_r)^n$

DCA $E(r_{DCA}) = 1/n \sum_{1=n}^{n} (1+r_f)^{(i-1)}(1+r_r)^{(n-i+1)}$

Modified LSI

w/o rebalancing $E(r_{w/o\ reb}) = \frac{n+1}{2n}(1+r_r)^n + \frac{n-1}{2n}(1+r_f)^n$

Modified LSI

w/ rebalancing $E(r_{w/\ reb}) = \left[\frac{n+1}{2n}(1+r_r) + \frac{n-1}{2n}(1+r_f)\right]^n$

We can substitute the arithmetic average of monthly investment returns from the Ibbotson Associates stocks and bills data series into the above formulas. For stocks, this is 0.9996% and for bills, 0.3050%. Table 2–9 details the results. While not exact matches, these numbers clearly indicate that the empirical observations reasonably coincide with our theoretical assumptions. Specifically, the evidence does not contradict our assumption that r_r and r_f do not change during the investment horizon in response to changes in market levels.

If we use simplified approximation formulas for the expected returns of the four strategies, we can see more clearly why DCA is riskier than either of the modified LSI strategies. Our previous formulas calculated expected return, with compounding. We can greatly simplify the formulas by removing the compounding element. For LSI, we can approximate the investment horizon expected return as simply the single-period expected return multiplied by the number of periods in the

TABLE 2–9 Expected Returns: Theoretical and Empirical

Strategy	Theoretical	Empirical
LSI	12.68%	12.78%
DCA	8.51%	8.51%
Modified LSI (w/o rebalancing)	8.57%	8.65%
Modified LSI (w/ rebalancing)	8.49%	8.51%

investment horizon, or $E(r_{LSI}) = nr_r$. In our model, this works out to $E(r_{LSI}) = (12)(0.9996\%)$, or 12.00%. For DCA, the expected return requires two separate LSI calculations, one for the risky investment and the other for the risk-free investment, weighted by the average investment in each asset. This works out to, $E(r_{DCA}) = n\left[\frac{(n+1)}{2n}r_r + \frac{(n-1)}{2n}r_f\right]$, or $\frac{(n+1)}{2}r_r + \frac{(n-1)}{2}r_f$. Since the two modified LSI formulas were created with the same exposure to the market, both modified LSI formulas have the same expected return as DCA. Therefore, $E(r_{DCA}) = E(r_{w/o\ reb}) = E(r_{w/\ reb}) = 13/2\,(0.9996\%) + 11/2\,(0.3050\%)$, or 8.18%. Again, these results are quite a bit lower than the previous results because they do not include compounding.

The expected returns produced by the simplified approximation formulas are not accurate enough to be very useful, but they do allow us to demonstrate why DCA is riskier than modified LSI. First, we assume that the single-period returns for the risky and risk-free investments are normally distributed and independent, with expected return of r_r and r_f, and standard deviation of σ_r and σ_f, respectively. Referring to the Ibbotson Associates data again, the monthly standard deviation has been 5.699% for stocks and 0.266% for bills. For our purposes, we will assume that the standard deviation of the risk-free investment is zero.

Our simplified approximation formula for LSI simply states that the investment horizon return is the sum of the individual single-period returns. Since we have assumed that the single-period returns are normally distributed with standard deviation σ_r, standard statistics formulas tell us that the investment horizon standard deviation is,

$$\sigma_{LSI} = \sqrt{n}\sigma_r .$$

For our model, this works out to (3.464)(5.699%), or 19.74%. This is significantly below the 22.24% standard deviation that we observed earlier. For now, we will assume this is because of imperfections created by using a simplified formula for expected return, which does not account for compounding of returns. Since the modified LSI strategy simply amounts to investing $\frac{(n+1)}{2n}$ of principal in the risky investment,

$$\sigma_{Mod.\ LSI} = \frac{(n+1)}{2n}\sqrt{n}\sigma_r, \text{ or } \frac{(n+1)}{2\sqrt{n}}\sigma_r .$$

For our model, this works out to $\frac{13}{2(3.464)}(5.699\%)$, or 10.69%. Again, this result is lower than the observed standard deviations. To the other possible causes, we can add that bill returns contribute a small amount of variance that we did not account for in the approximation formula.

As mentioned earlier, DCA is effectively a series of LSI investments, with ever shortening investment horizons. The first investment spans n periods. The second investment spans n-1 periods, etc. Thus, each investment contributes to strategy standard deviation, based on its own investment horizon. Complicating matters, each individual investment's return is dependent on the returns of the other individual investments. Therefore, strategy standard deviation includes a covariance component. For the simplest case, where n = 2, the variance of investment return is:

$$\left(\frac{1}{2}\right)^2 v[(1+r_1)(1+r_2)] + \left(\frac{1}{2}\right)^2 v[(1+r_2)] + 2\left(\frac{1}{2}\right)^2 Cov[(1+r_1)(1+r_2),(1+r_2)]$$

where v is the variance of the single-period rate of return and r_1 and r_2 are the single-period rates of return. We can generalize this formula for cases where n > 2 but, for our purposes, we will use another simplified approximation formula. We can approximate the variance of investment return under DCA, using Rozeff's formula, as $v_{DCA} = v\left[\frac{n}{3}+\frac{1}{2}+\frac{1}{6n}\right]$. Obviously, the standard deviation is simply the square root of the variance, or

$$\sigma_{DCA} = \sigma_r\sqrt{\left[\frac{n}{3}+\frac{1}{2}+\frac{1}{6n}\right]}.$$

For our model, this works out to $(5.699\%)\sqrt{\left[\frac{12}{3}+\frac{1}{2}+\frac{1}{72}\right]}$, or 12.11%. Again, this is lower than the empirical results, but significantly higher than the 10.69% predicted for the modified LSI strategies. Again, we must conclude that DCA produces lower investment returns than LSI and when we modify LSI to equalize investment returns, DCA results in a higher standard deviation.

The approximation formulas for expected return and standard deviation for each strategy are listed below.

$E(r_{LSI})$	nr_r	$E(r_{DCA}) = E(r_{w/o\ reb}) = E(r_{w/\ reb})$	$\frac{(n+1)}{2}r_r + \frac{(n-1)}{2}r_f$
σ_{LSI}	$\sqrt{n}\sigma_r$	$\sigma_{Mod.\ LSI}$ $\frac{(n+1)}{2\sqrt{n}}\sigma_r$	σ_{DCA} $\sigma_r\sqrt{\left[\frac{n}{3}+\frac{1}{2}+\frac{1}{6n}\right]}$

Perpetuating the Dollar Cost Averaging Myth

Now we can have a little fun with some well-intentioned sales pieces written to perpetuate the dollar cost averaging myth. These two examples are typical variations of the dollar cost averaging story. The key to spotting the flaw in logic is to constantly keep in mind the alternative of lump sum investing. Table 2–10 illustrates the first example.

> Dollar-cost averaging also works for you in a rising market. Let's assume you want to invest a total of $1,000. You begin by investing $200 in January and continue to invest $200 each month through May. During this period, while the average share price of the Fund is $12, your average share cost is only $9.66 and you have acquired 103.5 shares. Let's say, on the other hand, you waited until May to invest your $1,000, when the Fund's share price was $20. You would have acquired only 50 shares—less than half the amount of shares you would have acquired through the dollar-cost averaging strategy!

You might have seen that the author somehow forgot to mention one important fact. If you had invested all $1,000 in January, when the fund's share price was $5, you would have acquired 200 shares, nearly twice as many as under the DCA strategy. By dollar cost averaging, the investor underperformed the LSI investor by 48.25%.

Another reputable mutual fund family provided the second example. The fact that they use four real funds and real dollar amounts gives the advertisement a greater sense of authenticity. The funds have enjoyed great success and they have cleverly constructed the advertisement so that it appears that dollar cost averaging enhanced those returns. At first glimpse, it makes a very compelling case for dollar cost averaging. Chart 2–6 accompanies the text that follows.

Suppose you invested $100,000 into a money market fund and then made monthly investments of $1,000 for 25 months from that account into each of four XYZ Capital equity funds—Equity Income, Growth and

TABLE 2–10 Perpetuating the DCA Myth: Example 1

Month	Investment	Share Price	Shares Acquired
January	$200	$5.00	40.0
February	$200	$10.00	20.0
March	$200	$15.00	13.3
April	$200	$10.00	20.0
May	$200	$20.00	10.0
Total	$1,000	$60.00	103.3
Average Share Cost	$9.68		
Average Share Price	$12.00		

CHART 2–6 Perpetuating the DCA Myth: Example 2

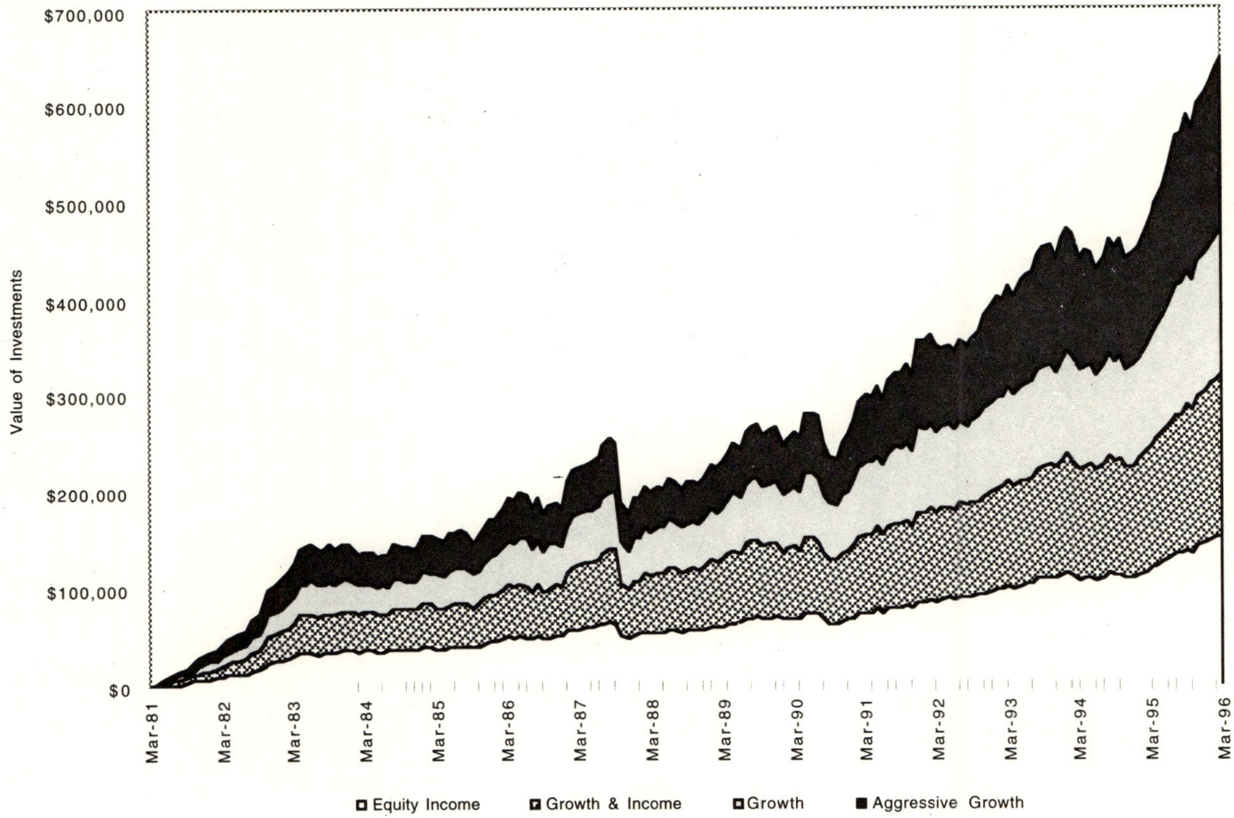

Income, Growth, and Aggressive Growth. If you had started this program on April 1, 1981, over fifteen years your equity portfolio value would have grown to $648,247—more than six times the original investment.

The final portfolio value of $648,247 is very impressive. A small table in the corner indicates that the average annual performance of each of the four funds ranged from 13.63% to 15.03%, with a blended average return of 14.26%. It is obvious that the funds have done well. However, the advertisement goes to a great deal of trouble to indicate that dollar cost averaging over the initial 25 month period created some additional gain for the investor. Fortunately, monthly returns on the funds are readily available so we can see if DCA did add value for the investor.

Chart 2–7 compares the 25-month DCA strategy with an LSI strategy that calls for the investment of all $100,000 on April 1, 1981. Contrary to what the advertiser would lead us to believe, the LSI strategy outperformed the DCA strategy. If all $100,000 had been invested on April 1, 1981, the result would be $678,016, or $29,769 more than under DCA. These are just a few of the ways in which the investment industry attempts to perpetuate the dollar cost averaging myth.

The Origins of Dollar Cost Averaging

With all the available evidence that clearly shows dollar cost averaging to be an inferior investment strategy, one might wonder how dollar cost averaging gained its popularity in the first place. To better understand this, we need to look back to the environment that existed in the U.S. equity market following the 1929 stock market crash. Unlike the stock market crash of 1987, from which a strong recovery was quick in coming, the 1929 crash preceded a great economic depression that lasted throughout the 30's. During the 30's, the stock market witnessed several precipitous declines, most notably from late 1929 through mid-1932 and in 1937 through early 1938. Partly offsetting these declines was a prolonged rally from mid-1932 through mid-1937. The 30's was a period of tremendous volatility in the markets, especially in comparison to the level of volatility in the U.S. equity market today. For example, investors in 1932 experienced consecutive monthly declines of 11.6%, 20.0%, and 22.0%, followed by monthly increases of 38.2% and 38.7%. In contrast, the S&P 500 has not seen a single monthly return outside the range of -5.0% to +5.0% since December 1991. To better illustrate just how wild 1932 was, two consecutive 38% monthly returns is equivalent to the Dow Jones Industrial Averaging increasing from 5000 to 9580 in just two months!

Chart 2–8 shows the Ibbotson Associates S&P 500 Cumulative Wealth Index for the period December 31, 1929 through December 31, 1946. As mentioned earlier, the cumulative wealth index measures the

CHART 2-7 DCA versus LSI: Example 2

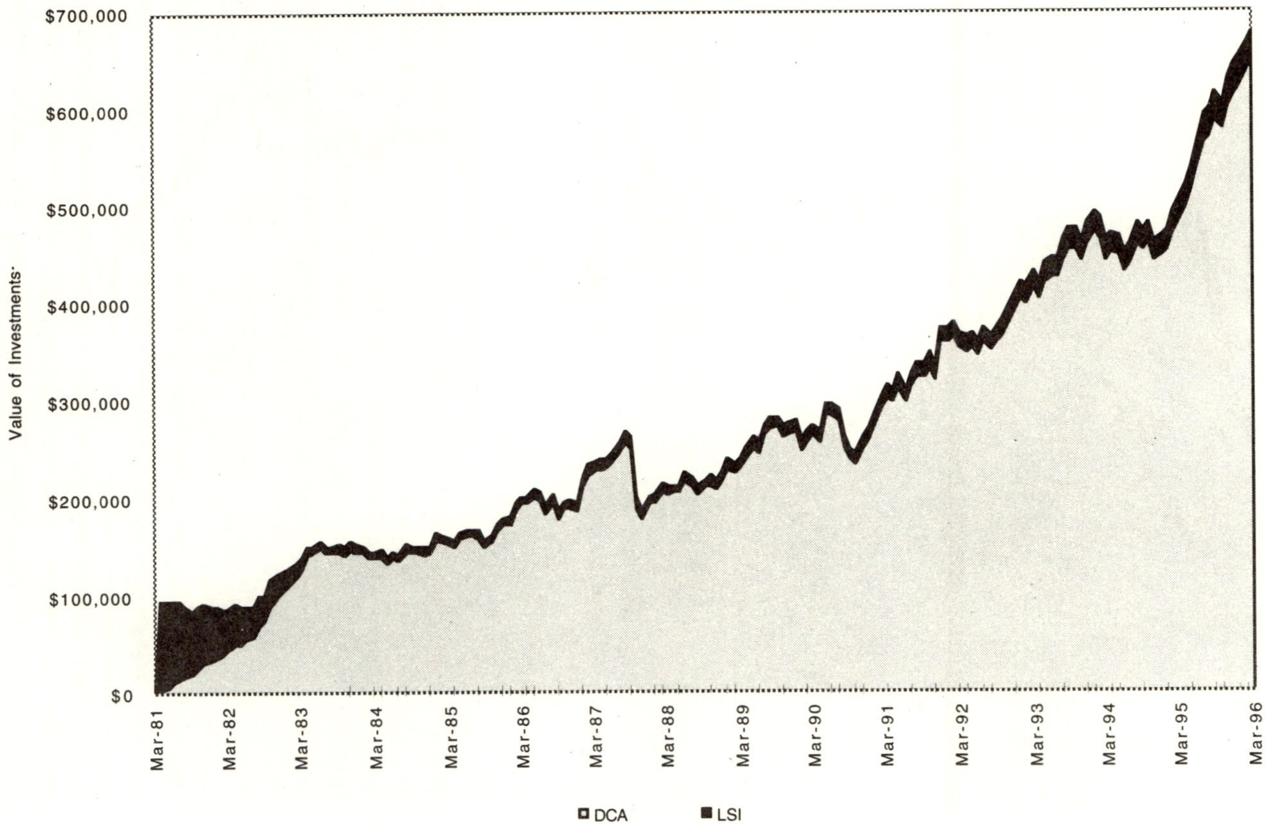

CHART 2–8 S&P 500 Cumulative Wealth Index: December 1929–December 1946

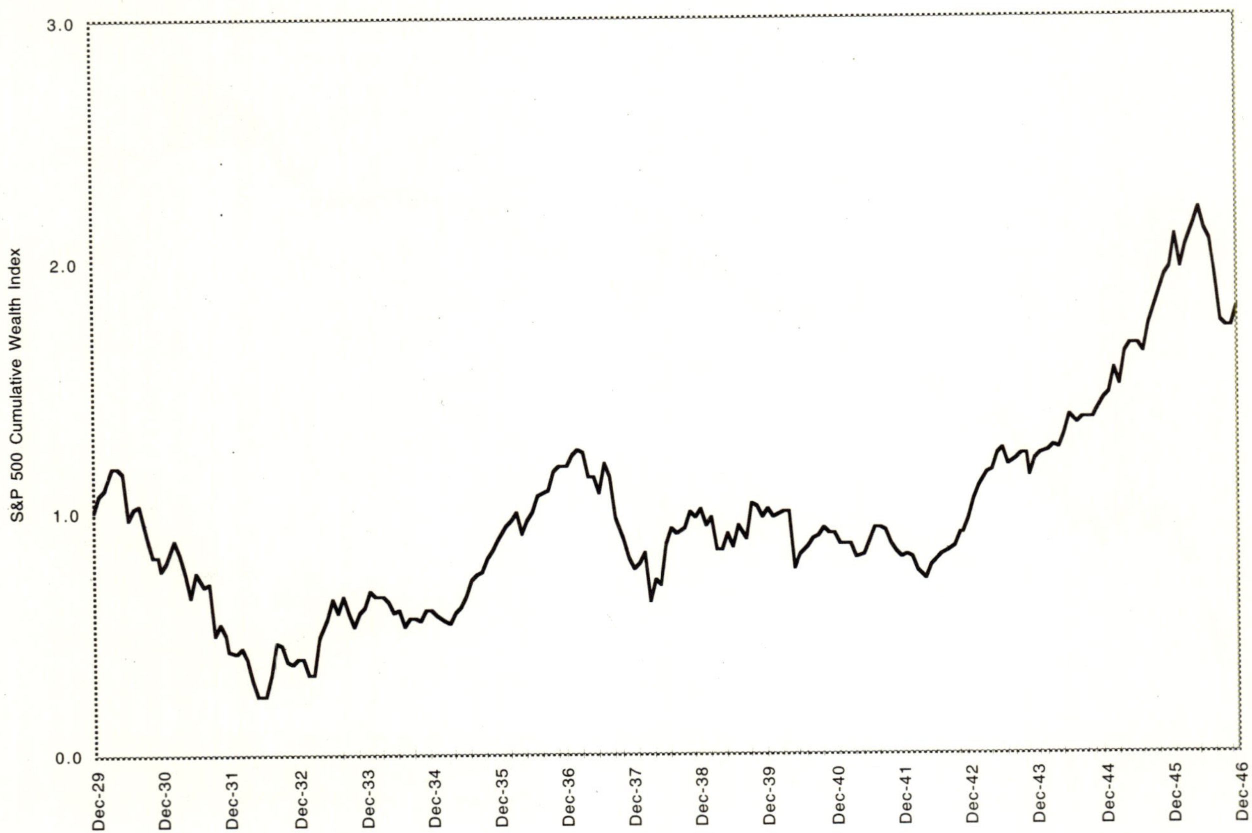

growth of a dollar invested in the S&P 500, including reinvestment of dividends. Obviously, Chart 2–8 presents a bleak investment scenario. At the market bottom, in mid 1932, the investor's portfolio was worth 24 cents on the dollar. By the end of the decade, he had only broken even. It took until January 1943, more than thirteen years, before the investor finally broke into positive ground for good. By the end of 1946, the cumulative wealth index was a paltry 1.80, which translates into an annualized return of 3.52%. The arithmetic mean of monthly returns was 0.68%, while the standard deviation of monthly returns was 8.92%.

Against this backdrop, researchers in the late 40's began to consider how the natural volatility exhibited by risky investments could work to the investor's advantage. In addition, they observed that periods of market declines were often followed by periods of increases, and vice versa. It seemed reasonable then that a strategy that encouraged buying when share prices were low and selling, or at least buying fewer shares, when share prices were high should increase the investor's return, if he could identify when prices were high and when prices were low. Ideally, there should exist a formula plan that would automatically force the purchase of shares when prices were low and the sale of shares when prices were high. The researchers set about to find it.

Weston and Ketchum's Search for Formula Plans

Some of the research revolved around identifying the various types of security price fluctuations. Weston divided them into two categories: cyclical fluctuations and secular fluctuations. Secular fluctuations describe the general direction of price movements: up, down, or horizontal. Cyclical fluctuations describe fluctuations above and below the general trend line of price movements as well as the relative amplitudes of price fluctuations. Weston provides a number of examples showing the performance of DCA under various types of cyclical and secular fluctuations. He concludes that "the success of the simplest type of formula-plan dollar averaging depends upon a favorable secular trend and a not too unfavorable cyclical pattern." It is interesting that he defines success as cases in which DCA provides a positive return. Nowhere does he address the issue of whether the strategy outperforms LSI. This is probably in large part due to the environment of generally horizontal, or down, stock price movements prevalent at the time. On the surface, their analysis of price fluctuation patterns seems distantly related to technical analysis. However, the difference is that these researchers were searching for a formula plan that would be automatic and would not require interpretation.

Ketchum explains the background and basic functionality of formula timing plans as follows.

> Attention has centered in recent years on attempts to protect investment funds against some of the losses from adverse fluctuations in security prices and to insure that such funds will retain some of the profits from favorable fluctuations through the use of formula timing plans. The essence of such plans is that the investment fund shall at all times consist of two portions—a defensive fund consisting of securities which have relatively small price fluctuations over the cycle and an aggressive fund made up of securities having considerable price volatility—and that as security prices rise, the defensive portion of the fund shall be enlarged relative to the aggressive segment, while as security prices decline, the aggressive portion shall be increased through transfer from the defensive section of the fund. Two important premises of these plans are (1) that security prices will continue to fluctuate and that the amplitude of fluctuation of some security types will be greater than that of others and (2) that the direction of security-price movements cannot be forecast accurately and consistently.

Three types of formula plans discussed by Weston and Ketchum are the constant ratio plan, constant stock fund plan, and the sliding scale plan. Under the constant ratio plan, they initially divided the total fund into determined percentages of aggressive and defensive securities. When subsequent price movement lead to portfolio drift, they rebalanced the portfolio to the original ratios. In practice, this plan results in the purchase of the aggressive securities following price declines and the sale of the aggressive securities following price increases. Under the constant stock fund plan, they initially divided the total fund into determined dollar amounts of aggressive and defensive securities. Later, when the portfolio drifted, they rebalanced it so that the dollar amount invested in the aggressive securities remained constant. Finally, the sliding scale plan utilizes rebalancing in response to changing security prices. Instead of rebalancing to either the determined percentage or dollar amount, they used a sliding scale. Specifically, as security prices rose, they reduced the percentage invested in the aggressive securities. As security prices fell, they raised the percentage invested in the aggressive securities. In all three types of plans, the underlying belief is that price movements imply imminent reversals and that it is better to own less of the aggressive security when prices are high and to own more of the aggressive security when prices are low.

While Weston provides a theoretical background on formula timing plans, Ketchum provides actual results obtained from each formula timing plan. In his study, Ketchum used the Dow Jones Industrial Average to represent the aggressive security and the Dow Jones 40 Bond Index to represent the defensive security. Since we have based our previous models on the S&P 500 stock index, we will also use that index when we look at the results obtained under the various formula plans. Probably the most interesting part of Ketchum's research is the meticulous simulations he created using a number of different sliding scale plans. We will briefly review his results and then see how his formula plans might have fared in the years since 1947.

In his study, Ketchum did not compare plain-vanilla DCA with a buy and hold strategy, but he did demonstrate that the sliding scale plans easily outperformed the buy and hold strategy over the seventeen year period from December 31, 1929, through December 31, 1946. His results indicated average (arithmetic mean, not geometric mean) annual rates of gain of +0.07% for the buy and hold strategy for stocks and +4.12% for bonds. He reported +7.86% and +8.12% average annual rates of gain, respectively, for the two sliding scale plans measured over this time period. Ketchum's calculations include an adjustment for transaction costs and management fees.

DCA versus LSI: December 1929–December 1946

Since Ketchum did not compare DCA with LSI, we created Chart 2–9. Chart 2–9 compares DCA and LSI over the seventeen year period from December 31, 1929 through December 31, 1946. As with our earlier models, the risky investment is the S&P 500 index and the risk-free investment is Treasury Bills. Furthermore, Chart 2–9 does not make any adjustment for transaction costs or management fees. Since this is a 204 month investment horizon, the LSI portfolio begins with an initial value of $204. We construct the DCA portfolio assuming the investor invests $1 every month for 17 years. Surprisingly, the final portfolio value under DCA is $458.57 versus $368.17 under LSI. The incredible 76% decline in the market from December 1929 through June 1932 devastated the LSI portfolio. At the market low, the LSI portfolio was worth only $49.18. In contrast, we had invested only $30 of the total $204 in the DCA portfolio during this time. So, although the $30 had declined in value to only $11.32, the remaining $174 were safely sheltered in Treasury Bills. As stock prices rebounded in the mid 30's and early 40's, the DCA portfolio surged past the LSI portfolio. The fact that DCA outperformed LSI by so much over such a long investment horizon indicates just how low returns were and how high volatility was throughout this period.

Chart 2–10 gives a long-term view of the U.S. equity market. In this view, the poor investment returns and high volatility of the highlighted seventeen year period are clear. The cumulative wealth index line is significantly straighter and more steeply positively angled after 1947 than it was before 1947. Compared to the market declines in the 30's, the market crash of 1987 looks like nothing more than a minor interruption of a steady, upward climb.

Chart 2–11 is similar to Chart 2–8 except that it covers the seventeen years ended December 31, 1995. In this case, the S&P 500 cumulative

CHART 2–9 DCA versus LSI: December 1929–December 1946

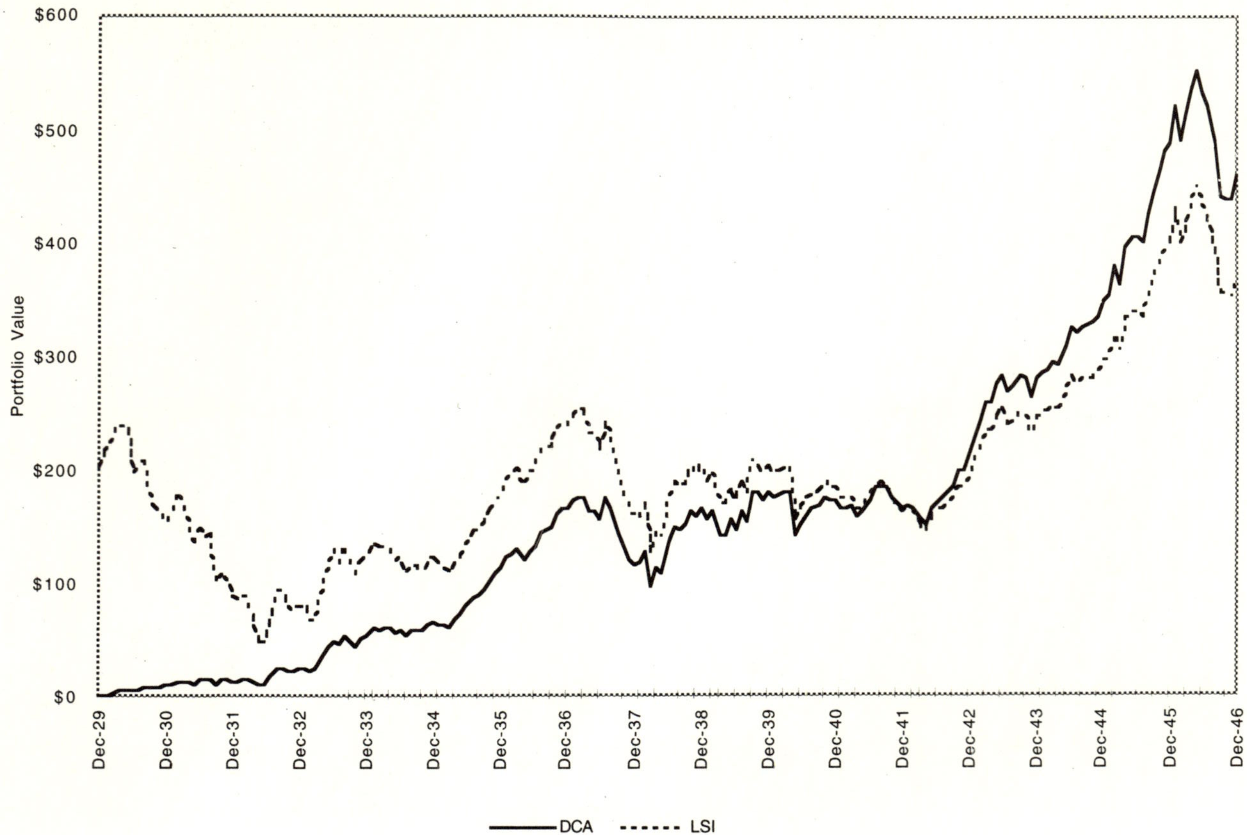

CHART 2–10 S&P 500 Cumulative Wealth Index: 1926–1995

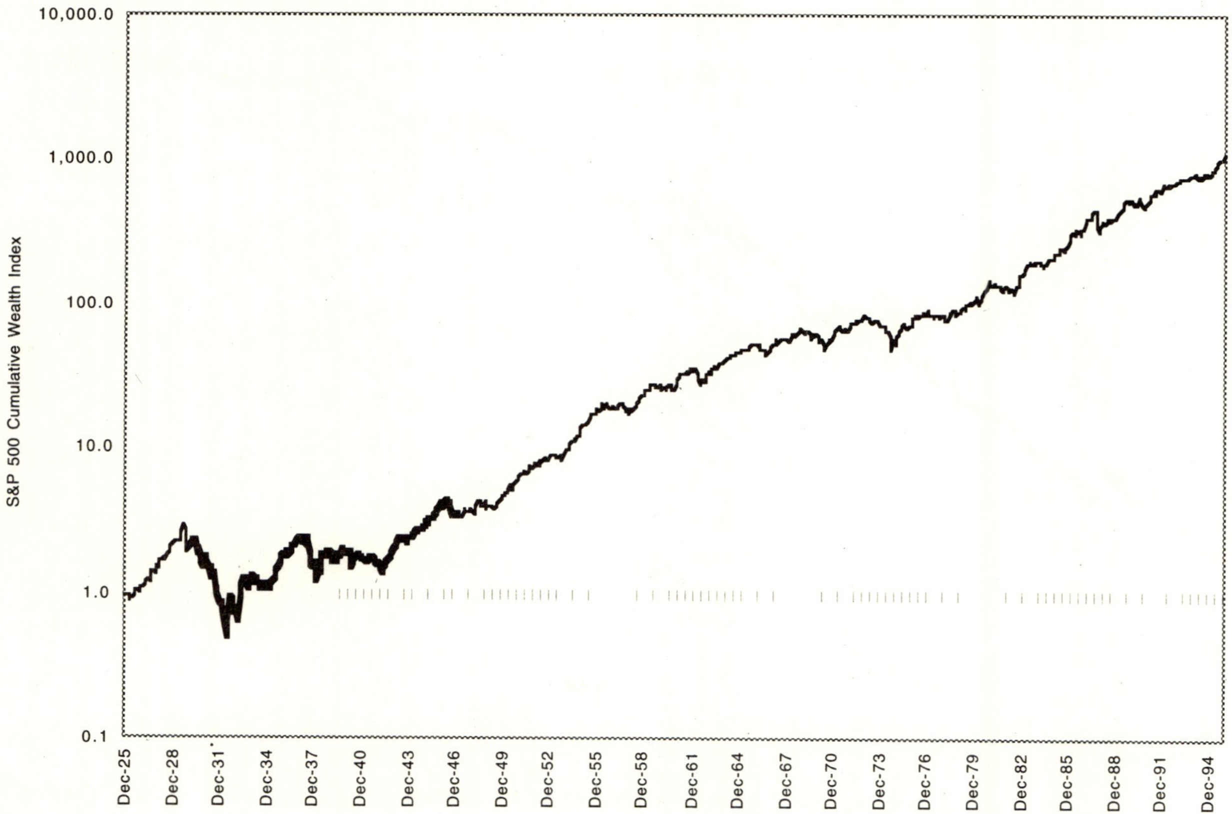

CHART 2–11 S&P 500 Cumulative Wealth Index: December 1978–December 1995

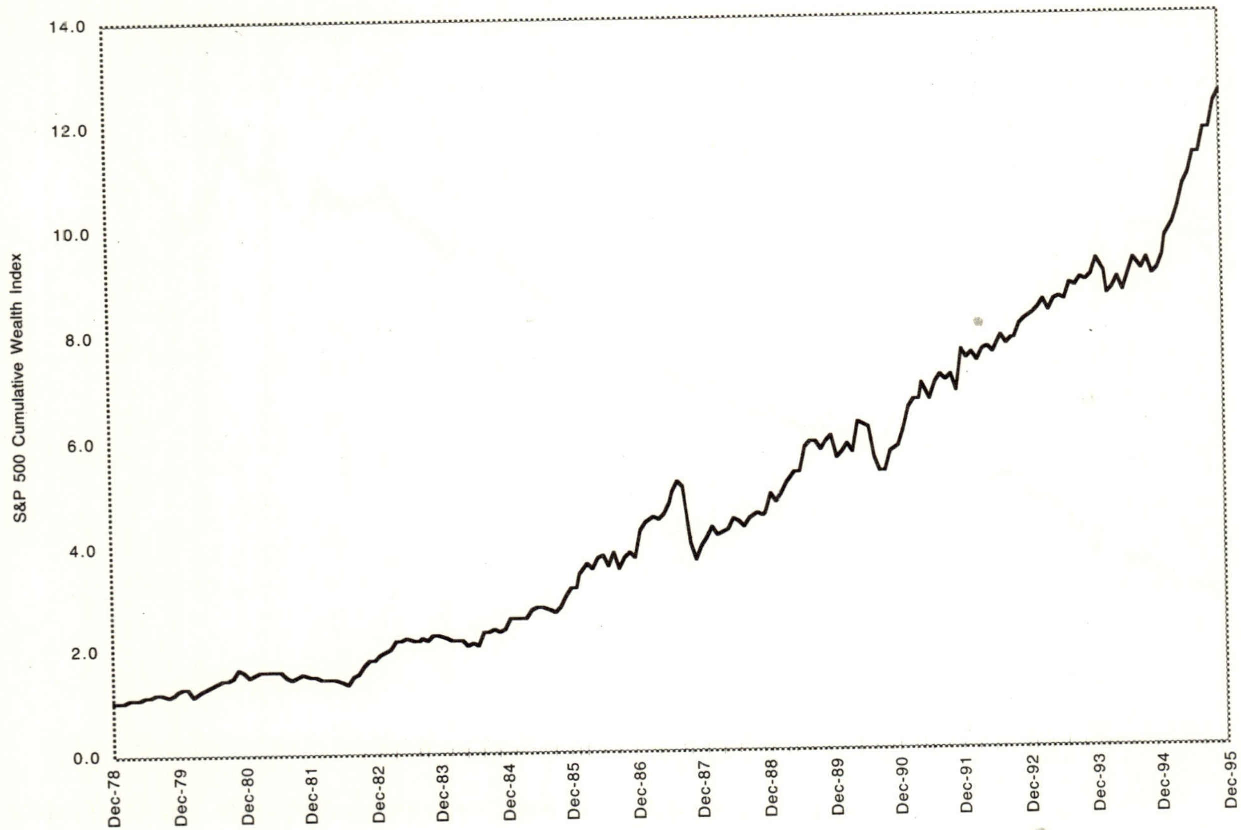

CHART 2–12 DCA versus LSI: December 1978–December 1995

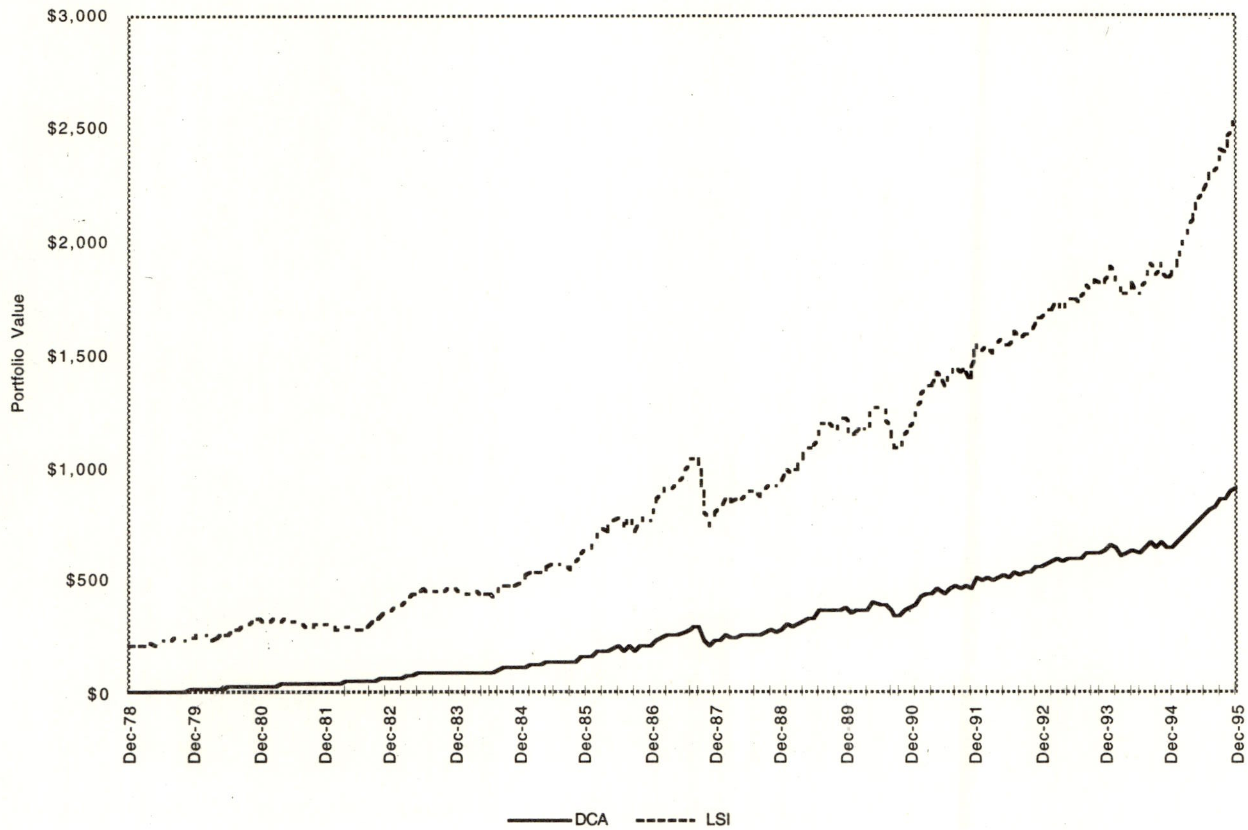

wealth index rises to 12.44, which translates into an annualized return of 15.98%. This is substantially better than the 1.80 cumulative wealth index produced during the earlier seventeen year period. Under these circumstances, we would suspect that LSI would far outperform DCA, which Chart 2–12 confirms. Beginning with $204, the LSI portfolio increased to $2,538.72, while the DCA portfolio managed only a meager $903.45. This result is more in line with our long-term empirical observations, but is divergent with research from the late 40's. Finally, the arithmetic mean of monthly returns during this period was 1.33%, while the standard deviation of monthly returns was 4.25%. Compared to the earlier period, returns doubled, while standard deviations were halved.

Sliding Scale Plans: Recent Performance

The sliding scale plans are interesting because they are primitive forms of tactical asset allocation. We know that Ketchum found that sliding scale plans added significantly to investment returns between 1929 and 1946. We would like to know if such simple formula plans can improve investment returns today. The investment environment today is significantly different than in 1947. Secular fluctuations are generally positive, unlike the horizontal and negative fluctuations of the past. Cyclical fluctuations are much less pronounced now. Volatility is much lower now. Investment management has become more sophisticated and markets have become more efficient. It is uncertain whether Ketchum's formula plans can still add value. To find out, we will devise a model similar to one described by Ketchum and test it over the period from 1947 through 1995.

Applying Ketchum's Sliding Scale Plan

There are four steps to implementing the sliding scale plan. First, we must divide a suitable index representative of the risky investment into a number of zones. Ketchum used the Dow Jones Industrial Average, but we will use the S&P 500. We will divide the price pattern of the index into seven zones. Zone 1 is the lowest zone and represents the market bottom and zone 7 is the highest zone and represents the market top. The second step is the selection of the sliding scale. The sliding scale should be based upon policy decisions that establish a target weighting for the risky investment as well as an acceptable range of weights. In our example, we will assume that the target weight for stocks is 50%, within a range of 20% to 80%. Table 2–11 provides one possible sliding scale schedule that we could use in this case. The basic idea is that when the market index is at a high level, the percentage invested in stocks is decreased and when the market index is at a low level, the percentage invested in stocks is increased. The third

TABLE 2–11 Sliding Scale Plan

Zone	Stocks	Bills
7	20%	80%
6	30%	70%
5	40%	60%
4	50%	50%
3	60%	40%
2	70%	30%
1	80%	20%

step is to establish a policy concerning rebalancing. Any time the market index moves into a different zone, the portfolio will always be rebalanced according to the determined schedule. However, we should decide whether the portfolio will be rebalanced when the zone does not change. This decision involves a tradeoff between the possibility that returns will improve by rebalancing against the transaction cost of rebalancing.

The fourth step is the implementation of special rules to counteract the basic tendency of the strategy to buy as the market goes into an extended decline or to sell as the market goes into an extended rally. In Ketchum's Plan C, he implemented a delaying rule that held the percentage invested in the risky investment constant whenever the market index reached one of the extreme zones, until the market index returned past the midway point. For example, if the market rose rapidly and the index reached Zone 7, the percentage invested in the risky investment would fall to 20%. The percentage would stay at 20% until the market index fell to Zone 4, at which time we would adjust the percentage invested in the risky investment to 50%. The logic behind the delaying rule makes sense. If the market index is falling from Zone 7 to Zone 4, it is highly likely that the market is experiencing either negative returns or positive returns that are significantly lower than the long-term trend. In that environment, it would be desirable to have the smallest percentage allowable under policy invested in the risky investment. Likewise, if the market index fell to Zone 1, the percentage invested in the risky investment would stay at 80% until the market index rose to Zone 4, at which time we would reduce the percentage invested in the risky investment to 50%.

We need a methodology for dividing the price movement of the market index into seven zones. Ketchum used the Dow Jones Industrial Average, which does not include dividends. We will use the Ibbotson Associates S&P 500 cumulative wealth index, except that in this case, we will not include dividends. Setting December 31, 1925, at 1.00, the index rises to 48.30 by December 31, 1995. Typically, charts of cumulative wealth indices use a logarithmic scale. This is because the compounding effect usually causes cumulative wealth indices to rise slowly at first, then explode upward towards the end of the time period. Chart 2–10 is an example of a cumulative wealth index illustrated using a logarithmic scale. Chart 2–13 shows those data without using a logarithmic scale. In this view, all the declines and rallies and general market volatility that occurred in the 30's and early 40's are invisible. Incredibly, the S&P 500 cumulative wealth index rose more in the last 4 1/2 years than it did in the first 65 1/2 years.

Finding the Zone

Our goal is to plot a trend line against the price movement of the S&P 500 index. To do this, we will use the logarithms of the cumulative wealth index values instead of the values themselves. As we can see from Chart 2–10, the logarithmic scale features a more steadily upwardly sloping line. Equivalent slopes, at any place on the line, translate into equivalent investment returns. Chart 2–14 plots the logarithm of the S&P 500 cumulative wealth index, without dividends, covering the ten year period from December 31, 1985, through December 31, 1995. Ten years will be the default measurement period in all calculations. On December 31, 1985, the index had a value of 2.81, then gradually sloped upward, reaching a final value of 3.88 on December 31, 1995. The heavy line in the middle represents the least-squares regression line. We determine the upper limit and lower limits by finding the lines that run parallel to the regression line and are tangent to the point that lies farthest above and below the regression line, respectively. In this example, the upper limit occurs on August 31, 1987, and the lower limit occurs on November 30, 1987. Once we establish the upper and lower limits, we divide the region into seven zones. We determine the upper limits of Zones 4, 5, and 6 by multiplying the difference between the upper and central trend lines by 1/7, 3/7, and 5/7, respectively, and adding the result to the central trend line. We determine the upper limits of Zones 3, 2, and 1 by multiplying the difference between the central and lower trend lines by 1/7, 3/7, and 5/7, respectively, and subtracting the result from the central trend line. The widths of the zones above are generally not the same as the widths of the zones below the central trend line.

Chart 2–14 shows that the market index was in Zone 6 on December 31, 1995. It is important to understand that Chart 2–14 does not show the zone in which any of the other data points lie. We use the ten year regression to calculate the zone of the final point only. To calculate the zones for each of the other data points we must produce a separate regression analysis for each one. Chart 2–15 is the composite result of 792 regression analyses. The heavy line in the center is the logarithm of the S&P 500 cumulative wealth index, without dividends. The borders of the seven

CHART 2–13 S&P 500 Cumulative Wealth Index: Non-Logarithmic Scale

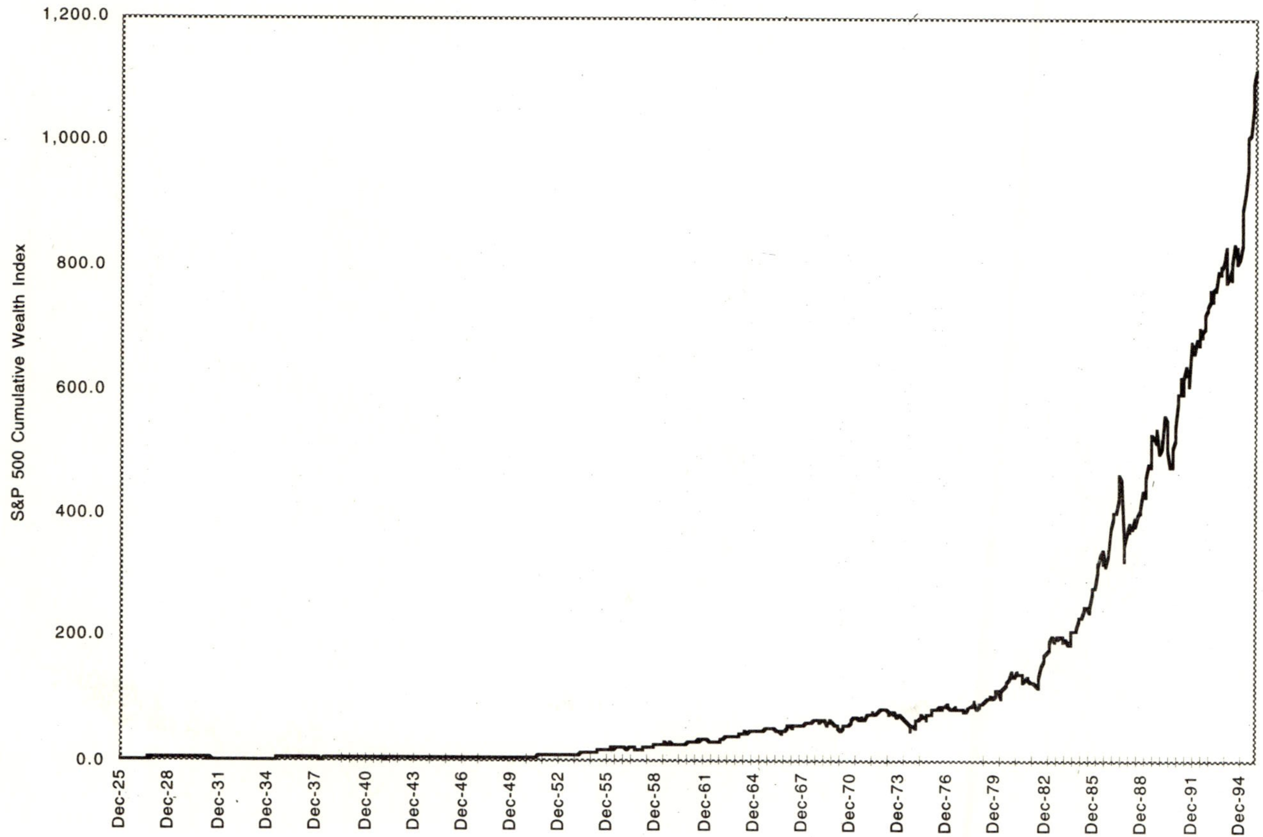

CHART 2–14 Finding the Zone

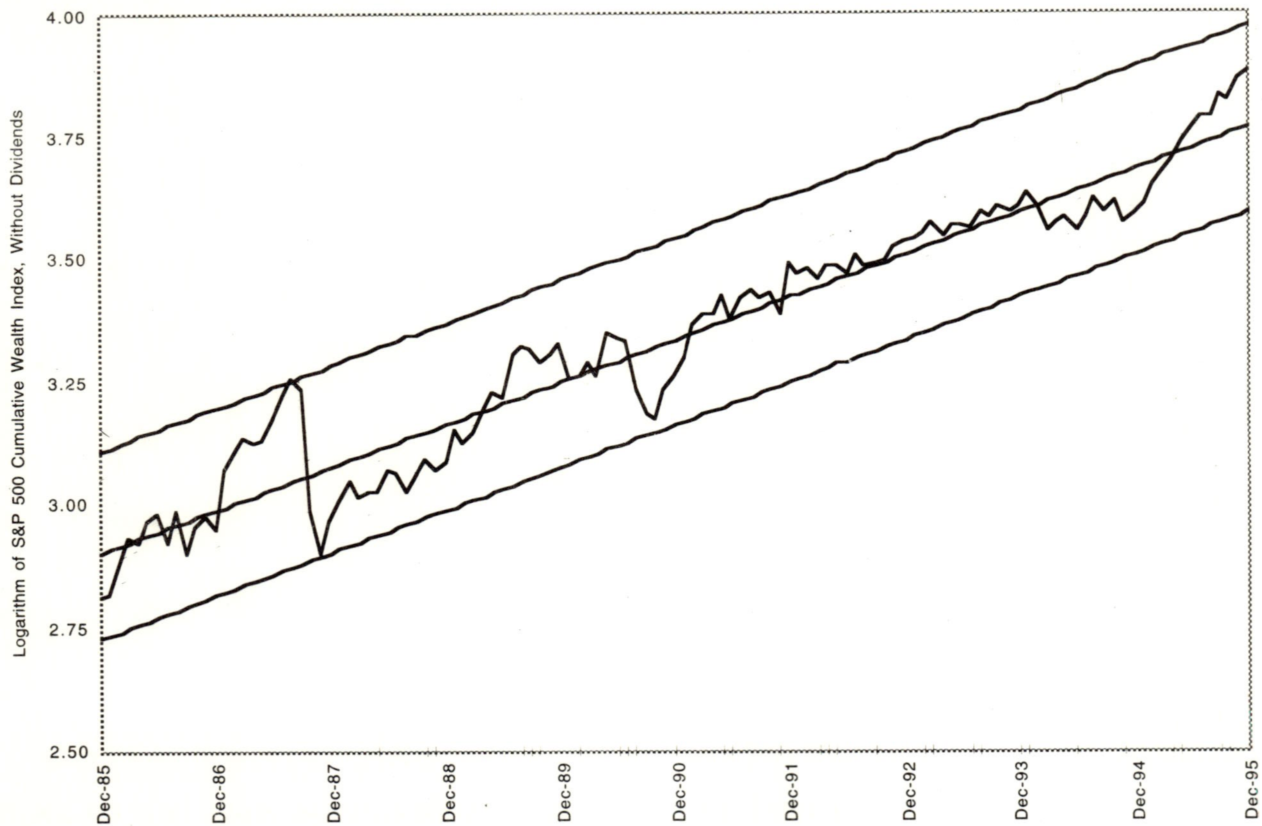

CHART 2–15 Historical Zones: December 1929–December 1995

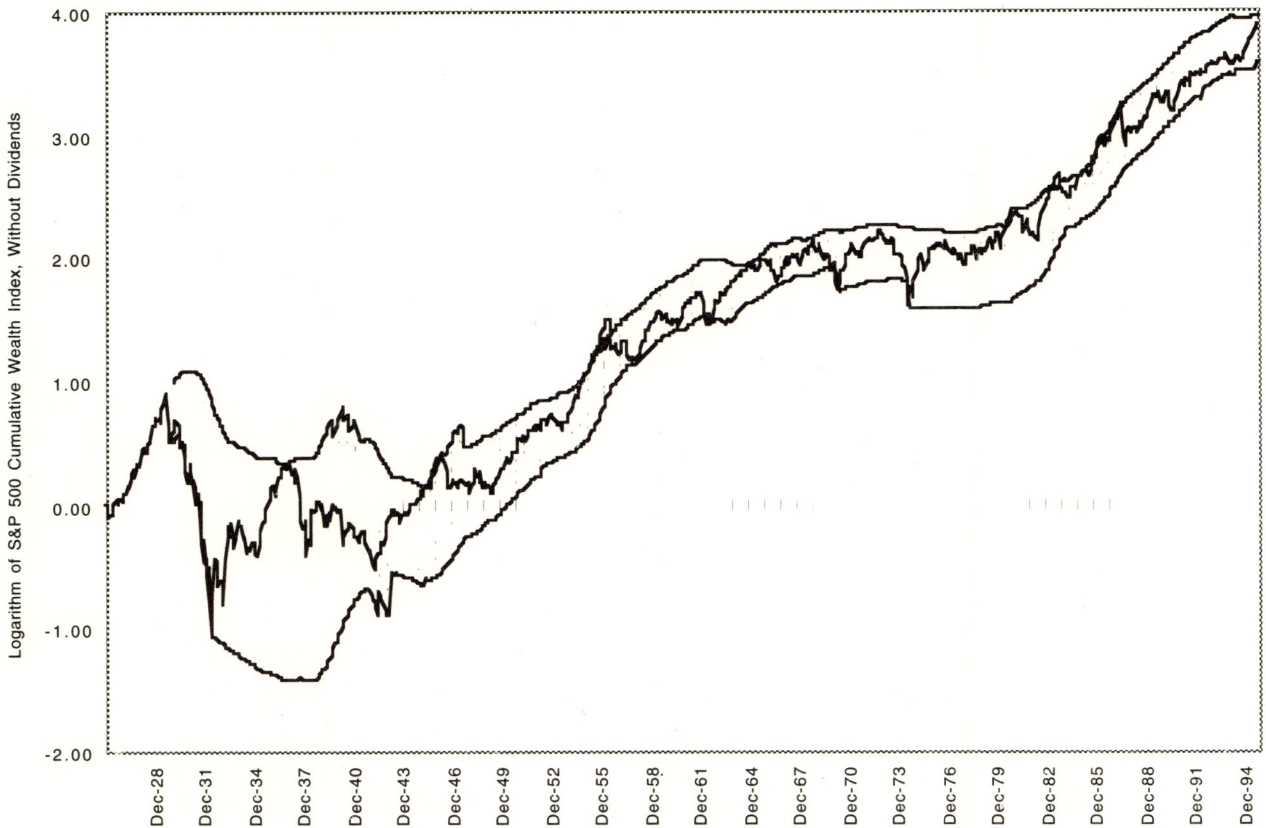

zones surround the price level line. Interestingly, the market bottom in November 1987, which determined the minimum line in Chart 2–14, lies in Zone 2. The decline in the market that took place in September and October 1990 did cause the index to fall to Zone 1, although this decline was less severe than the 1987 decline, both absolutely and relatively.

The Results

The results for the sliding scale plan, as shown in Table 2–12, are surprisingly good. The sliding scale plan, with rebalancing, produced an annualized investment return of 9.57%. The average exposure to stocks was 49.116%, very near the target allocation of 50%. Monthly returns had an arithmetic mean of 0.789% and a standard deviation of 2.195%. In comparison, a strategy of holding a constant portfolio invested 49.116% in stocks, with rebalancing, produced an annualized investment return of only 8.78%, significantly less than under the sliding scale plan. The standard deviation of monthly returns is 1.973%, much less than under the sliding scale plan. In short, the constant 49.116% stock exposure strategy produced a lower return, but with lower risk. With trial and error, we can arrive at the percentage allocation in stocks that will equalize the monthly standard deviations of the constant stock exposure strategy with the sliding scale plan. A constant 54.636% stock exposure strategy produces an identical 2.195% monthly standard deviation as the sliding scale plan, with rebalancing. The annualized investment return of 9.20% still falls short of the return generated by the sliding scale plan, despite having 5 1/2% more invested in the risky investment. While these results might indicate a valid starting point for a tactical asset allocation discipline, we must treat them with caution. A t-test on these data indicates that these results are not statistically significant. As Chart 2–16 shows, the sliding scale plan

TABLE 2–12 Sliding Scale Plans: Results

				Monthly Returns	
Plan	**Wealth Index**	**Annualized Return**	**Stock Exposure**	**Arithmetic Mean**	**Standard Deviation**
Sliding Scale Plan, With Rebalancing	88.25	9.57%	49.116%	0.789%	2.195%
Sliding Scale Plan, Without Rebalancing	89.50	9.61%		0.791%	2.208%
Constant 49.116% Stock Exposure, With Rebalancing	61.85	8.78%	49.116%	0.723%	1.973%
Constant 54.636% Stock Exposure, With Rebalancing	74.49	9.20%	54.636%	0.760%	2.195%

CHART 2–16 Sliding Scale Plan versus Buy-and-Hold Strategies: December 1946–December 1995

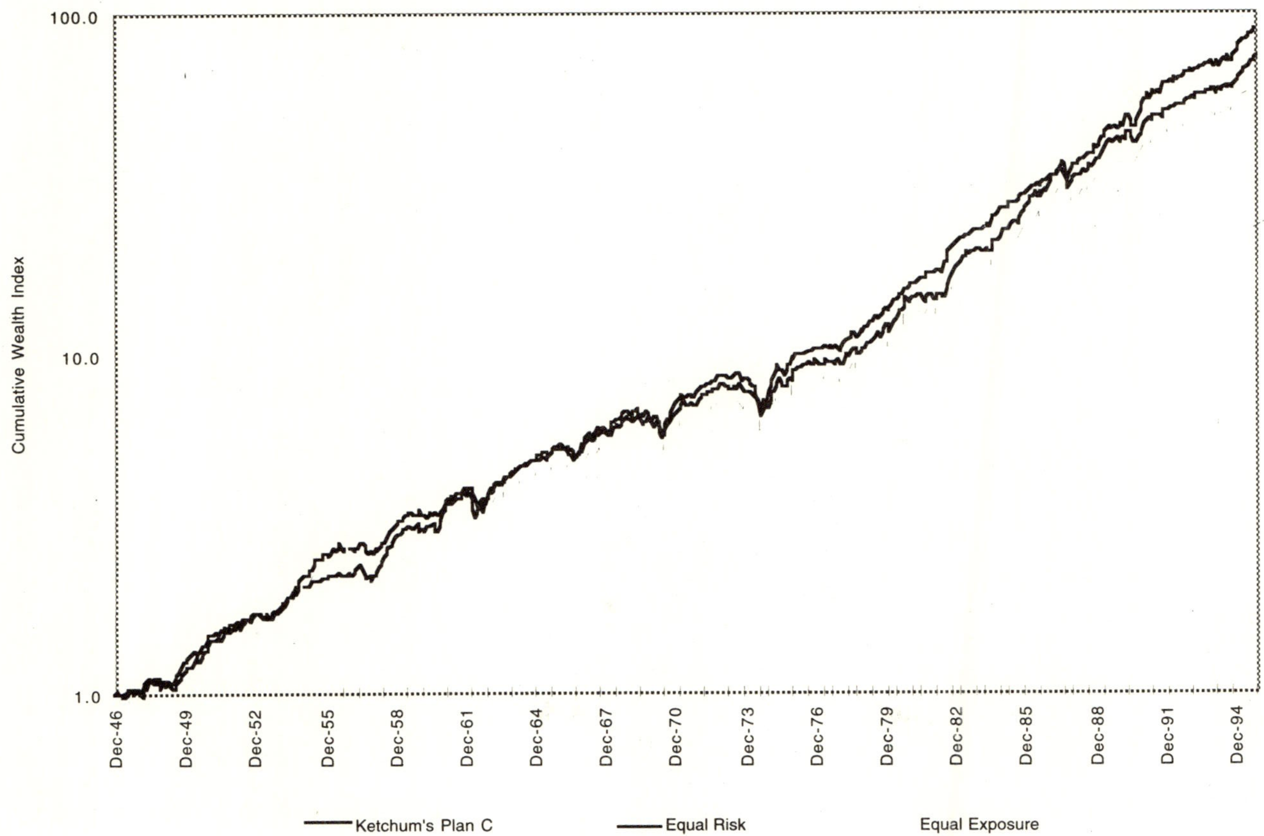

did not finally separate from the other strategies until the stock market crash of 1987.

Having completed a review of some of the historical research on dollar cost averaging, we now have an idea why the investment profession took dollar cost averaging seriously. Explaining its continuing popularity is more difficult.

Dollar Cost Averaging: A Psychological Perspective

Let us consider the possibility that human beings treat gains and losses differently. Specifically, we will assume that losses are more painful than equivalent gains are pleasurable. One veteran portfolio manager claims, "my clients love to make money, but they hate to lose money even more." By definition, the investor who engages in a dollar cost averaging program has at least a reasonable expectation that the investment will decline in value. More to the point, he is afraid that soon after investing all of his investable cash into an investment, it will decline, and he seeks a way to minimize the regret he would feel if a decline did happen. That is why he is willing to use a dollar cost averaging strategy that is clearly suboptimal in a mean-variance framework. He believes that dollar cost averaging may reduce the likelihood and the magnitude of a loss on his investment due to a future price decline. In exchange for that piece of mind, he is sacrificing investment return, knowingly or not. Is the price for piece of mind too high or is it reasonable?

To help understand how humans process probabilities and outcome values, let us consider some games of chance. If you had the chance to play a fair game in which you would flip a coin and win a dollar for heads and lose a dollar for tails, you would probably play. The stakes are low so the perceived risk of the game is minimal. You would probably quit playing because of boredom before you would quit because of a financial consideration. If we raised the stakes so that each flip was worth ten times your annual salary, the game would be entirely different. Chances are, the risk of losing ten years' salary would be too great for almost anybody to consider playing. Yet, the game is exactly the same as the first one. The probabilities are the same. Only the dollar payouts are different. The difference is that losing one dollar does not cause much regret, but the regret caused by losing ten years' salary is significant. It would far outweigh the joy of winning ten years' salary. The probabilities of winning and losing in the two games are equal, but the values of the payouts are unequal, at least psychologically. Now, suppose that you had the chance to play a fair game in which you would roll one die and win a dollar if you rolled a one through five and lose a dollar if you rolled a six. In this case, the odds are distinctly stacked in your favor. You will win five dollars for every one dollar that you lose. You would play this game for as long as you wanted to produce a constant stream of dollars. Any losses that occur are insignificant and easily recouped because wins occur more frequently than losses. The probabilities are unequal, but tilted in your favor, and the payouts are equal. Now, we will change the game slightly. Instead of rolling a die, you will play Russian Roulette. If you aim the gun at your head, pull the trigger, and nothing happens, you win a dollar. If you lose, you are dead. The probability of winning the game has not changed, but the relative value of the outcomes is far different. Nobody would play this game because we recognize that the positive value of a favorable outcome is far exceeded by the negative value of an unfavorable outcome. In processing this kind of decision, the human mind determines the probabilities of favorable and unfavorable outcomes and then assigns a value to each outcome. Research in human decision making has uncovered a number of facts that have important implications for investment management. Most importantly, humans assign a higher negative value to a loss than they do to an equivalent gain.

We have compared DCA with LSI from a number of different angles, but we have not examined the traits that affect the probability of one strategy outperforming the other or the probability that a strategy will result in a gain or a loss. If we examine a hypothetical investment and assume that monthly returns are normally distributed, we can estimate the likelihood that a DCA strategy will outperform an LSI strategy. The two necessary variables are the monthly expected return and the monthly standard deviation. Chart 2–17 shows the likelihood that DCA outperforms LSI under a variety of expected return and standard deviation assumptions. Three simple rules summarize the results of Chart 2–17. The likelihood of LSI outperforming DCA is a function of the expected return of the risky investment. All else being equal, the higher the expected return of the investment, the higher the likelihood that LSI will outperform. At the same time, the higher the level of volatility of the risky investment, the higher the likelihood that DCA will outperform, given that more volatility leads to a greater range of possible results as well as a greater differential between the average cost per share and average of the share prices. Finally, the effect of expected return on the likelihood of DCA outperforming is much more pronounced for low levels of volatility than it is for high levels of volatility.

It is important to realize that a higher likelihood of one strategy outperforming the other does not impact the relative expected returns of the strategies. The expected returns of the two strategies depend only on the single-period expected returns and the number of investment periods. Standard deviation does not impact expected return. The reason standard deviation affects the likelihood of one strategy outperforming the other is

CHART 2–17 DCA Likelihood of Outperforming for Various Expected Return and Risk Estimates

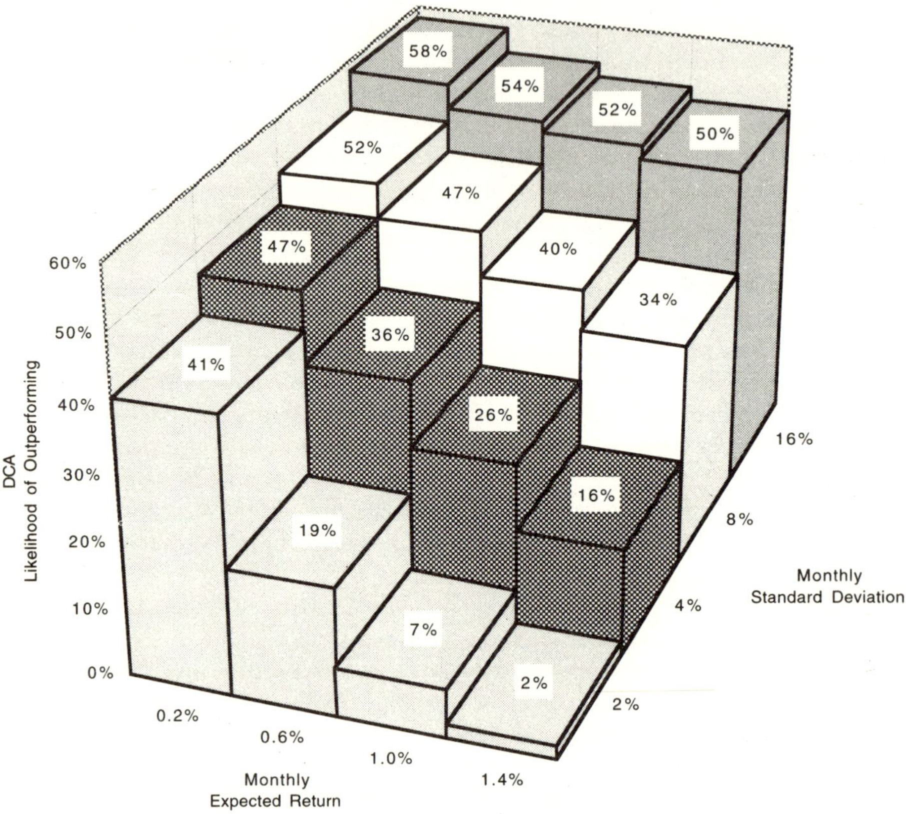

because the volatility causes the final probability distribution curve to be positively skewed. The more volatility, the more positively skewed the probability distribution curve becomes. Nevertheless, it seems reasonable that if the probability that DCA outperforms LSI increases with higher levels of volatility, seasoned investment professionals would have observed this over the course of their careers. Thus, we use DCA almost exclusively with riskier investments, which typically exhibit higher levels of volatility. DCA is "unnecessary" when investing in low risk investments, because both the likelihood and magnitude of a decline in the security's price are sufficiently small. From the investor's point of view, if he uses a DCA strategy with a risky investment and the investment declines in value during the investment period, he feels joy that he avoided the full magnitude of the loss that would have occurred if he had invested all at once. If the investment increases in value, his return will generally be lower than if he had invested all at once, but he will still have a gain. The loss from using the DCA strategy is not really a loss, but an opportunity cost. The mind processes the two outcomes as (1) avoiding a large loss and (2) producing a gain. The mind attaches a positive value to each result. Under LSI, the mind processes the two outcomes as (1) a large loss and (2) a gain. In this case, the mind attaches a negative value to the large loss and a positive value to the gain.

Adjusting DCA and LSI Outcomes to Account for Psychological Perception

Given that losses are weighted more heavily than gains in the natural mental accounting system, it would be instructive to divide the results for DCA and LSI into three categories: gains, losses, and big losses. Within each category, gains will be unweighted, losses will be double-weighted, and losses greater than 10% will be triple-weighted. In other words, the positive value of a 30% gain will be equivalent to the negative value of a 10% loss. Table 2–13 summarizes the results of DCA and LSI over the seventy year period from December 31, 1925, through December 31, 1995. Table 2–14 presents the same concept, but covers the period from December 31, 1946, through December 31, 1995, thus eliminating a period of extreme volatility in the U.S. stock market not likely to be repeated in the future. The three rows correspond with the DCA results, while the three columns correspond with the LSI results. Within each grid, the table gives the average return of DCA and LSI, the number of observations, and the weight-adjusted average return figures for each strategy. For example, the third row and first column represent the situation where DCA produces a gain and LSI produces a loss greater than 10%. Out of 829 total observations, this situation has occurred 16 times. When it did occur, the average return for the DCA strategy was 5.96% and the average return for the LSI strategy was -17.23%. Since gains are unweighted, the adjusted value for DCA is 5.96%, the same as the actual observed gains. Losses greater than 10% are triple-weighted so the adjusted value for LSI is -51.69%, triple the actual observed losses. In aggregate, LSI produces a loss greater than 10% 104 times versus 52 times for DCA. LSI also produces 114 small losses compared with 130 for DCA. Overall, DCA produces fewer observations of losses than LSI and the average loss for DCA is significantly smaller on average than under LSI. These data are consistent with our expectations.

On the other hand, the most common observation, a gain for both strategies, occurs 582 times out of 829 total observations. In those cases, LSI has a clear advantage over DCA. When both strategies record a gain, LSI averages a gain of 22.96% against 14.29% for DCA. In short, DCA pro-

TABLE 2–13 Weighted Results for DCA and LSI: 1926–1995

DCA		LSI							
		Loss > 10%		**Loss**		**Gain**		**Grand Total**	
Loss > 10%	DCA - Average	-21.95%	-65.85%	-13.24%	-39.73%			-20.61%	-61.83%
	LSI - Average	-32.75%	-98.26%	-6.77%	-13.53%			-28.75%	-85.22%
	Count	44		8		0		52	
Loss	DCA - Average	-5.67%	-11.35%	-3.56%	-7.13%	-2.73%	-5.46%	-4.09%	-8.18%
	LSI - Average	-14.98%	-44.93%	-5.53%	-11.07%	5.77%	5.77%	-6.21%	-18.77%
	Count	44		57		29		130	
Gain	DCA - Average	5.96%	5.96%	5.04%	5.04%	14.29%	14.29%	13.38%	13.38%
	LSI - Average	-17.23%	-51.69%	-3.83%	-7.66%	22.96%	22.96%	19.94%	18.79%
	Count	16		49		582		647	
Grand Total	DCA - Total Average	-10.77%	-31.74%	-0.55%	-4.19%	13.48%	13.35%	8.51%	5.28%
	LSI - Total Average	-22.84%	-68.53%	-4.89%	-9.78%	22.14%	22.14%	12.78%	6.38%
	Count	104		114		611		829	

TABLE 2–14 Weighted Results for DCA and LSI: 1947–1995

		LSI							
DCA		**Loss > 10%**		**Loss**		**Gain**		**Grand Total**	
Loss > 10%	DCA - Average	-14.65%	-43.95%	-12.47%	-37.42%			-14.25%	-42.76%
	LSI - Average	-23.64%	-70.92%	-6.58%	-13.17%			-20.54%	-60.42%
	Count	9		2		0		11	
Loss	DCA - Average	-5.63%	-11.26%	-2.94%	-5.88%	-1.99%	-3.99%	-3.47%	-6.95%
	LSI - Average	-13.44%	-40.31%	-5.08%	-10.15%	3.07%	3.07%	-5.53%	-15.55%
	Count	23		40		19		82	
Gain	DCA - Average	4.41%	4.41%	4.23%	4.23%	13.02%	13.02%	12.21%	12.21%
	LSI - Average	-12.81%	-38.44%	-3.38%	-6.76%	19.68%	19.68%	17.38%	16.70%
	Count	8		37		439		484	
Grand Total	DCA - Total Average	-5.65%	-15.48%	0.18%	-1.94%	12.40%	12.32%	9.47%	8.44%
	LSI - Total Average	-15.61%	-46.82%	-4.32%	-8.64%	18.99%	18.99%	13.40%	10.65%
	Count	40		79		458		577	

tects the investor from large losses when the investment does poorly at a cost of some participation on the upside when the investment does well. The final totals, in the lower right hand total, are equivalent to those shown in Table 2–6. The arithmetic mean of returns for DCA is 8.51% and for LSI, 12.78%. When adjusted to account for the asymmetrical value assigned to gains and losses, the gap narrows considerably. The weight-adjusted value for DCA is 5.28% versus 6.38% for LSI. Although this still indicates an advantage for LSI, the margin over DCA appears to be smaller than under a simple comparison of arithmetic means. We will continue to develop the concept of weight-adjusting for "human" factors in a coming chapter.

CHAPTER 3

The Importance of Asset Allocation

History has witnessed its share of revolutions—major events that have completely uprooted prior ways of doing things and replaced them with completely new systems. Most of the time we associate revolutions with civil upheavals that have changed the course of history by resulting in the overthrow of governments and their subsequent replacement with wholly new forms of government. However, on a smaller scale, an event can also be considered revolutionary if it so thoroughly changes the current way of looking at or doing things that it is impossible to move forward again without considering the new perspective. For example, Albert Einstein revolutionized modern physics with his theory of relativity. Babe Ruth revolutionized major league baseball when he started repeatedly hitting home runs into the right field bleachers in New York. More recently, Bill Gates revolutionized office and home productivity when he developed an operating system and software that enabled the personal computer industry to flourish, effectively making PCs available worldwide.

Within the investment field, Harry Markowitz revolutionized modern portfolio theory when he published *Portfolio Selection* in 1952. Prior to that time, a nebulous idea that diversification improved investment portfolios existed, but no disciplined approach to quantifying the relative efficiency of portfolios was available to help investment managers construct portfolios. Since then, Markowitz's theory has served as a foundation from which others have been able to make numerous important contributions.

Brinson, Hood, and Beebower made a revolutionary contribution to the science of asset allocation when they wrote *Determinants of Portfolio Performance*, published in the July-August 1986 issue of the *Financial Analysts Journal*. Their findings stunned the investment profession by focusing attention on the issues of the importance of asset allocation and the ability of active investment management to add to investment returns. In the 10 years that have passed since its publication, a tremendous variety of asset allocation services and products have appeared. Index funds and other types of passively managed funds, in particular, have burst forth in large part because of the finding that professional investment managers generally subtract value, rather than add value, in the areas of market timing and security selection, while adding to overall portfolio risk. Assets invested using passive management continue to grow both absolutely and as a percentage of total assets under management. Furthermore, within the research community, asset allocation has become a hot topic. Several researchers have developed important new ideas in the area of asset allocation in the last decade, whereas the topic of asset allocation was comparatively unknown prior to 1986. So influential was the Brinson, Hood, and Beebower article that it recently appeared in the *Journal's* fiftieth anniversary issue, commemorating the most important works of their first 50 years. (For purposes of simplicity, we will refer to Brinson, Hood, and Beebower as BHB throughout the next two chapters.)

Revisiting the Determinants of Portfolio Performance

In their seminal work, BHB made three outstanding contributions to the science of asset allocation. First, they observed that pension plan sponsors and investment managers needed a clear method of attributing investment returns to three distinct components—investment policy, market timing, and security selection. In response to this need, they built a three-level framework in order to decompose investment returns. The bottom level was a passive, benchmark portfolio representing the plan's long-term asset allocation weights. The second level combined policy with one of the other two components of investment return—market timing and security selection. The market timing component was a passive, benchmark index return based on the actual asset allocation decisions of the plan. The security selection component considered actual asset class returns, together with the plan's long-term asset allocation weights. The top level was the return of the total portfolio, including all components of its return. Their general framework enabled them to analyze the results of 91 large pension plans covering the 1974 through 1983 period. From this analysis followed two other critically important contributions. First, they observed that investment policy return explained on average 93.6 percent of the total variance in actual plan return. Returns due to policy and market timing resulted in average variance explained of 95.3 percent. Returns due to policy and security selection resulted in average variance explained of 97.8 percent. The implication is that market timing and security selection are far less influential factors in determining total plan return than asset allocation policy. In their words, these results "clearly show that total return to a plan is dominated by investment policy decisions. Active management, while important, describes far less of a plan's returns than investment policy." Second, they found that active investment management resulted in a reduction in total plan return of 1.10 percent annually on average. Market timing cost the average plan 0.66 percent annually. Security selection cost the average plan 0.36 percent annually. The remaining 0.07 percent lost was the result of a cross-product term that measures the interaction of the market timing and security selection decisions. Furthermore, they found that while active management led to lower returns compared to the passive, benchmark index, active management also led to higher levels of risk. With regard to their finding that active management did not add to returns, BHB made the same observation that others had already reported in numerous prior studies.

In the next two chapters, we will address two of the issues covered in *Determinants of Portfolio Performance*: the importance of asset allocation and the construction of a general framework for the decomposition of investment returns. We will not address the issue of whether active investment management adds to investment return. Our general purpose is not to refute the BHB results, but rather to clarify their results where they may have been misinterpreted, expand upon their results, and provide an alternative viewpoint by looking at the data in a different way.

In this chapter, we will examine the claim that asset allocation explains 93.6 percent of investment returns and explain exactly what it means. After reviewing the methodology used by BHB, we will present two alternative ways of looking at the importance of asset allocation. In our opinion, asset allocation policy is a vitally important aspect of investment management, but not nearly as large a factor as one might think based on the usual interpretation of the BHB research. Before building upon the BHB results, it would be helpful to review in detail their work.

A Review of the BHB Results

Basically, we can divide the research into four parts: development of the general framework, a description of the data, the plans' investment results, and the relative importance of each of the three components of return. The BHB study focused on U.S. pension plans, so all references made to stocks, bonds, and cash refer to U.S. stocks, bonds, and cash. Later, when we expand our discussion to include foreign stocks, we refer to them from the perspective of the U.S. investor, denominated in U.S. dollars. In general, the concepts described by BHB and the ideas we present here can be generalized for the non-U.S. investor. In addition, Singer and Karnosky have done an excellent job expanding upon the original BHB framework to account for foreign market and currency attribution.

The BHB general framework is really a three-level framework, although the authors did not present it that way. It contains four quadrants set up in a two-by-two grid, as shown in Figure 3–1. The two axes correspond to timing and selection. Each axis contains an actual and a passive element. The lower right-hand quadrant, Policy Return, represents the bottom of the three levels. For policy return, both timing and selection are passive. The returns in this quadrant represent the passive, benchmark index weighted according to the plan's long-term average asset allocations. BHB used the S&P 500, Shearson Lehman Government/

FIGURE 3–1 The Brinson, Hood and Beebower Framework: Concept

		Selection: Actual	Selection: Passive
Timing	Actual	(IV) Actual Portfolio Return	(II) Policy and Timing Return
	Passive	(III) Policy and Security Selection Return	(I) Policy Return (Passive Portfolio Benchmark)

Active Returns Due to:

Timing	II - I
Selection	III - I
Other	IV - III - II + I
Total	IV - I

Corporate Bond Index (now the Lehman Brothers Government/Corporate Bond Index), and 30-day Treasury bills as the benchmark indices. Quadrants II and III, Policy and Timing and Policy and Security Selection, respectively, represent the middle of the three levels. In both cases, one axis is actual and the other is passive. For the former, the timing axis is actual and the selection axis is passive; it measures the results from strategic shifts among asset classes, relative to the normal weight. For the latter, the selection axis is actual and the timing axis is passive; it measures the ability of the investment manager to outperform within an asset class, by calculating the actual asset class return against the passive, benchmark index for that asset class. The topmost of the three levels is the Actual Portfolio, which naturally consists of both the actual selection and the actual timing results. As the name implies, this is the plan's actual return, taking into consideration all components of investment return.

Figure 3–2 provides the mathematical equations for calculating the returns for each of the four quadrants. It looks complicated, but a simple example should make it clearer. Table 3–1 presents a hypothetical plan's returns over a three-month period. The top section gives general results, while the bottom section gives the calculations for each of the four quadrants in the BHB general framework. The plan made tactical asset alloca-

FIGURE 3–2 The Brinson, Hood and Beebower Framework: Formulas

		Selection	
		Actual	Passive
Timing	Actual	(IV) $\Sigma_i\ (W_{ai} \cdot R_{ai})$	(II) $\Sigma_i\ (W_{ai} \cdot R_{pi})$
	Passive	(III) $\Sigma_i\ (W_{pi} \cdot R_{ai})$	(I) $\Sigma_i\ (W_{pi} \cdot R_{pi})$

W_{pi} = policy (passive) weight for asset class i

W_{ai} = actual weight for asset class i

R_{pi} = passive return for asset class i

R_{ai} = actual return for asset class i

TABLE 3–1 The BHB Framework: An Example

		Month 1	Month 2	Month 3	Policy
Asset Class Weights	Stocks	55.0%	60.0%	50.0%	55.0%
	Bonds	40.0%	30.0%	35.0%	35.0%
	Cash	5.0%	10.0%	15.0%	10.0%
Passive Index Returns	Stocks	4.0%	1.0%	-3.0%	
	Bonds	1.0%	2.5%	-1.5%	
	Cash	0.5%	0.5%	0.5%	
Actual Plan Returns	Stocks	3.0%	2.0%	-1.0%	
	Bonds	1.5%	3.0%	-2.0%	
	Cash	0.5%	0.5%	0.5%	
		Month 1	**Month 2**	**Month 3**	
Policy Return	Stocks	2.20%	0.55%	-1.65%	
	Bonds	0.35%	0.88%	-0.53%	
	Cash	0.05%	0.05%	0.05%	
	Total	2.60%	1.48%	-2.13%	
Policy and Timing	Stocks	2.20%	0.60%	-1.50%	
	Bonds	0.40%	0.75%	-0.53%	
	Cash	0.03%	0.05%	0.08%	
	Total	2.63%	1.40%	-1.95%	
	Contribution	0.03%	-0.07%	0.18%	
Policy and Selection	Stocks	1.65%	1.10%	-0.55%	
	Bonds	0.53%	1.05%	-0.70%	
	Cash	0.05%	0.05%	0.05%	
	Total	2.23%	2.20%	-1.20%	
	Contribution	-0.38%	0.73%	0.93%	
Actual Portfolio Return	Stocks	1.65%	1.20%	-0.50%	
	Bonds	0.60%	0.90%	-0.70%	
	Cash	0.03%	0.05%	0.08%	
	Total	2.28%	2.15%	-1.13%	
	Contribution	-0.33%	0.68%	1.00%	

tion moves in each of the three months. Stock weights moved from 55 percent to 60 percent to 50 percent; bond weights moved from 40 percent to 30 percent to 35 percent; and cash weights moved from 5 percent to 10 percent to 15 percent. The average weights for stocks, bonds, and cash were 55 percent, 35 percent, and 10 percent, respectively, as indicated in the Policy column. In the equations in Figure 3–2, the average asset class weights, or policy weights, are simply the long-term average of the actual weights, or w_p. The actual asset class weights in each month are w_a.

The next two rows in Table 3–1 compare the passive index returns with the actual asset class returns. In the equations in Figure 3–2, the passive asset class return is r_p and the actual asset class return is r_a. Conceptually, we would expect that where the plan's asset class weights differ from the policy weights, the investment manager adds value through timing, or active asset allocation, whenever he overweights an asset class that outperforms the others or underweights an asset class that underperforms. Following the terminology in Figure 3–2, when r_p for an asset class is greater than r_p for the other asset classes, the investment manager adds value if $w_a > w_p$ for that asset class. Likewise, when r_p for an asset class is less than r_p for the other asset classes, the investment manager adds value if $w_a < w_p$ for that asset class. Simply put, the investment manager wants to have more of the good-performing asset class and less of the poor-performing asset class. The contribution to return from timing is quadrant II minus quadrant I. We would also expect that where the active returns, either for a particular asset class or the plan as a whole, exceed the passive returns, the investment manager has added value through security selection. Similarly, where the active returns are less than the passive returns, the investment manager has subtracted value. In Figure 3–2 terminology, the investment manager adds value if $r_a > r_p$. The contribution to return from security selection is quadrant III minus quadrant I. The contribution to return from active management is quadrant IV minus quadrant I.

Using the data in Table 3–1, we will work through the four calculations for Month 1. We calculate policy return by multiplying the policy asset class weights by the passive index returns: stocks (55 percent)(4.0 percent), bonds (35 percent)(1.0 percent), and cash (10 percent)(0.5 percent), for a total of 2.60 percent. We calculate policy and timing the same way as policy return, except that we use the actual asset class weights instead: stocks (55 percent)(4.0 percent), bonds (40 percent)(1.0 percent), and cash (5 percent)(0.5 percent), or 2.63 percent. We calculate policy and selection the same as policy return, except that we use the actual asset class returns instead: stocks (55 percent)(3.0 percent), bonds (35 percent)(1.5 percent), and cash (10 percent)(0.5 percent), or 2.23 percent. Finally, the actual portfolio return uses the actual asset class weights and the actual asset class returns: stocks (55 percent)(3.0 percent), bonds (40 percent)(1.5 percent), and cash (5 percent)(0.5 percent), or 2.28 percent.

BHB used quarterly data from 91 pension plans in the SEI Corp. Large Plan Universe covering the 10-year period from 1974 through 1983 to develop their results. They divided the assets held in the plans into stocks, bonds, cash, and "other." Table 3–2 summarizes the averages, minimums, maximums, and standard deviations of the holdings in the 91 pension plans. When they removed the "other" asset class, the average asset class weights for all 91 plans were stocks 62.9 percent, bonds 23.4 percent, and cash 13.6 percent. The range of asset class weights was quite wide, as indicated by the minimums, maximums, and standard deviations in Table 3–2.

When analyzed using the BHB framework, the 91 pension plans produced the results shown in Table 3–3. The average plan had an annualized 10-year return of 9.01 percent. The average passive, benchmark

TABLE 3–2 Summary of Asset Class Weights

All Holdings	Average	Minimum	Maximum	Std. Deviation	Policy Benchmark
Common Stocks	57.5%	32.3%	86.5%	10.9%	S&P 500 Index
Bonds	21.4%	0.0%	43.0%	9.0%	Shearson Lehman Gov't / Corp. Bond Index
Cash Equivalents	12.4%	1.8%	33.1%	5.0%	30 Day Treasury Bills
Other	8.6%	0.0%	53.5%	8.3%	None
	100.0%				

Stocks, Bonds, and Cash Only	Average	Minimum	Maximum	Std. Deviation
Common Stocks	62.9%	37.9%	89.3%	10.6%
Bonds	23.4%	0.0%	51.3%	9.4%
Cash Equivalents	13.6%	2.0%	35.0%	5.2%
	100.0%			

TABLE 3–3 Annualized 10-Year Returns and Risk by Activity

Portfolio Total Returns	Avg. Return	Minimum Return	Maximum Return	Std. Deviation
Policy	10.11%	9.47%	10.57%	0.22%
Policy and Timing	9.44%	7.25%	10.34%	0.52%
Policy and Selection	9.75%	7.17%	13.31%	1.33%
Actual Portfolio	9.01%	5.85%	13.40%	1.43%
Active Returns				
Timing Only	-0.66%	-2.68%	0.25%	0.49%
Security Selection Only	-0.36%	-2.90%	3.60%	1.36%
Other	-0.07%	-1.17%	2.57%	0.45%
Total Active Return	-1.10%	-4.17%	3.69%	1.45%

index return was 10.11 percent, indicating that active management cost the average plan 1.10 percent. The policy and timing return averaged 9.44 percent, indicating that timing cost the average plan 0.66 percent. The policy and selection return averaged 9.75 percent, indicating that selection cost the average plan 0.36 percent. Results among individual plans varied widely. Policy returns ranged from 9.47 percent to 10.57 percent. Contributions from timing ranged from -2.68 percent to +0.25 percent. Contributions from selection ranged from -2.90 percent to +3.60 percent. Overall active management contributed between -4.17 percent to +3.69 percent. BHB noted that the standard deviation of policy returns was quite low, 0.22 percent, versus the standard deviations of the results from the other three quadrants. The standard deviation of actual portfolio returns was 1.43 percent, prompting BHB to conclude that active investment not only subtracted value, but also increased risk.

Next, BHB looked at the variance explained by policy, policy and timing, and policy and selection. Variance explained, as shown in Table 3–4, is equivalent to the R-squares of 91 regression equations using each quadrant's return as the independent variable and the plan's actual return as the dependent variable. Astonishingly, BHB found that policy explained on average a whopping 93.6 percent of total plan variance. policy and timing explained 95.3 percent of total plan variance, while policy and selection explained 97.8 percent of total plan variance. These results were the strongest argument ever developed for the importance of asset allocation.

In a follow-up article published in the May-June 1991 issue of the *Financial Analysts Journal*, BHB found nearly identical results. Tables 3–5, 3–6, and 3–7 provide the 1991 results that correspond with Tables 3–2, 3–3, and 3–4, respectively. In the second study, the average asset class weights, excluding "other," were stocks 59.6 percent, bonds 26.9 percent, and cash 13.6 percent. Active investment management cost the plan only 0.08 percent, but the standard deviations of the actual portfolio returns were much higher than the standard deviations of the passive, benchmark index returns, indicating again that active investment management increased risk. Finally, policy explained 91.5 percent of total plan variance, demonstrating yet again the importance of asset allocation.

TABLE 3–4 Variance Explained

	Average	**Minimum**	**Maximum**	**Std. Deviation**
Policy	93.6%	75.5%	98.6%	4.4%
Policy and Timing	95.3%	78.7%	98.7%	2.9%
Policy and Selection	97.8%	80.6%	99.8%	3.1%

TABLE 3–5 Summary of Asset Class Weights

All Holdings	Average	Minimum	Maximum	Std. Deviation	Policy Benchmark
Common Stocks	53.0%	26.0%	79.1%	10.8%	S&P 500 Index
Bonds	24.5%	4.0%	53.1%	10.4%	Shearson Lehman Gov't / Corp. Bond Index
Cash Equivalents	12.1%	3.0%	24.1%	4.6%	30 Day Treasury Bills
Other	10.5%	0.1%	65.4%	12.0%	None
	100.0%				

Stocks, Bonds, and Cash Only	Average	Minimum	Maximum	Std. Deviation
Common Stocks	59.6%	36.5%	83.9%	10.5%
Bonds	26.9%	5.6%	54.0%	10.2%
Cash Equivalents	13.6%	3.5%	24.3%	4.9%
	100.0%			

TABLE 3–6 Annualized 10-Year Returns and Risk by Activity

Portfolio Total Returns	Avg. Return	Minimum Return	Maximum Return	Std. Deviation
Policy	13.49%	12.43%	14.56%	0.49%
Policy and Timing	13.23%	11.26%	15.09%	0.68%
Policy and Selection	13.75%	10.52%	19.32%	1.66%
Actual Portfolio	13.41%	10.34%	19.95%	1.75%
Active Returns				
Timing Only	-0.26%	-1.81%	0.86%	0.47%
Security Selection Only	0.26%	-3.32%	6.12%	1.52%
Other	-0.07%	-3.50%	1.33%	0.80%
Total Active Return	-0.08%	-3.43%	6.73%	1.67%

TABLE 3–7 Variance Explained

	Average	Minimum	Maximum	Std. Deviation
Policy	91.5%	67.7%	98.2%	6.6%
Policy and Timing	93.3%	69.4%	98.3%	5.2%
Policy and Selection	96.1%	76.2%	99.8%	5.2%

Measuring the Importance of Asset Allocation

One important question is, what do BHB mean when they say asset allocation policy explains 93.6 percent of total returns? This has been a source of great misunderstanding and misrepresentation over the years. One way to begin to answer that question is to discuss what it does *not* mean. The usual interpretation of the BHB results is to assume that since policy explains 93.6 percent of total returns and policy and timing explains 95.3 percent of total returns, timing must explain 1.7 percent of total returns. Likewise, since policy and selection explains 97.8 percent of returns, selection must explain 4.2 percent of total returns. Usually, this relationship is shown in a pie chart like Chart 3–1. The implication is that asset allocation policy is 55 times more important than timing and 22 times more important than selection. No matter how you slice it, that is hard to believe.

It is a mathematical fact that the sum of the R-squares of two regressions using two separate variables will be different from the R-square of a multiple regression using the same two variables. Thus, it is incorrect to say that timing and selection explain 1.7 percent and 4.2 percent of total plan return, respectively. A simple example illustrates why. In Table 3–8, we show the results of a random sample of 40 men in which we recorded their heights, waist sizes, and weights. In addition, the table shows the

CHART 3–1 The Usual Interpretation

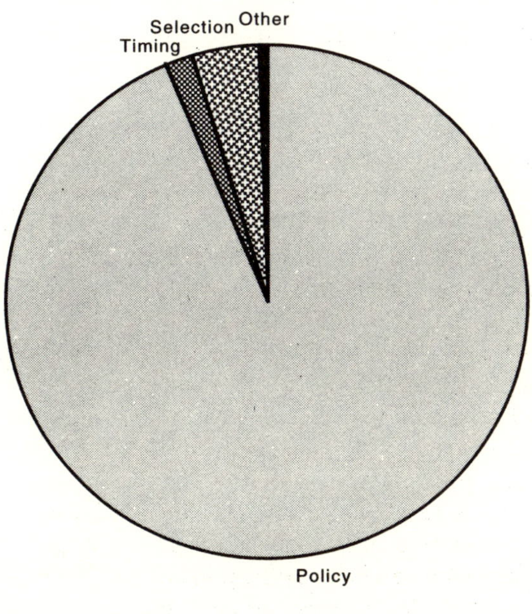

TABLE 3–8 Multiple Regression: An Example

			Height Only Regression		Waist Only Regression		Height and Waist Regression	
			alpha	(208.6)	alpha	(87.2)	alpha	(299.7)
			beta	5.5	beta	7.5	beta 1	3.9
							beta 2	5.8
Height	**Waist**	**Weight**		**Prediction**		**Prediction**		**Prediction**
67.0	29.0	133		162.6		130.7		129.8
64.5	40.5	183		148.7		217.2		186.2
72.0	35.0	188		190.3		175.8		183.9
72.0	34.0	181		190.3		168.3		178.2
69.0	32.0	149		173.7		153.3		154.9
71.5	38.0	195		187.5		198.4		199.2
71.5	32.5	170		187.5		157.0		167.6
70.0	36.0	184		179.2		183.3		181.8
64.5	33.5	151		148.7		164.5		145.9
67.0	31.5	142		162.6		149.5		144.2
81.5	37.0	231		242.9		190.8		232.7
74.0	39.5	220		201.4		209.6		217.7
72.0	34.5	183		190.3		172.1		181.0
68.0	34.0	178		168.1		168.3		162.5
71.5	34.0	185		187.5		168.3		176.2
71.5	38.5	195		187.5		202.1		202.1
72.0	37.0	188		190.3		190.8		195.4
74.0	38.0	207		201.4		198.4		209.0
72.0	38.0	201		190.3		198.4		201.2
71.5	31.5	154		187.5		149.5		161.8
76.0	38.5	227		212.5		202.1		219.7
65.0	32.5	145		151.5		157.0		142.1
73.5	36.5	191		198.6		187.1		198.4
72.0	38.0	202		190.3		198.4		201.2
67.0	32.0	150		162.6		153.3		147.1
71.0	37.5	198		184.8		194.6		194.4
62.0	32.5	129		134.9		157.0		130.4
70.5	32.0	151		182.0		153.3		160.8
67.0	40.5	208		162.6		217.2		196.0
73.5	37.0	216		198.6		190.8		201.3
71.5	39.0	200		187.5		205.9		205.0
72.0	34.5	180		190.3		172.1		181.0
69.5	39.5	197		176.4		209.6		200.0
68.0	35.5	175		168.1		179.6		171.1
71.0	37.0	187		184.8		190.8		191.5
71.0	37.5	197		184.8		194.6		194.4
64.5	32.0	134		148.7		153.3		137.3
65.5	37.0	160		154.3		190.8		170.0
70.0	36.5	173		179.2		187.1		184.7
70.5	34.5	175		182.0		172.1		175.2
	Total	7,213		7,213.0		7,213.0		7,213.0
	Variance	683.8		404.1		467.3		643.7
	R-Squared			59.1%		68.3%		94.1%

results of least-squares regression analyses using each independent variable separately, as well as a multiple regression analysis using both independent variables. The results indicate that we correctly assumed that both height and waist size are important determinants of weight. The height-only regression analysis indicates an alpha of -208.6 and a beta of 5.5, meaning that the prediction for weight is (5.5)(height)-208.6. For the first man in the sample, we would predict a weight of 162.6 pounds, based on a height of 67.0 inches. This turns out to be a poor estimate because we have not considered that he has a waist size of only 29.0 inches. The waist-only regression analysis indicates an alpha of -87.2 and a beta of 7.5, meaning that the prediction for weight is (7.5)(waist size)-87.2. For the second man in the sample, we would predict a weight of 217.2 pounds, based on a waist size of 40.5 inches. Again, this is a poor estimate because we have not considered that he is only 64.5 inches tall. The multiple regression analysis using both variables gives us much better estimates. In cases where one of the variables gives a poor prediction, the other variable will often provide sufficient information so that a prediction based on both variables is more accurate. Using both variables, the prediction for weight is (3.9)(height)+(5.8)(waist size)-299.7. For the first man in the sample, the predicted weight is 129.8 pounds, just slightly less than the actual weight of 133 pounds. For the second man, the predicted weight is 186.2 pounds, just slightly over the actual weight of 183 pounds. The multiple regression using both variables produces an R-square of 94.1 percent. The regression using only height results in an R-square of 59.1 percent. If we erroneously assumed that the R-square for waist size was the difference between the height and waist size R-square and the height R-square, we would conclude that the R-square for waist size would be 35.0 percent. Instead, the R-square for waist size was 68.3 percent. Thus, we can see that the regression equation using both variables explains significantly more variance than the regression equations using either of the variables alone, but the R-squares for each individual variable sum to more than the R-square for the multiple regression. We will probably never know what the average R-squares for timing and selection alone were in the BHB study, but we do know that they were not 1.7 percent and 4.2 percent, respectively.

If asset allocation policy explains 93.6 percent of total plan variance, it stands to reason that policy must be important. BHB themselves claim, "because of its relative importance, investment policy should be addressed carefully and systematically by investors." Yet their own data show that the range of policy returns for the 91 plans was a mere 1.10 percent; the minimum policy return was 9.47 percent and the maximum policy return was 10.57 percent. The standard deviation of policy returns was only 0.22. If policy is so important, why was there so little difference in the policy returns of the 91 plans? It does not appear that there was a significant penalty for bad asset allocation policy or a substantial reward for good asset allocation policy. At the same time, there was a much bigger range in results for timing and security selection. The range of timing returns was 2.93 percent. The range of selection returns was 6.50 percent. Overall, returns from active management had a range of 7.86 percent. There was a very big penalty for bad active management and a very big reward for good active management but because, in aggregate, the results from active management were not statistically different from zero, active management was deemed to be less important than asset allocation policy. These observations would lead us to believe that further investigation into the relative importance of asset allocation and active management are in order.

Simulating the Original BHB Data

Although we do not have access to the original BHB data, we can closely replicate the data using Monte Carlo simulation techniques. Fortunately, BHB described their results in great detail, making simulating their results easier. Our model is somewhat complex, so a brief description of how we constructed it would be helpful. We began by arbitrarily deciding that our model would use 30 "pension plans" instead of the 91 used by BHB. We determined the policy asset mix for each portfolio. From Table 3–2, we can see the average allocation to stocks, bonds, and cash, as well as the minimums, maximums, and standard deviations. We simply selected from a normal distribution to assign policy asset class weights to each of the portfolios. Technically, we assigned the policy weights to bonds and cash and calculated the policy weight for stocks as stocks = 100 percent - bond weight - cash weight.

Once we had established the policy weights, we simulated the tactical shifts in asset class weights over the 40 quarters comprising the test period. The key considerations were the ranges and standard deviations of the policy and timing and timing results reported in Table 3–3. The standard deviations of policy and timing and timing results were 0.52 percent and 0.49 percent, respectively. Our simulation had to strategically shift assets on a quarter-by-quarter basis in order to produce this range of results. There were three variables used to control quarter-by-quarter shifts in asset class weights: a base standard deviation, a divisor to control trending, and an adjustment to the base standard deviation, based on the policy asset class weight. The base standard deviation for bonds and cash was 6 percent, meaning that from one quarter to another, the weight for those asset classes would change by less than 6 percent with 68.3 percent probability and would change by less than 12 percent with 95.4 percent probability. We made each quarter's adjustment to policy weight based on the previous quarter's adjustment to allow for trending. However, we controlled trending using a divisor. For bonds and cash the divisor was 2.0. So if the prior quarter's weight was 10 percent below the policy weight, we selected the next quarter's weight based on a weight of 5 percent below the policy weight. Finally, since the average policy weight for bonds and cash was occasionally close to zero, we wanted to make an adjustment in those cases to reduce the magnitude of asset class shifts when the weight neared zero. This led to the implementation of a standard deviation adjustment, based on the individual plan's asset class policy weights compared with BHB's average observed asset class weights. The lower the plan's asset class policy weight, the smaller the standard deviation used. The higher the plan's asset class policy weight, the higher the standard deviation used. The multiplier was the plan's asset class policy weight divided by the BHB's average plan's asset class weight.

For example, if the plan's policy weight for bonds was 11.7 percent and the average bond weight was 23.4 percent, the multiplier would be 0.50. Thus, we would make quarterly shifts in bond weights based on a standard deviation of (0.50)(6.0 percent), or 3.0 percent. This adjustment helped reduce the volatility of asset class weight shifts when their averages were low and allow for higher volatility when their averages were high. Specifically, this reduced the likelihood that an asset class's weight would fall below zero. Although there was no comment in BHB's paper as to whether leveraged and/or short positions existed in their data, we tried to keep asset class weights below zero to a minimum. Since we take no position on the issue of whether active management adds value, we were content to allow the aggregate contribution from timing to gravitate toward zero rather than try to force it to an average of -0.66 percent.

For security selection, the key considerations were the ranges and standard deviations of the policy and selection and selection results reported in Table 3–3. The standard deviations of policy and selection and selection results were 1.33 percent and 1.36 percent, respectively. Our simulation had to allow for both variation among plans and consistency within plans. Two variables were used to control selection: a base standard deviation and a selection magnifier. The base standard deviations for stocks, bonds, and cash were 2.8 percent, 0.3 percent, and 0.1 percent, respectively. So for stocks, we would expect the investment manager to perform within 2.8 percent of the benchmark index 68.3 percent of the time and within 5.6 percent of the benchmark index 95.4 percent of the time. We used the selection magnifier to account for the fact that different plans would have different strategies with regard to deviation from the benchmark index. In the extreme, a plan that indexed 100 percent of plan assets would have no deviation from the index, meaning that a 0 percent quarterly standard deviation would be appropriate. On the other end of the spectrum, some plans might have more exposure to mid- and small-cap stocks, which would have lower correlations with S&P 500 returns, or allow their investment managers more freedom to deviate from benchmark returns. We used a magnifier to account for this possibility. We set the plan's stock selection magnifier as (random number between 0 and 1)(1.5)+0.25. The range of magnifiers was 0.25 to 1.75. Once we had established the plan's magnifier, it stayed constant for the entire 10-year period. By implementing the magnifier, we were able to individualize the quarterly standard deviation for stock selection. Instead of a fixed 2.8 percent, it ranged from 0.7 through 4.9 percent.

On the bond side, we used the magnifier differently. We established that deviations from the index return could come from two sources, straight security selection and deviations between plan duration and index duration. We used the magnifier to account for the amount by which security selection returns differed from the index because of a differing duration strategy. In computing the bond magnifier, we also considered that there would be a relationship between the stock magnifier and the bond magnifier. In other words, there would be a positive relationship between the extent to which a plan indexed its stock returns and how closely its bond duration would match the index. We calculated the bond magnifier by selecting from a normal distribution with a mean of 1.0, and a standard deviation of (0.15)(stock magnifier). Once we had determined the bond magnifier, we calculated quarterly bond returns by selecting from a normal distribution with a mean of (benchmark index return)(bond selection magnifier) and standard deviation of (0.30 percent)(bond selection magnifier). We simply took the cash return from a normal distribution with a mean equal to the benchmark return and standard deviation of 0.10 percent. We targeted the average selection effect to be zero rather than attempting to force it to -0.36 percent.

While intended to be fairly comprehensive, this model is not and does not have to be perfect. We could probably incorporate further refinements to make the data match the BHB results even closer but, for our purposes, the results obtained are sufficient. We have assembled these data so that we can look at the BHB research from a slightly different viewpoint. Table 3–9 briefly summarizes the results from our simulations, combining all elements of Tables 3–2, 3–3, and 3–4. The average weights for stocks, bonds, and cash were 62.4 percent, 23.6 percent, and 13.4 percent, respectively. These figures are very close to those obtained by BHB, as we would expect given the manner in which we generated them. The range of asset class weights are narrower than the BHB observations, indicating that the BHB study included some distant outliers not ade-

TABLE 3–9 Summary of Results

Summary of Asset Class Weights

	Average	Minimum	Maximum	Std. Deviation
Stocks	62.4%	42.4%	81.7%	10.6%
Bonds	23.6%	7.7%	40.5%	8.9%
Cash	13.4%	1.0%	24.5%	5.6%

Annualized 10-Year Returns and Risk by Activity

	Average	Minimum	Maximum	Std. Deviation
Policy	10.11%	9.65%	10.42%	0.22%
Policy and Timing	10.11%	8.74%	11.14%	0.59%
Policy and Selection	10.13%	7.04%	12.67%	1.44%
Actual Portfolio	10.14%	6.88%	12.56%	1.52%
Timing	0.02%	-0.87%	0.78%	0.45%
Selection	0.03%	-3.07%	2.18%	1.36%
Other	0.03%	-0.20%	0.28%	0.10%

Variance Explained

	Average	Minimum	Maximum	Std. Deviation
Policy	93.0%	80.5%	98.7%	5.2%
Policy and Timing	94.1%	81.2%	99.5%	4.7%
Policy and Selection	98.5%	95.6%	99.8%	1.2%

quately handled by our model. Overall, the standard deviations for the asset class weights are consistent with the BHB data.

The average policy return was 10.11 percent, with a minimum return of 9.65 percent and a maximum return of 10.42 percent. The standard deviation among policy returns was 0.22 percent, an exact match with the BHB data. For policy and timing, the range of returns was slightly wider than under policy: The average return was 10.11 percent, but the minimum return was 8.74 percent and the maximum return was 11.14 percent. The standard deviation was 0.59 percent. The range was significantly lower than shown in the BHB data, even though the standard deviation was slightly higher. Our interpretation of this effect is that the BHB data was not normally distributed, but more centrally distributed with one or two extreme outliers. This is not just the case for policy and timing, but for all their results to some extent. For policy and selection, the range of returns was even wider still: The average return was 10.13 percent, while the minimum return was 7.04 percent, and the maximum return was 12.67 percent. The standard deviation was 1.44 percent. Finally, the actual portfolio had an average return of 10.14 percent, a minimum return of 6.88 percent, a maximum return of 12.56 percent, and a standard deviation of 1.52 percent. All of these data are reasonably close to those reported by BHB. We can make the same conclusion BHB made—active management did not add value, although in our case we do not say active management subtracted value; and active management increased risk, if we define risk as the standard deviations of the results among plans.

Finally, under variance explained, our results closely matched the BHB results. The average variance explained for policy, policy and timing, and policy and selection were 93.0 percent, 94.1 percent, and 98.5 percent, respectively. While true that our minimums under variance explained were higher than those found by BHB, this is likely caused by the fact that BHB did not remove the "other" asset class from total plan returns, and in some cases the "other" component was relatively large. We feel that if BHB had removed the "other" component from their analysis, their results would have been closer to those we obtained. Overall, the results closely match the BHB results and provide us with the information we need to make some important observations.

Table 3–10 provides the benchmark index returns for stocks, bonds, and cash over the 10-year period from 1974 through 1983. Table 3–11 provides quarter-by-quarter results for one portfolio out of our sample of 30. The actual asset class weights are in the first three rows. Stocks ranged

TABLE 3–10 Benchmark Index Returns: 1974–1983

	1Q74	2Q74	3Q74	4Q74	1Q75	2Q75	3Q75	4Q75	1Q76	2Q76
Stocks	-2.8%	-7.6%	-25.2%	9.4%	22.9%	15.4%	-11.0%	8.6%	15.0%	2.5%
Bonds	-1.8%	-3.5%	0.1%	5.6%	3.7%	2.8%	-1.1%	6.4%	3.9%	1.1%
Cash	1.8%	2.1%	2.1%	1.8%	1.4%	1.3%	1.5%	1.5%	1.2%	1.2%

	3Q76	4Q76	1Q77	2Q77	3Q77	4Q77	1Q78	2Q78	3Q78	4Q78
Stocks	1.9%	3.1%	-7.4%	3.3%	-2.8%	-0.1%	-4.9%	8.5%	8.7%	-4.9%
Bonds	4.3%	5.5%	-0.8%	3.0%	0.8%	0.0%	0.5%	-0.3%	2.6%	-1.6%
Cash	1.3%	1.2%	1.1%	1.2%	1.3%	1.5%	1.5%	1.6%	1.8%	2.2%

	1Q79	2Q79	3Q79	4Q79	1Q80	2Q80	3Q80	4Q80	1Q81	2Q81
Stocks	7.1%	2.7%	7.5%	0.1%	-4.1%	13.4%	11.2%	9.5%	1.3%	-2.3%
Bonds	2.6%	3.9%	-1.1%	-3.0%	-8.3%	18.1%	-6.2%	1.5%	0.7%	0.0%
Cash	2.3%	2.4%	2.4%	2.8%	2.9%	2.7%	1.9%	3.3%	3.4%	3.6%

	3Q81	4Q81	1Q82	2Q82	3Q82	4Q82	1Q83	2Q83	3Q83	4Q83
Stocks	-10.2%	7.0%	-7.3%	-0.5%	11.5%	18.3%	10.0%	11.0%	-0.2%	0.4%
Bonds	-3.4%	10.3%	3.6%	2.8%	13.8%	8.3%	3.1%	1.6%	1.5%	1.5%
Cash	3.8%	3.2%	2.7%	3.2%	2.3%	1.9%	2.0%	2.1%	2.3%	2.2%

TABLE 3–11 One Simulated Portfolio

	1Q74	2Q74	3Q74	4Q74	1Q75	2Q75	3Q75	4Q75	1Q76	2Q76	3Q76	4Q76	1Q77	2Q77	3Q77	4Q77
Actual Stock Weight	49.9%	62.6%	64.0%	57.1%	60.3%	47.9%	52.4%	64.1%	63.2%	58.2%	49.5%	58.0%	44.5%	62.3%	61.0%	70.8%
Actual Bond Weight	36.4%	30.5%	24.0%	28.3%	32.7%	32.3%	32.9%	25.3%	25.8%	24.6%	35.9%	30.4%	35.7%	19.9%	22.2%	16.2%
Actual Cash Weight	13.7%	7.0%	12.1%	14.6%	7.0%	19.8%	14.6%	10.6%	11.0%	17.3%	14.7%	11.5%	19.8%	17.8%	16.8%	13.0%
Actual Stock Return	-4.2%	-10.2%	-26.6%	11.4%	24.9%	14.7%	-13.0%	6.2%	15.4%	1.8%	-0.9%	2.8%	-8.3%	4.2%	-2.4%	-2.7%
Actual Bond Return	-1.5%	-3.3%	0.0%	5.5%	3.5%	2.9%	-0.6%	5.7%	4.0%	0.9%	3.6%	5.0%	-0.2%	2.8%	0.5%	0.0%
Actual Cash Return	1.7%	2.1%	2.2%	1.8%	1.4%	1.5%	1.6%	1.3%	1.3%	1.1%	1.4%	1.1%	1.1%	1.1%	1.3%	1.5%
Policy	-1.9%	-5.2%	-14.6%	7.3%	14.8%	10.0%	-6.6%	7.1%	10.1%	1.9%	2.5%	3.5%	-4.5%	3.0%	-1.3%	0.1%
Policy and Timing	-1.8%	-5.6%	-15.8%	7.2%	15.1%	8.5%	-5.9%	7.3%	10.6%	1.9%	2.7%	3.6%	-3.4%	2.9%	-1.3%	0.1%
Policy and Selection	-2.7%	-6.7%	-15.4%	8.5%	15.9%	9.7%	-7.6%	5.4%	10.4%	1.4%	0.7%	3.2%	-4.9%	3.4%	-1.1%	-1.4%
Actual Portfolio	-2.4%	-7.3%	-16.8%	8.3%	16.3%	8.3%	-6.8%	5.6%	10.9%	1.4%	1.1%	3.3%	-3.6%	3.3%	-1.1%	-1.7%
Timing	0.1%	-0.5%	-1.3%	-0.1%	0.4%	-1.5%	0.7%	0.2%	0.5%	0.0%	0.2%	0.1%	1.1%	-0.1%	-0.1%	0.0%
Selection	-0.7%	-1.5%	-0.9%	1.2%	1.1%	-0.4%	-1.0%	-1.7%	0.3%	-0.5%	-1.8%	-0.3%	-0.4%	0.4%	0.2%	-1.5%
Active Management	-0.5%	-2.1%	-2.2%	1.0%	1.5%	-1.8%	-0.2%	-1.5%	0.8%	-0.5%	-1.4%	-0.3%	0.9%	0.4%	0.1%	-1.8%
Passive Policy	-1.9%	-5.3%	-15.4%	7.4%	15.4%	10.4%	-6.9%	7.1%	10.4%	2.0%	2.4%	3.4%	-4.7%	2.9%	-1.4%	0.1%
Active Policy	0.0%	0.1%	0.8%	-0.1%	-0.6%	-0.4%	0.3%	0.0%	-0.3%	0.0%	0.1%	0.1%	0.2%	0.0%	0.1%	0.0%

	1Q78	2Q78	3Q78	4Q78	1Q79	2Q79	3Q79	4Q79	1Q80	2Q80	3Q80	4Q80	1Q81	2Q81	3Q81	4Q81
Actual Stock Weight	58.7%	58.6%	58.5%	43.1%	56.7%	43.0%	58.5%	46.7%	53.5%	60.1%	67.6%	51.9%	67.9%	65.5%	74.0%	63.8%
Actual Bond Weight	30.2%	16.7%	25.4%	32.7%	31.2%	37.8%	27.5%	35.2%	37.7%	28.6%	29.1%	30.8%	26.4%	25.7%	14.9%	32.1%
Actual Cash Weight	11.2%	24.7%	16.1%	24.2%	12.1%	19.2%	14.0%	18.1%	8.7%	11.4%	3.3%	17.2%	5.7%	8.8%	11.0%	4.1%
Actual Stock Return	-5.5%	10.4%	10.2%	-4.2%	7.6%	2.0%	6.9%	-2.5%	-6.2%	13.6%	11.1%	9.2%	2.6%	-1.5%	-7.8%	6.3%
Actual Bond Return	0.3%	-0.1%	2.3%	-1.3%	2.3%	3.5%	-1.4%	-3.4%	-7.3%	16.4%	-5.5%	1.3%	1.0%	0.2%	-2.9%	9.0%
Actual Cash Return	1.6%	1.5%	1.9%	2.1%	2.2%	2.4%	2.4%	2.9%	2.9%	2.7%	2.0%	3.2%	3.3%	3.7%	3.9%	3.1%
Policy	-2.6%	5.1%	6.1%	-3.1%	5.2%	3.0%	4.5%	-0.4%	-4.4%	13.3%	5.1%	6.4%	1.4%	-0.9%	-6.5%	7.4%
Policy and Timing	-2.6%	5.3%	6.0%	-2.1%	5.1%	3.1%	4.4%	-0.5%	-5.1%	13.5%	5.8%	5.9%	1.3%	-1.2%	-7.7%	7.9%
Policy and Selection	-2.9%	6.3%	6.9%	-2.6%	5.4%	2.4%	4.0%	-2.1%	-5.3%	13.0%	5.3%	6.2%	2.3%	-0.3%	-4.9%	6.6%
Actual Portfolio	-3.0%	6.4%	6.9%	-1.7%	5.3%	2.6%	4.0%	-1.8%	-5.8%	13.2%	6.0%	5.7%	2.2%	-0.6%	-5.8%	7.0%

TABLE 3–11 *(Continued)*

	1Q78	2Q78	3Q78	4Q78	1Q79	2Q79	3Q79	4Q79	1Q80	2Q80	3Q80	4Q80	1Q81	2Q81	3Q81	4Q81
Timing	0.0%	0.2%	-0.1%	1.0%	-0.1%	0.1%	0.0%	-0.1%	-0.7%	0.2%	0.7%	-0.5%	-0.1%	-0.3%	-1.2%	0.5%
Selection	-0.4%	1.1%	0.8%	0.5%	0.2%	-0.6%	-0.4%	-1.7%	-1.0%	-0.4%	0.2%	-0.2%	0.9%	0.6%	1.6%	-0.8%
Active Management	-0.4%	1.3%	0.8%	1.3%	0.1%	-0.4%	-0.4%	-1.4%	-1.4%	-0.2%	0.9%	-0.7%	0.8%	0.3%	0.7%	-0.4%
Passive Policy	-2.8%	5.4%	6.3%	-3.2%	5.3%	3.0%	4.8%	-0.2%	-4.1%	13.0%	5.8%	6.7%	1.4%	-1.0%	-6.7%	7.2%
Active Policy	0.2%	-0.3%	-0.2%	0.1%	-0.1%	0.1%	-0.3%	-0.2%	-0.2%	0.3%	-0.7%	-0.3%	0.0%	0.1%	0.2%	0.2%

	1Q82	2Q82	3Q82	4Q82	1Q83	2Q83	3Q83	4Q83	Avg.	RSquare
Actual Stock Weight	49.2%	62.5%	64.6%	74.1%	61.2%	69.8%	61.5%	63.2%	59.0%	
Actual Bond Weight	31.7%	30.8%	21.8%	15.7%	33.5%	18.5%	31.4%	24.0%	28.1%	
Actual Cash Weight	19.0%	6.6%	13.6%	10.2%	5.3%	11.7%	7.1%	12.9%	12.9%	
Actual Stock Return	-6.5%	-1.6%	11.1%	20.9%	8.1%	10.4%	-1.7%	-0.2%		
Actual Bond Return	2.8%	2.5%	13.0%	7.5%	2.9%	1.5%	1.4%	1.6%		
Actual Cash Return	2.5%	3.2%	2.3%	1.9%	2.0%	2.1%	2.2%	2.1%		
Policy	-3.0%	0.9%	11.0%	13.3%	7.0%	7.2%	0.6%	1.0%	10.04%	97.3%
Policy and Timing	-1.9%	0.7%	10.8%	15.0%	7.3%	8.2%	0.5%	0.9%	10.29%	98.2%
Policy and Selection	-2.7%	0.2%	10.5%	14.7%	5.8%	6.8%	-0.3%	0.6%	8.94%	99.1%
Actual Portfolio	-1.8%	0.0%	10.3%	16.8%	6.0%	7.8%	-0.5%	0.5%	9.32%	100.0%
Timing	1.0%	-0.1%	-0.2%	1.7%	0.2%	1.0%	-0.1%	0.0%	0.27%	13.6%
Selection	0.2%	-0.7%	-0.5%	1.3%	-1.2%	-0.4%	-1.0%	-0.3%	-0.97%	14.2%
Active Management	1.1%	-0.9%	-0.6%	3.5%	-1.0%	0.6%	-1.1%	-0.4%	-0.58%	23.6%
Passive Policy	-3.4%	0.7%	10.7%	13.6%	7.2%	7.5%	0.6%	0.9%	10.1%	97.3%
Active Policy	0.4%	0.1%	0.2%	-0.3%	-0.2%	-0.3%	0.1%	0.0%	-0.1%	36.9%

from 43.0 percent to 74.1 percent. Bonds ranged from 14.9 percent to 37.8 percent. Cash ranged from 3.3 percent to 24.7 percent. The policy weights were 59.0 percent, 28.1 percent, and 12.9 percent for stocks, bonds, and cash, respectively. Chart 3–2 shows in graphical form the quarterly shifts in asset class weights. With a bond policy weight for this portfolio of 28.1 percent, slightly higher than the BHB average bond policy weight of 23.4 percent, the adjustment to standard deviation for quarter-by-quarter shifts in bond weights is 120 percent. Likewise, with a cash policy weight of 12.9 percent, slightly lower than the BHB average cash policy weight of 13.6 percent, the adjustment for cash is 95 percent. The actual asset class returns are in the next three rows. The stock selection magnifier was 59 percent, meaning that this portfolio's stock investments were managed in such a way that returns would deviate much less from the benchmark index than the average portfolio. The bond selection magnifier was 90 percent, meaning that we would expect bond returns to be 90 percent less volatile than the benchmark index returns.

The calculations for each quadrant in the BHB framework are in the next four rows. Refer to the discussion accompanying Table 3–1 for a review of how we calculated these figures. The annualized policy return was 10.04 percent. Policy return explained 97.3 percent of actual portfolio variance. Similarly, the policy and timing return was 10.29 percent, while explaining 98.2 percent of portfolio variance. The policy and selection return was 8.94 percent, while explaining 99.1 percent of portfolio variance. Finally, the actual portfolio return was 9.32 percent.

The next data section in Table 3–11, which BHB did not provide, contains the quarter-by-quarter contributions to returns from timing, selection, and active management alone. As BHB noted, each level of active management adds to overall portfolio risk. Our results confirm this observation. Chart 3–3 shows the quarter-by-quarter contributions from timing. Overall, timing added 0.27 percent to returns annually, with annualized standard deviation of 0.62 percent. Some quarters, such as the second quarter of 1975 and the fourth quarter of 1982, added significantly to overall plan risk. There were 5 quarters out of 40 with contributions from timing outside the range of -1.0 percent and +1.0 percent. Chart 3–4 shows the quarter-by-quarter contributions from selection. Selection cost the plan 0.97 percent annually. Even though the stock selection magnifier was only 0.59 and the bond selection magnifier was 0.90—both below average—the annualized standard deviation from selection returns was 0.89 percent. For selection, the third quarter of 1976 and the third quarter of 1981 were the biggest contributors to plan risk, but there were several others. There were 11 quarters with contributions from selection outside the range of -1.0 percent and +1.0 percent. As noted by BHB, the risk from

CHART 3–2 Quarterly Shifts in Asset Class Weights

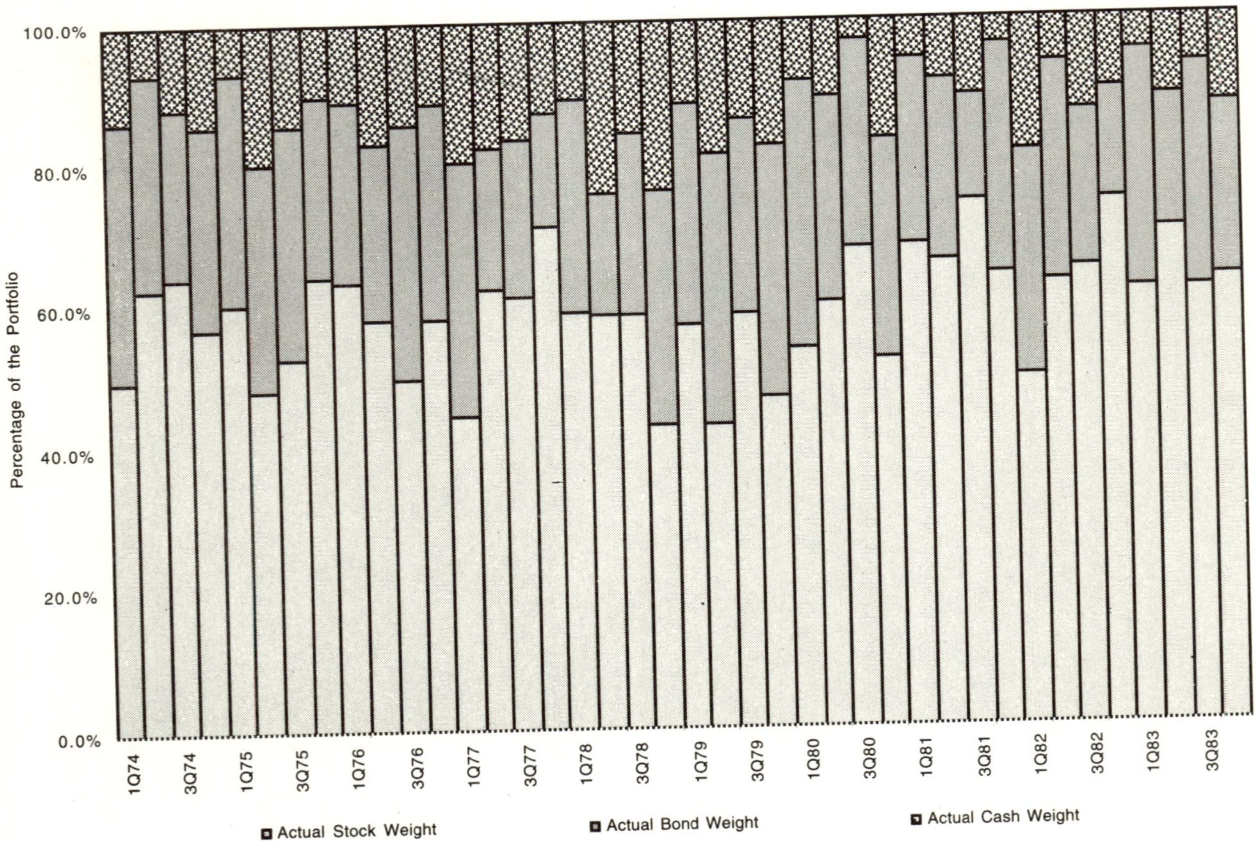

CHART 3–3 Quarter-by-Quarter Contributions from Timing

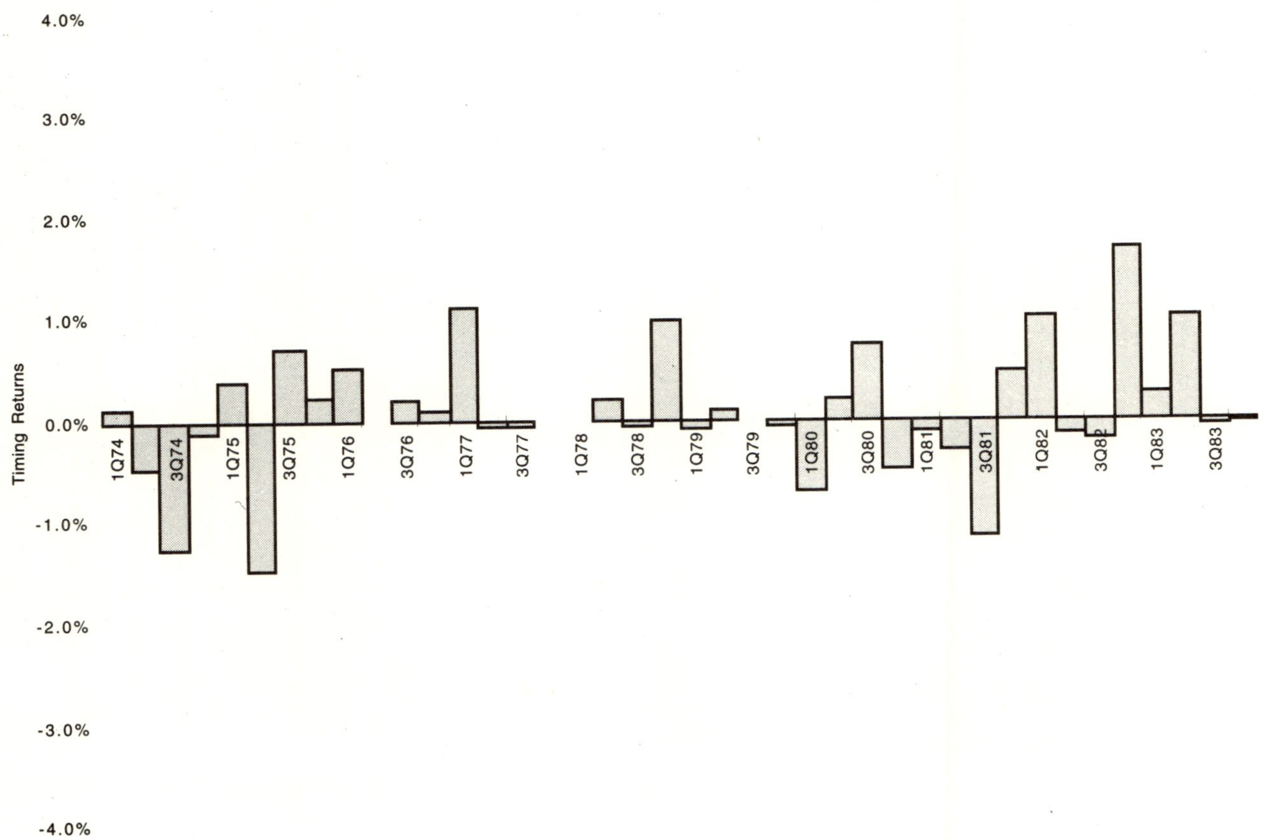

CHART 3–4 Quarter-by-Quarter Contributions from Selection

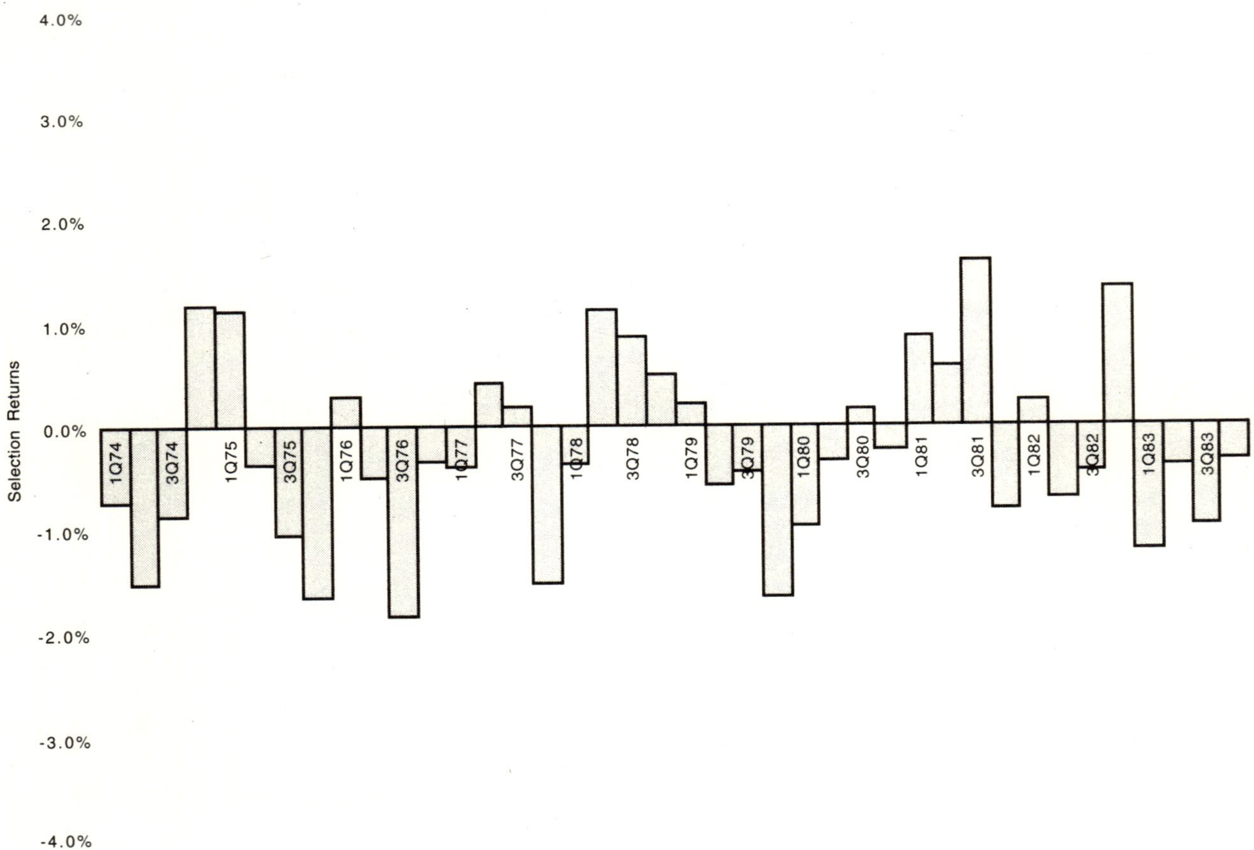

the individual components of investment return are somewhat additive, so the risk from overall active management is very high when compared with the passive, benchmark index. Our data also produce a similar observation. Chart 3–5 shows the quarter-by-quarter contributions from active management. Active management resulted in an annualized loss of 0.58 percent to the plan versus the passive, benchmark return. In addition, the standard deviation of active management returns was 1.18 percent. Clearly, in this sample, active management subtracted value while increasing risk, if we define risk in this way. There were 14 quarters with active management returns outside the range of -1.0 percent and +1.0 percent and 3 quarters outside the range of -2.0 percent and +2.0 percent. The fourth quarter of 1982 produced a whopping +3.49 percent return.

Absolute Risk *versus* Relative Risk

The issue of whether this is a valid measure of risk falls somewhat outside the scope of this analysis, but it is worth pointing out that the annualized standard deviation of quarterly policy returns was 6.20 percent, while the standard deviation of the quarterly actual portfolio returns was 6.69 percent, a difference of only 0.49 percent. The difference lies in the fact that the first measure, 1.18 percent, calculates the standard deviation relative to the target benchmark return, and the second measure, indicating added standard deviation of 0.49 percent, calculates the standard deviation relative to zero. Conceivably, the portfolio could be managed using securities less volatile than the market, in which case we would expect the standard deviation of actual portfolio returns to be even lower than the standard deviation of the passive, benchmark index returns. In general, this is not likely to be the case, but in our sample of 30 portfolios, 7 produced actual portfolio standard deviations lower than the benchmark index. Obviously, the standard deviation of active management returns considered alone cannot be negative, because by definition standard deviation is a positive number.

In summary, this illustrates the difference between absolute risk and relative risk. A portfolio managed to produce lower variance in return must add incrementally to risk when measured against the benchmark index, but when viewed absolutely it can produce lower variance than the benchmark index. Before claiming that active management increases risk, it is important to define exactly what we mean by risk and then defend whether it is a valid measure thereof. We have looked at two ways in which we could define the riskiness of a portfolio, both of which are different from the way in which BHB defined risk when they claimed that active management added to risk. However, since we share general

CHART 3–5 Quarter-by-Quarter Contributions from Active Management

agreement that active management increases risk, we will not spend more time on this issue. Suffice it to say that the subject of risk, and how we define risk, is complex. It is important to understand how risk is being defined in any instance in which something is claimed to be riskier than something else.

Timing, Selection, and Active Management

Earlier, we discussed an example where we performed regression analyses using height and waist size as independent variables and weight as the dependent variable. We found that the R-squares for height and waist size alone when added together surpassed the R-square for height and waist size taken together. With our simulated data, we can now look at the R-squares for timing, selection, and active management alone. The results show that the importance of timing, selection, and active management is much higher than would be implied by the usual interpretation of the BHB data.

For the sample portfolio as that shown in Table 3–11, timing alone resulted in an R-square of 13.6 percent. This is not a high value but it is much higher than 0.9 percent, the amount implied by subtracting the R-square for policy from the R-square for policy and timing. Selection alone resulted in an R-square of 14.2 percent. Again, this is not a high value, but it is higher than the implied amount. Finally, active management produced an R-square of 23.6 percent. Table 3–12 summarizes these figures for all 30 portfolios in our simulation. On average, timing explains 9.5 percent of total portfolio variance, selection 9.8 percent, and active management 14.1 percent. While these figures are very low relative to the 93.0 percent for policy, they are not inconsequential.

Before continuing, it will be helpful to define two important concepts, cause and reflection, and how they relate to the BHB data. One interpretation of the finding that policy asset allocation explains 93.6 percent of total plan variance is that it is important to carefully consider policy asset allocation because that decision will greatly impact the overall plan return. Underpinning this interpretation is causality: Certain asset allocation decisions will cause certain portfolio results. Another interpre-

TABLE 3–12 Variance Explained

	Average	Minimum	Maximum	Std. Deviation
Timing	9.5%	0.0%	34.2%	9.7%
Selection	9.8%	0.1%	44.9%	10.9%
Active Management	14.1%	0.0%	49.4%	14.6%

tation is that it just happens to be, in aggregate, that 91 large pension plans managed their portfolios in such a way that 93.6 percent of total plan variance was explained by policy asset allocation. The number, 93.6 percent, simply is a reflection of an aggregate investment policy. We know, from Table 3–4, that plans engaged in many different investment policies. In one case, policy explained only 75.5 percent of plan return. In another case, policy explained 98.6 percent of plan return. Individual plans seem to have some control over the importance of policy asset allocation to their overall return.

Theoretically, plan sponsors could establish a particular asset allocation policy and never deviate from it. They would continuously rebalance and index all investments in stocks, bonds, and cash. They would never use any "other" assets. If a plan adopted this policy, its policy return would be identical to the total plan return. Policy return would explain 100 percent of total plan variance.

On the other hand, the plan sponsors could establish a policy where they would invest 100 percent of plan assets in the asset class that they determined would be the best-performing asset class every quarter, based on their evaluation of the prospects for stocks, bonds, and cash. They would invest nothing in the two asset classes expected to underperform for the quarter. Quarter after quarter, they would liquidate the entire portfolio and reinvest in response to their ever-changing outlook for the three asset classes. After 10 years, the policy mix, as determined by taking the average of each asset class's weight, might be something like one-third stocks, one-third bonds, and one-third cash. In any given quarter, the portfolio would always be invested 100 percent in one asset class and 0 percent in the other two asset classes, so it stands to reason that a passive, benchmark index created using an asset mix of one-third stocks, one-third bonds, and one-third cash would not explain very much of the variance of this particular plan. We would expect that policy and timing or timing alone would explain a very high percentage of total plan return.

If the plan had chosen to index its security selection, policy and timing would explain 100 percent of plan return. Similarly, plan sponsors can control the importance the security selection with their investment policy. A policy to index the three asset classes to the S&P 500 Index, Lehman Brothers Government/Corporate Bond Index, and the 30-day Treasury Bill Index would eliminate any contribution to return from security selection. To the extent that investment policy allows for deviation from these indices, security selection will contribute incrementally more to total plan return.

The plan sponsor controls the extent to which policy, timing, selection, and active management contribute to return. Table 3–12 reflects this.

While we have discussed the average variance explained by timing, selection, and active management, we have not explored the implications of the wide range of results in this table. The near-zero minimum value for timing reflects policy decisions to allow a narrow range of deviation from the policy asset mix. Likewise, the near-zero minimum value for selection reflects policy decisions to index asset class returns, or at least to allow for a much lower level of deviation from the index than other plans. The maximum values for timing, selection, and active management were 34.2 percent, 44.9 percent, and 49.4 percent, respectively—much higher than the averages. These extreme values reflect policy decisions to allow for wider ranges of deviation from the policy asset mix and passive asset class returns. Investment policy causes the relative importance of asset allocation policy and active management. The BHB results merely reflect the aggregate policies of 91 large pension plans.

Active Policy *versus* Passive Policy

Another important concept that we would like to introduce is the difference between active asset allocation policy and passive asset allocation policy. We have noted that BHB defined a plan's asset allocation policy as the average observed quarterly asset class weights, primarily due to lack of more information from the plans themselves. While we will probably never know how accurate their estimates of the plans' asset allocation policies were, they were probably very close and their estimates were certainly reasonable proxies for the actual target asset class weights. In any case, we know that each plan undoubtedly had an asset allocation policy. We define the asset allocation policy established by each plan as the active asset allocation policy, because they had to undergo some kind of an active process to establish it.

Now, suppose that a pension plan did not wish to establish an asset allocation policy. Suppose they preferred a passive approach. We have seen earlier that active timing can be removed by not allowing for deviations from the policy asset mix. We have also seen that active selection can be eliminated by indexing all investments within an asset class. We would like to allow for passive asset allocation policy. As we saw in Table 3–2, BHB found that the average asset class weight, excluding "other" assets, was 62.9 percent stocks, 23.4 percent bonds, and 13.6 percent cash. It seems reasonable that if a plan wanted to avoid an active asset allocation decision, they might choose to set their target asset class weights according to the average asset allocation policy of their peers.

We define passive asset allocation policy as the average asset class weights for all the plans. With so many new terms, some clarification would be helpful. BHB defined asset allocation policy as the average asset class weights over the investment horizon. We have effectively divided this into two components: an active component and a passive component. The passive component represents the case where no asset allocation policy decision is made. Some asset allocation decision must exist, and we simply have defined the lack of a decision to be the average asset class weights. The active component represents the extent to which a plan chooses to differ from the average in its asset allocation policy. Mathematically, the return attributable to active policy, when separated from passive policy, is the passive, benchmark index return calculated using the plan's specific policy weights less the passive, benchmark index return calculated using the average plan's weightings. For simplification, we will refer to these three concepts as policy, active policy, and passive policy.

One practical disadvantage of this definition of passive policy is that a plan sponsor could not know ahead of time what the average asset class weights were for all the other plans. However, the plan sponsor could estimate passive policy and then make active policy decisions based on decisions to overweight or underweight asset classes relative to the passive policy. The distinction between active policy and market timing is important. A plan might determine that passive policy would be 60 percent stocks, 30 percent bonds, and 10 percent cash., then decide that they preferred to overweight stocks and underweight bonds and cash. Their resulting active policy might be 70 percent stocks, 25 percent bonds, and 5 percent cash. This would be a conscious decision, based upon an analysis of the needs of the plan and how they might differ from the average plan. Once asset allocation policy had been established, timing policy would follow. For example, the plan sponsor might establish asset class ranges of 55-85 percent stocks, 15-35 percent bonds, and 0-10 percent cash. Decisions to shift asset class weights within these ranges are timing decisions. The decision to establish the 70 percent stock, 25 percent bond, and 5 percent cash normal weights is the active policy decision.

Looking back to the bottom two rows of Table 3–11, our sample taken from 30 simulated portfolios shows a passive policy return of 10.07 percent and an active policy return of -0.08 percent. In this case, we would compute the passive policy return using the three benchmark indices weighted 62.4 percent stocks, 23.6 percent bonds, and 13.4 percent cash, in accordance with the results in Table 3–9. Amazingly, the passive policy return explains 97.3 percent of this plan's return, even though the passive policy has nothing to do with this particular plan whatsoever. This plan's policy happens to also explain exactly 97.3 percent of its returns. The fact that these two numbers are identical is a coincidence.

This plan has an asset allocation policy with target weights of 56.7 percent stocks, 31.2 percent bonds, and 12.1 percent cash, fairly close to the passive mix, but not as close as we would expect given the R-square of 97.3 percent. We would expect that for plans with target asset class weights more distant from the passive mix, the explanatory power of the passive policy return would be lower. Table 3–13 indicates that passive policy explains on average 92.0 percent of portfolio return, a mere 1.0 percent less than the 93.0 percent reported for policy. The minimum variance explained is 76.9 percent, while the maximum variance explained is 98.7 percent. This is somewhat in line with what we would expect.

The extent to which passive policy explains portfolio return is highly dependent upon the extent to which active policy differs from passive policy. Nevertheless, it is somewhat alarming that passive asset allocation policy explains on average 92.0 percent of variance. BHB concluded that the asset allocation decision is important because it explains 93.6 percent of total portfolio variance, but no asset allocation decision explains 92.0 percent of total portfolio variance. It appears that simply existing, without making any investment decisions at all, dominates all of the actions of the investment professional. Fortunately, for the continued existence of the investment management profession, active management is more important than these data would imply. This result sheds some light on the danger of equating variance explained with importance.

If we were to interpret this data in the same manner as the BHB data has typically been interpreted with regard to timing and selection, we would conclude that active asset allocation policy explains only 1.0 percent of portfolio returns, making it significantly less influential than either timing or policy. However, we saw earlier that timing, selection, and active management alone explain far more of a plan's return than would be implied from that interpretation. We would expect the same to be true of active policy when viewed apart from passive policy. From Table 3–9, we can see that for our one sample, active policy, when separated from passive policy, explains 36.9 percent of portfolio variance. From Table 3–13, we see that active policy explains on average 58.0 percent of plan variance, but the range is very wide. The minimum observa-

TABLE 3–13 Variance Explained

	Average	**Minimum**	**Maximum**	**Std. Deviation**
Passive Policy	92.0%	76.9%	98.7%	6.0%
Active Policy	58.0%	6.4%	95.5%	25.8%

tion was 6.4 percent, the maximum was 95.5 percent, and the standard deviation was 25.8 percent.

Based on our simulated data, we can state that the average variance explained due to active policy is roughly six times greater than both timing and selection and four times greater than active management. It is impossible to know how closely our simulated data approximate the results that BHB would have obtained using their data. We expect that active policy must explain between two and six times the variance of active management. While certainly significant, this figure is much lower than the usual interpretation of the BHB data would imply. To repeat, we cannot safely imply importance from variance explained. These results are merely reflective of the aggregate results of a number of pension plans. The relative importance of any component of investment return can be controlled to a large extent through investment policy. The actual importance of asset allocation, or every other component of investment return, is a function of a number of important policy decisions made by the plan sponsor as well as the abilities of their investment managers.

An Alternative to the BHB Model

Up to now we have focused exclusively on the assumption that variance explained denoted importance. Now, we will look at the importance of asset allocation from another perspective, based on the observation we made earlier that there does not appear to be a significant penalty for bad asset allocation policy or a significant reward for good asset allocation policy. Active management exhibited a wide range of possibilities, both bad and good, which tended to cancel each other out. The fact that net contribution from active management was near zero was partly responsible for the conclusion that active management contributed less to overall portfolio return than asset allocation policy. Because we have defined passive policy as the average asset class weights for all plans, it must be true that, in aggregate, active policy returns must be near zero as well. Thus, the task confronting each plan is to produce positive return contributions within each active management component, including active asset allocation policy. We would expect that, in aggregate, the net contribution from each active management component would be about zero. We can define the importance of each component as its range of possible outcomes or, relative to passive asset allocation policy, the range of possible penalties for bad decisions and rewards for good decisions.

Another important element of portfolio return analysis that does not figure in the BHB framework is risk. There is no adjustment made to account for the plan that weights the riskiest asset class, typically stocks, lower than the average plan. There is no mechanism to reward the plan that reduces risk by allowing narrower ranges in their asset class weights. There is no allowance for the general riskiness of security selection within a given asset class. We report results for an equity component with a 1.20 beta exactly the same as the results for the 0.80 beta equity component. Within the BHB framework, a positive-alpha, low-beta return could easily translate into a negative contribution to plan return. It seems logical that we should consider the risk dimension when analyzing the contributions from active management.

Another way that we can define the importance of policy, timing, and selection is to look at the possible ranges of returns within their respective quadrants. We noted earlier that policy returns exhibited a low standard deviation, 0.22 percent, in the BHB study, while timing, selection, and active management exhibited both wider ranges of returns and higher standard deviations. There did not seem to be a particularly large penalty for bad asset allocation policy or a large reward for good asset allocation policy. In addition to range of returns, we will also want to consider the ranges of riskiness for policy, timing, and selection.

Based on these ideas, we designed an alternative model to describe the relative importance of each component of investment return. The idea behind the model is to define specific parameters for policy, timing, and selection, from which we will select return data, allowing one component to fluctuate while holding the other two constant. Once we have selected the return data, we can plot a scatter diagram and observe the distribution of points. As an alternative definition, we can define the relative importance of policy, timing, and selection as the range of possible results obtained in this manner.

For asset allocation policy, we defined passive policy to be stocks 50 percent, bonds 30 percent, cash 10 percent, and foreign stocks 10 percent. The indices for the asset classes were the S&P 500, Lehman Brothers Government/Corporate Bond Index, Salomon Brothers 30-Day Treasury Bill Index, and the MSCI Europe, Australia, and Far East (EAFE) Index. We allowed three different asset class ranges, then randomly selected 3,998 samples using each range. The three ranges were: 0-100 percent stocks, 0-60 percent bonds, 0-20 percent cash, and 0-20 percent foreign stocks; 20-80 percent stocks, 10-50 percent bonds, 5-15 percent cash, and 5-15 percent foreign stocks; and 40-60 percent stocks, 20-40 percent bonds, 7.5-12.5 percent cash, and 7.5-12.5 percent foreign stocks.

We obtained data points by first randomly selecting asset class weights for stocks, bonds, cash, and foreign stocks within the ranges specified above, then dividing each weight by the sum of all the weights, so that they would sum to 100 percent. In some cases, the process of dividing by the sum of all the weights would cause some the asset class weights to deviate outside their allowable range. We discarded those samples. The net effect was that mixes with asset class weights near the outside of their respective ranges were more likely to be discarded than those with asset class weights near the middle of their respective ranges. Since we would expect a tendency for asset class weights to gravitate toward the middle in the real world, we were content with this selection process.

Table 3–14 shows the calculations for our passive 50/30/10/10 stocks/bonds/cash/foreign stocks mix. We used annual returns for each asset class, covering the 10-year period from 1986 through 1995. The weighted contribution to return is calculated by multiplying each asset class's benchmark index return by its policy weight. The 10-year investment return was 226.4 percent, or 12.56 percent annualized. The standard deviation was 9.69 percent. Chart 3–6 shows the distribution of the 3,998 randomly selected data points using the range of weights, stocks 20-80 percent, bonds 10-50 percent, cash 5-15 percent, and foreign stocks 5-15 percent. The x-axis represents the annualized standard deviation; the y-axis the 10-year investment return. Of principal interest is the wide range of possible investment returns. The highest return was 270.x percent, and the lowest 190.x percent—a range of 85.x percent. However, for any given level of risk, there is very little difference between the highest and the lowest observed returns; generally about 5 percent. In other words, there is very little difference between the efficient frontier and the inefficient frontier (those portfolios that provide the least return for a given amount of risk).

To test the relative importance of timing, we selected asset class weights for each individual year using the three different asset class weight ranges and selection method described earlier for policy. The average asset class weight naturally tended toward the 50/30/10/10 stocks/bonds/cash/foreign stocks mix, but we did not make any adjustments to ensure that it was exactly that mix. Thus, we cannot say that we held policy perfectly constant, but the difference should be immaterial.

Table 3–15 shows the calculations allowing each year's asset class weights to fluctuate but holding the average asset class weights to our passive 50/30/10/10 stocks/bonds/cash/foreign stocks mix. The weighted contribution to return is calculated by multiplying each year's benchmark index return by that year's asset class weight. Decisions to over- or underweight asset class weights, relative to policy targets, affects both return and risk. In this case, the investment return was 222.4 percent, or 12.42 percent annualized. The standard deviation was 10.07 percent.

TABLE 3–14 Passive Return Calculations

	Weights	Asset Class Passive, Benchmark Index Returns									
		1986	**1987**	**1988**	**1989**	**1990**	**1991**	**1992**	**1993**	**1994**	**1995**
S&P 500	50.0%	18.21%	5.17%	16.50%	31.44%	-3.19%	30.55%	7.68%	10.00%	1.33%	37.51%
Lehman Bros. Gov't / Corp.	30.0%	15.60%	2.30%	7.59%	14.24%	8.28%	16.13%	7.58%	11.03%	-3.51%	19.24%
Treasury Bills-3 Month	10.0%	6.17%	5.91%	6.76%	8.65%	7.90%	5.75%	3.61%	3.07%	4.22%	5.74%
EAFE	10.0%	69.94%	24.93%	28.59%	10.80%	-23.20%	12.50%	-11.85%	32.95%	8.06%	11.55%

	Weighted Contribution to Plan Return									
	1986	**1987**	**1988**	**1989**	**1990**	**1991**	**1992**	**1993**	**1994**	**1995**
S&P 500	9.11%	2.59%	8.25%	15.72%	-1.60%	15.27%	3.84%	5.00%	0.66%	18.75%
Lehman Bros. Gov't / Corp.	4.68%	0.69%	2.28%	4.27%	2.48%	4.84%	2.27%	3.31%	-1.05%	5.77%
Treasury Bills-3 Month	0.62%	0.59%	0.68%	0.86%	0.79%	0.57%	0.36%	0.31%	0.42%	0.57%
EAFE	6.99%	2.49%	2.86%	1.08%	-2.32%	1.25%	-1.19%	3.29%	0.81%	1.16%
	21.40%	6.36%	14.06%	21.93%	-0.64%	21.94%	5.29%	11.91%	0.84%	26.25%

10-Year Investment Return	226.4%
10-Year Annualized Return	12.56%
Standard Deviation	9.69%

CHART 3–6 Distribution: Policy

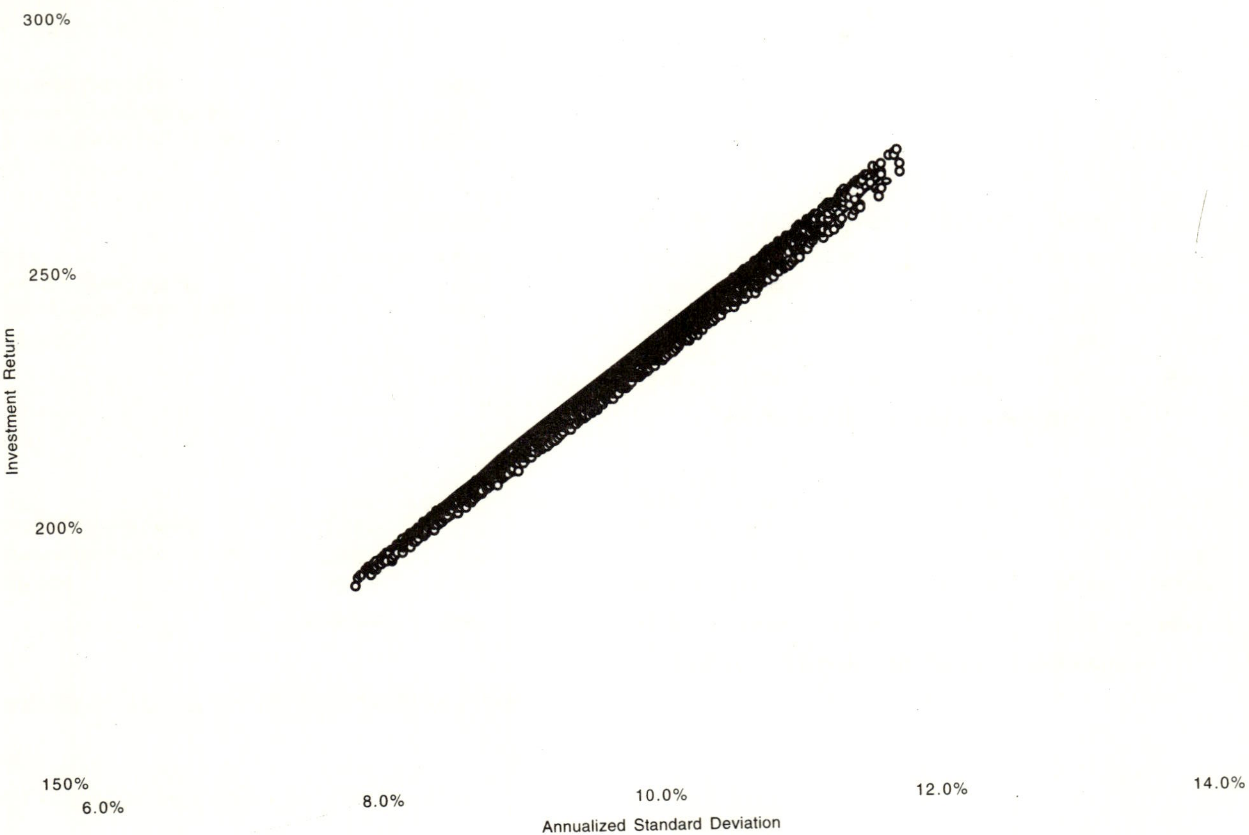

TABLE 3–15 Return Calculations: Actual Timing

Weights

	Avg. Weights	1986	1987	1988	1989	1990	1991	1992	1993	1994	1995
S&P 500	50.0%	37.30%	63.91%	54.77%	50.02%	54.73%	38.16%	42.33%	51.74%	48.06%	58.98%
Lehman Bros. Gov't / Corp.	30.0%	41.30%	21.20%	25.11%	33.31%	23.35%	39.12%	33.77%	26.44%	29.82%	26.59%
Treasury Bills-3 Month	10.0%	11.36%	7.41%	10.84%	9.79%	11.20%	8.03%	9.64%	10.35%	12.93%	8.46%
EAFE	10.0%	10.04%	7.48%	9.29%	6.88%	10.72%	14.70%	14.27%	11.46%	9.19%	5.97%

Asset Class Passive, Benchmark Index Returns

	1986	1987	1988	1989	1990	1991	1992	1993	1994	1995
S&P 500	18.21%	5.17%	16.50%	31.44%	-3.19%	30.55%	7.68%	10.00%	1.33%	37.51%
Lehman Bros. Gov't / Corp.	15.60%	2.30%	7.59%	14.24%	8.28%	16.13%	7.58%	11.03%	-3.51%	19.24%
Treasury Bills-3 Month	6.17%	5.91%	6.76%	8.65%	7.90%	5.75%	3.61%	3.07%	4.22%	5.74%
EAFE	69.94%	24.93%	28.59%	10.80%	-23.20%	12.50%	-11.85%	32.95%	8.06%	11.55%

Weighted Contribution to Plan Return

	1986	1987	1988	1989	1990	1991	1992	1993	1994	1995
S&P 500	6.79%	3.31%	9.04%	15.72%	-1.75%	11.66%	3.25%	5.17%	0.64%	22.12%
Lehman Bros. Gov't / Corp.	6.44%	0.49%	1.91%	4.74%	1.93%	6.31%	2.56%	2.92%	-1.05%	5.12%
Treasury Bills-3 Month	0.70%	0.44%	0.73%	0.85%	0.89%	0.46%	0.35%	0.32%	0.55%	0.49%
EAFE	7.03%	1.87%	2.66%	0.74%	-2.49%	1.84%	-1.69%	3.78%	0.74%	0.69%
	20.96%	6.10%	14.33%	22.06%	-1.41%	20.26%	4.47%	12.19%	0.88%	28.41%

10-Year Investment Return	222.4%
10-Year Annualized Return	12.42%
Standard Deviation	10.07%

Relative to the earlier example where we made no timing decisions, return was lower and risk was higher.

Chart 3–7 shows the distribution of the 3,998 randomly selected data points, again using the range of weights, stocks 20-80 percent, bonds 10-50 percent, cash 5-15 percent, and foreign stocks 5-15 percent. Compared with the policy data, the range of investment returns is smaller and the range of risk is larger. For any given level of risk, there is up to a 50 percent range in observed returns. There is a much wider range between the efficient and inefficient frontiers.

We used the returns from mutual funds to test the relative importance of selection. To allow for different ranges of selection freedom, we took samples using varying numbers of funds for each asset class. The three ranges were three stock, two bond, and one foreign stock funds; five stock, three bond, and two foreign stock funds; and ten stock, five bond, and three foreign stock funds. We selected the mutual funds from the 200, 100, and 25 largest stock, bond, and foreign stock funds, respectively, with full 10-year return records through 1995. We recognize that this selection system suffers from various selection biases, most notably survivorship bias (i.e., funds that have failed are no longer available for selection) and sample bias (i.e., the largest funds in 1995 would likely have been more successful than the others over the past 10 years). Both of these biases would tend to cause us to record overstated returns from selection.

The flip side is that mutual funds report returns net-of-management fees, whereas the passive, benchmark index does not include fees. This bias would tend to cause returns from selection to be understated. Since we do not address the issue of whether active management adds to return, we are content with this selection method. Rather than select from money market funds for the cash component, we used the 30-day Treasury bill return. We calculated the weightings for each fund by taking a random number between one-third and one and one-third for each fund within an asset class and dividing by the sum of the random numbers. This allows a particular fund to be weighted up to four times as heavily as another fund.

Table 3–16 shows the calculations for one random selection using five stock, three bond, and two foreign stock funds. Once we had determined the weights for each fund within an asset class, we held them constant for the entire 10-year period. We held the weights constant at our policy mix of 50/30/10/10 stocks/bonds/cash/foreign stocks. We calculated returns for each asset class by multiplying the fund's weighting by its return, then weighting the asset class returns 50/30/10/10. In this case, the 10-year investment return was 235.3 percent, or 12.86 percent annualized. The standard deviation was 12.05 percent. Compared to the

CHART 3–7 Distribution: Timing

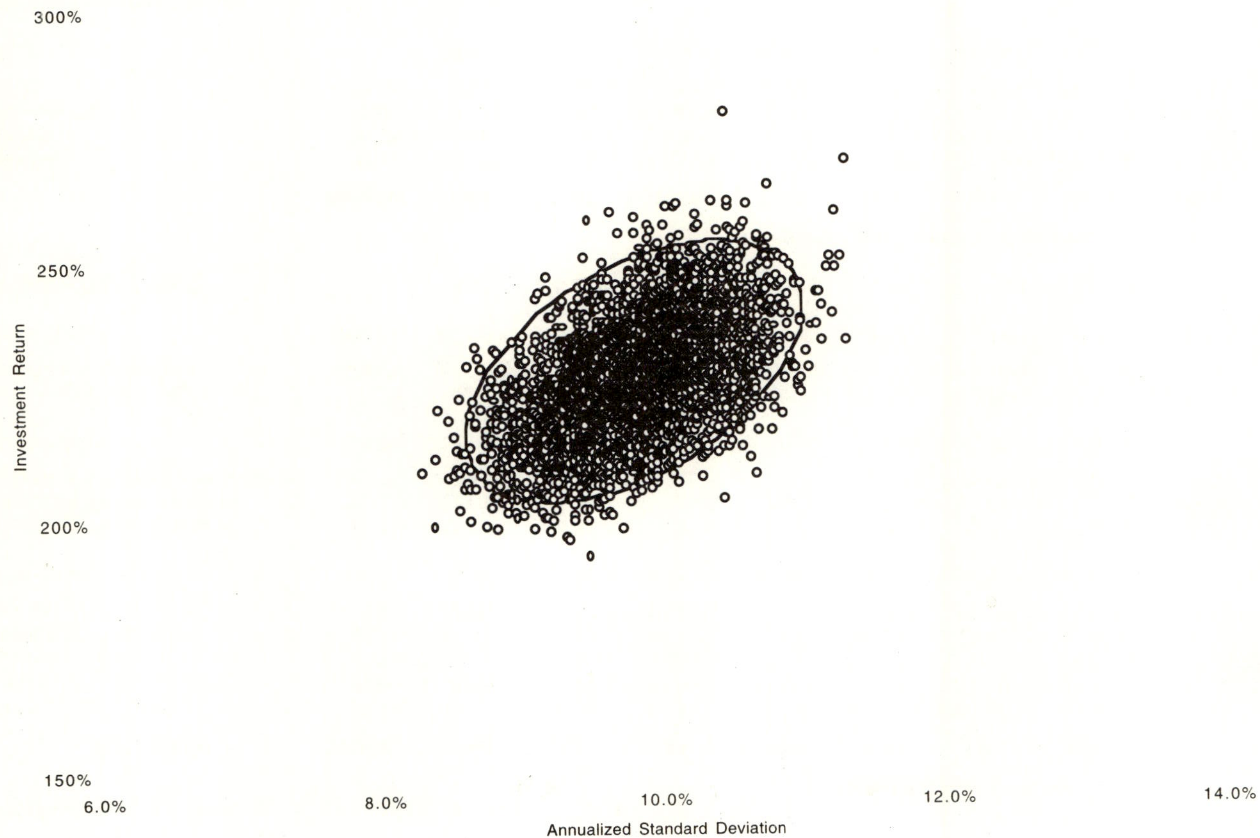

TABLE 3–16 Return Calculations: Actual Selection

Fund Name	Weight	1986	1987	1988	1989	1990	1991	1992	1993	1994	1995
		Investment Returns by Fund									
Strong Opportunity	17.5%	59.90%	11.85%	16.47%	18.49%	-11.30%	31.69%	17.35%	21.16%	3.18%	27.27%
Delaware Trend	35.5%	5.28%	-7.80%	26.83%	49.69%	-24.61%	74.49%	22.40%	22.37%	-9.97%	42.51%
Safeco Equity	16.9%	12.71%	-4.80%	25.30%	35.79%	-8.57%	27.91%	9.26%	30.91%	9.94%	25.26%
Vanguard/Windsor II	16.2%	21.41%	-2.14%	24.73%	27.83%	-9.98%	28.69%	11.99%	13.60%	-1.16%	38.83%
Ivy Growth	13.9%	17.06%	-1.87%	12.40%	27.24%	-3.82%	30.76%	5.21%	12.29%	-2.97%	27.34%
Total Stocks	100.0%	20.32%	-2.12%	22.41%	35.23%	-14.31%	45.65%	15.22%	20.78%	-1.91%	34.23%
Oppenheimer U.S. Gov't	36.4%	11.86%	3.52%	6.81%	11.93%	7.66%	15.24%	5.04%	8.00%	-1.28%	14.94%
Putnam U.S. Gov't Income	28.4%	11.01%	4.57%	7.55%	12.80%	9.90%	11.87%	6.60%	5.64%	-2.47%	16.23%
Wright U.S. Treasury Near Term	35.1%	13.12%	2.34%	5.75%	11.17%	8.23%	13.08%	6.26%	7.94%	-3.09%	11.93%
Total Bonds	100.0%	12.06%	3.40%	6.65%	11.91%	8.50%	13.52%	5.91%	7.31%	-2.26%	14.25%
G.T. Global New Pacific	50.2%	70.04%	5.95%	22.86%	48.12%	-10.96%	13.07%	-7.96%	60.61%	-19.73%	7.45%
Scudder International	49.8%	50.69%	0.85%	18.84%	26.95%	-8.92%	11.78%	-2.64%	36.50%	-2.99%	12.22%
Total Foreign	100.0%	60.40%	3.41%	20.86%	37.58%	-9.95%	12.43%	-5.31%	48.60%	-11.39%	9.82%
Treasury Bills-3 Month		6.17%	5.91%	6.76%	8.65%	7.90%	5.75%	3.61%	3.07%	4.22%	5.74%

	Weights	1986	1987	1988	1989	1990	1991	1992	1993	1994	1995
		Weighted Contribution to Plan Return									
Stocks	50.0%	10.16%	-1.06%	11.21%	17.62%	-7.16%	22.82%	7.61%	10.39%	-0.95%	17.11%
Bonds	30.0%	3.62%	1.02%	1.99%	3.57%	2.55%	4.06%	1.77%	2.19%	-0.68%	4.27%
Foreign Stocks	10.0%	6.04%	0.34%	2.09%	3.76%	-0.99%	1.24%	-0.53%	4.86%	-1.14%	0.98%
Cash	10.0%	0.62%	0.59%	0.68%	0.86%	0.79%	0.57%	0.36%	0.31%	0.42%	0.57%
Total		20.43%	0.89%	15.96%	25.81%	-4.81%	28.70%	9.21%	17.75%	-2.35%	22.94%
10-Year Investment Return		235.3%									
10-Year Annualized Return		12.86%									
Standard Deviation		12.05%									

passive, benchmark return, selection resulted in higher return and higher risk. Chart 3–8 shows the distribution of the 3,998 data points using five stock funds, three bond funds, and two foreign stock funds. The ranges of both investment returns and standard deviations are very wide. For a particular risk level, the range of returns approaches 100 percent. In this case, there is a huge difference between the efficient and inefficient frontiers.

We can observe that each distribution is roughly elliptical in shape. In order to describe each distribution, we have fit each with an ellipse, containing exactly 3,816 points, the percentage out of 3,998 observations that corresponds with the number of observations that we would expect would fall within two standard deviations of the mean if drawn from a normal distribution. We plotted them along with the data points in Charts 3–6, 3–7, and 3–8, although it is hard to see in Chart 3–6. Each ellipse represents those observations that fall within two standard deviations of the center. All points outside the ellipse are greater than two standard deviation events. In order to prevent extreme outliers from clouding our analysis, we use the two standard deviation ellipses to represent the shapes of the distributions.

Within this framework, we consider the relative importance of policy, timing, and selection to be the area of their respective ellipses. The general equation for an ellipse is $\frac{x^2}{a^2} + \frac{y^2}{b^2} = 1$, where a is the distance from the center of the ellipse to the outer point of the ellipse on the long axis, and b is the distance from the center of the ellipse to the outer point of the ellipse on the perpendicular axis. The area of the ellipse is πab.

Our ellipses also exhibit translation and rotation of axis. The formulas for translation of axis are $x = x' + h$, where h is the average standard deviation of return, and $y = y' + k$, where k is the average 10-year investment return. The formulas for rotation of axis are $x = x' \cos\theta - y' \sin\theta$ and $y = x' \sin\theta + y' \cos\theta$, where θ is the angle of rotation, measured in radians. Table 3–17 shows the values for a, b, h, k, θ, and the area for each ellipse representing the various combinations of return component and ranges. From Table 3–17, we see that the area of the policy ellipse in Chart 3–6 was 0.171. The area for the timing ellipse in Chart 3–7 was 0.840, and the area for the selection ellipse in Chart 3–8 was 2.465. The area for the timing ellipse is 4.9 times greater than the area for the policy ellipse. The area for the selection ellipse is 14.4 times greater than the area for the policy ellipse. Although not shown here, when ellipses are fitted using annualized investment return rather than cumulative investment return, the relative areas of the ellipses are not materially different.

CHART 3-8 Distribution: Selection

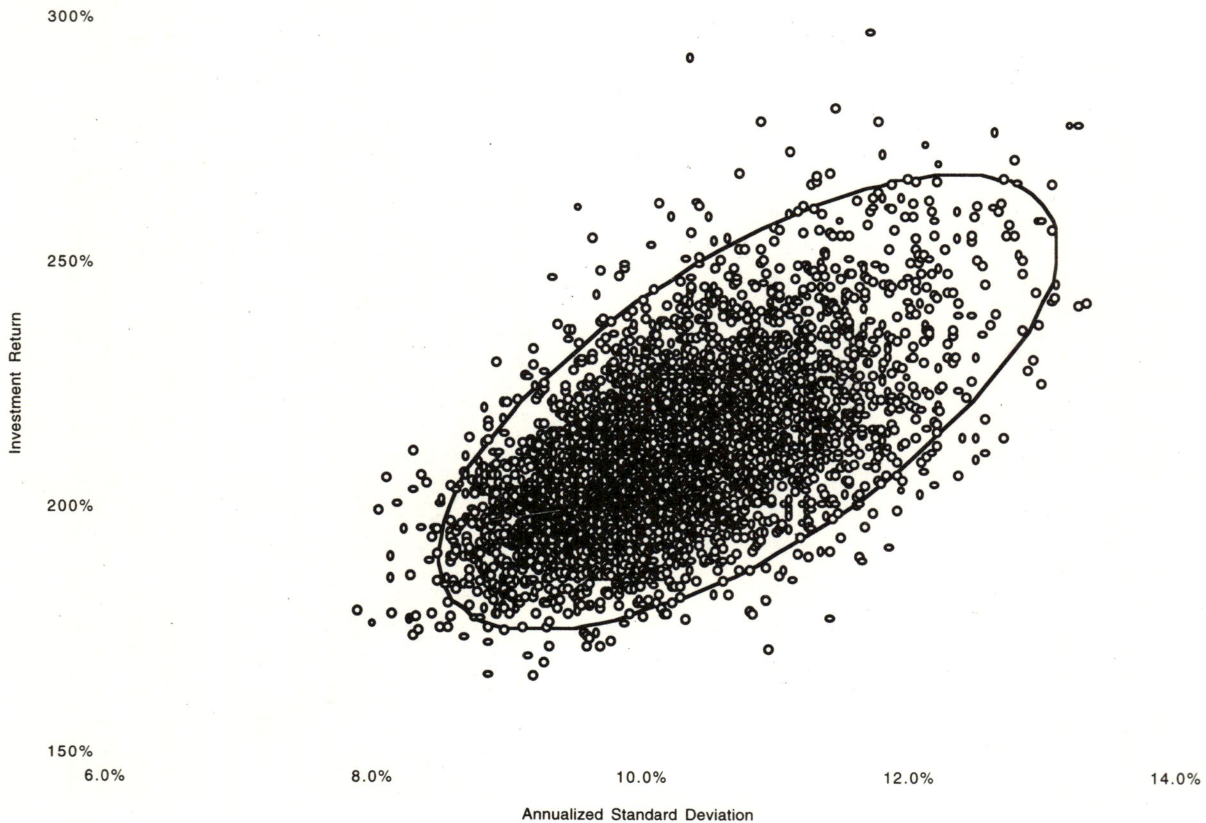

TABLE 3–17 Ellipse Parameters

Component	Range	a	b	h	k	q	area (%^{2})
Policy	S:0-100, B:0-60, F:0-20, C:0-20	64.50%	0.401%	10.08%	230.2%	-0.049	0.813
Policy	S:20-80, B:10-50, F:5-15, C:5-15	37.60%	0.145%	9.82%	228.0%	-0.049	0.171
Policy	S:40-60, B:20-40, F:7.5-12.5, C:7.5-12.5	17.98%	0.054%	9.70%	226.2%	-0.049	0.031
Timing	S:0-100, B:0-60, F:0-20, C:0-20	50.05%	1.550%	10.21%	234.0%	-0.021	2.437
Timing	S:20-80, B:10-50, F:5-15, C:5-15	25.50%	1.048%	9.80%	228.5%	-0.023	0.840
Timing	S:40-60, B:20-40, F:7.5-12.5, C:7.5-12.5	13.45%	0.430%	9.68%	226.1%	-0.025	0.182
Selection	S:3, B:2, F:1	72.43%	2.420%	11.62%	237.0%	-0.032	5.507
Selection	S:5, B:3, F:2	46.40%	1.691%	10.80%	221.4%	-0.034	2.465
Selection	S:10, B:5, F:3	37.67%	1.220%	10.45%	218.0%	-0.035	1.444

Just as it is not appropriate to say that asset allocation policy is 55 times more important than timing and 22 times more important than selection, it is not appropriate to say that timing is 4.9 times more important than policy and selection is 14.4 times more important than policy. Under certain circumstances it might be, but the range of possibilities is very wide. Table 3–17 reveals that under different ranges of freedom within the components of return the areas of the ellipses vary dramatically. Thus, we conclude that the relative importance of policy, timing, and selection is completely a function of the range of freedom allowed in a plan's investment policy. However, it is clear that to underestimate the importance of timing and selection decisions could be very detrimental to a plan's results.

Furthermore, since the ratio a/b is much higher for policy than for either timing or selection, we can say that policy decisions are likely to have a greater impact on return than on risk, relative to timing and selection. For timing and selection, which both exhibit larger b's, indicating a rounder ellipse, bad or good decisions are likely to manifest themselves in either return, risk, or both. In a return-based framework like that of BHB, this could distort the importance of policy relative to timing and selection. We suspect that in a risk-based framework, timing and selection would emerge as being more important than under the BHB framework.

In this chapter, we have explored the implications of Brinson, Hood, and Beebower's *Determinants of Portfolio Performance* in great detail. In the next chapter, we incorporate some of the ideas from this chapter in formulating an expanded version of the BHB framework.

CHAPTER 4

General Framework for Performance Attribution

In the previous chapter, we discussed in detail Brinson, Hood, and Beebower's general framework for performance attribution. In that chapter, we introduced the concept of passive asset allocation policy and active asset allocation policy. We also noted that general framework of BHB does not account for the overall level of portfolio risk. In this chapter, we expand upon the BHB general framework to include passive and active policy as well as risk. In addition, we will break down each asset class into smaller subcomponents, based on their style characteristics and incorporate style analysis within our general framework. Singer and Karnosky's expansion upon the BHB general framework provides the necessary modifications to account for returns due to country and currency weighting decisions. Allen also provides an interesting framework for global investment return attribution. The global investor can utilize the proposed modifications although focus is on the basic BHB framework, which serves the single country, single currency investor.

Performance Analysis—A Brief History

Performance analysis has become a very important component of the investment management process in recent years. This has been due in part to the sheer amount under management, the sophistication available in analysis methods, and the ever-increasingly competitive investment management business. The subject of performance analysis has an interesting history, some of which we will discuss here because it is relevant to establishing our general framework for performance analysis.

The earliest works that still enjoy current usage were born in the mid-60's. This period immediately followed the development of CAPM and most of the theories from this time build upon the CAPM foundation. Each method of performance analysis that we will discuss considers both return and risk, although none go much further than that.

Treynor's Measure

In 1965, Treynor described a method of fund performance analysis that captured the return and risk of a fund, and provided a measure that could be easily calculated and used to compare the performance of one fund against another. Central to his measure was the fund's "characteristic line." He found the characteristic line by regressing the fund's period returns against a general market average. The slope of the characteristic line measures the fund's volatility relative to the general market average. The higher the slope, the higher the volatility, and vice versa. The slope of the characteristic line is equivalent to beta, which as a definition of risk, includes only systematic risk, while ignoring unsystematic risk. Treynor does note that observations that deviate from the characteristic line indicate either a lack of efficient diversification or either an accidental or deliberate effort on the part of fund management to alter the volatility of the fund during the measurement period. Treynor defined his measure for management rating as the "rate of return for the general market at which the fund in question will produce the same return as that produced by a fund consisting solely of riskless investment."

Chart 4–1 illustrates the use of the characteristic line and the determination of *r*, Treynor's Measure. In Chart 4–1, the x-axis is the market index return and the y-axis is the fund's return. The heavy diagonal line, the characteristic line, is determined by regressing the fund's returns against the market index's return. Treynor's Measure, *r*, is found at the point where the characteristic line intersects the line $y = \mu_*$, where μ_* is the risk-free rate. Contrary to intuition, a lower value of *r* is better than a higher value of *r*. In Treynor's diagram, the angle formed by the characteristic line and the horizontal line passing through μ_* was called B. Furthermore, Treynor defined σ as tan B, although in current usage we now refer to tan B as beta and use σ to signify standard deviation. When we define h as the y-intercept of the characteristic line, $r = \dfrac{\mu_* - h}{\sigma}$.

CHART 4–1 Treynor's Measure

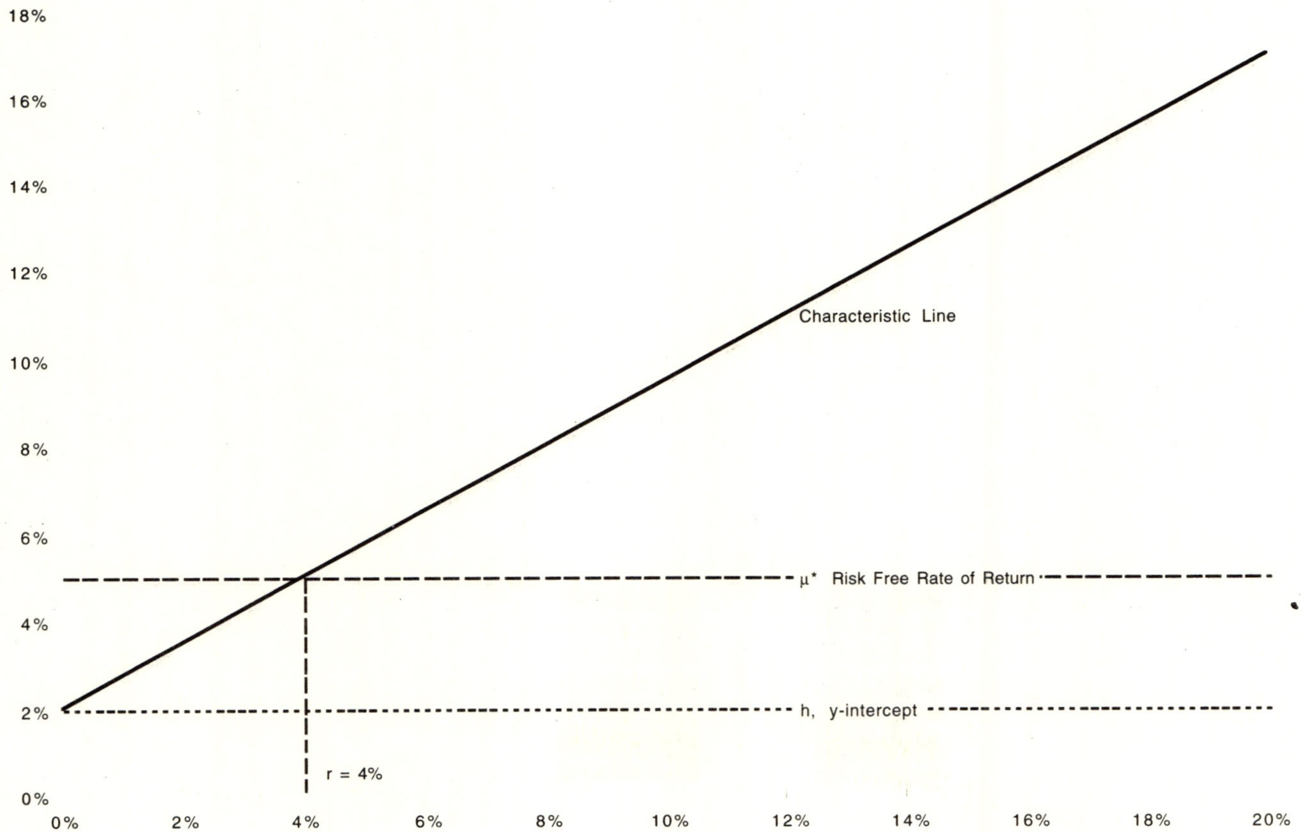

The Sharpe Ratio

A short time later, Sharpe rearranged the terms in some of Treynor's equations to develop the now quite familiar Treynor Index, $TI = \frac{R_p - R_f}{\beta}$, where R_p is the return on the portfolio, R_f is the risk-free rate of return, and B is the portfolio's beta. The Treynor Index measures the incremental return on a fund per unit of systematic risk. Essentially, Sharpe tied Treynor's work into his recent CAPM development. At the same time he developed his own Sharpe Ratio, $SI = \frac{R_p - R_f}{\sigma}$, where R_p is the return on the portfolio, R_f is the risk-free rate of return, and σ is the portfolio's standard deviation. Sharpe defined this as a reward-to-variability ratio, as opposed to the Treynor Index which is a reward-to-volatility ratio. Both are essentially bang-to-buck ratios—the higher the ratio, the better. Which measure is better? Sharpe concluded that the Treynor Index "is an inferior measure of *past* performance, but it may be a superior measure for predicting *future* performance." He considered that variability of returns is likely due to "transitory effects." He felt that the systematic part of a fund's variability—its volatility—was a more permanent relationship. For our purposes, we are looking for a way to evaluate past performance, so we will go along with Sharpe's notion that variability is a better proxy for risk than volatility when evaluating past performance.

Alpha

Shortly afterwards, Jensen followed-up with his own measure of investment performance that is now referred to as Jensen's alpha. Jensen postulated that a fund's return was made up of the risk-free rate, the market return adjusted for the fund's volatility, the investment manager's value-added, which he called alpha, and an error term. In equation form, the return on the portfolio was,

$$R_p = \alpha_p + R_f + \beta_p[R_m - R_f] + \mu_p,$$

where R_p is the return on the portfolio, α is the alpha, or the incremental value-added, R_f is the risk-free rate, B is the beta, or volatility, R_m is the market return, and μ_p is the error term. Jensen's alpha purports to measure the amount to which the portfolio return exceeded the return that would be expected given the risk-free rate, the market return, and the portfolio's volatility. The higher the alpha, the better.

In his discussion that followed Jensen's article, Treynor pointed out the close relationship between the Treynor measure and alpha. Specifically, the Treynor measure $= R_F - \frac{\alpha}{\beta}$. Treynor also pointed out that Sharpe's comment that the Treynor Index does not capture the portion of variability due to lack of diversification also applies to Jensen's alpha. A portfolio manager can improve his Jensen or Treynor rating without improving in the quality of his selection skills merely by departing further from perfect diversification.

Farrar's Argument

In another discussion following Jensen's article, Farrar noted that Jensen's alpha assumes that risk is market-related alone and that it is constant over time. Furthermore, he noted that risk can be subdivided as "market-related" and "item-related." Likewise, managerial skill can be subdivided as "market-related" and "item-related." This means that managers can add value by "adjusting their overall portfolio's risk in anticipation of general market movements" or by "the careful selection of individual stocks," which in the BHB framework, correspond with timing and selection.

Lastly, Farrar discussed, "instances in which judicious decisions to accumulate cash near market peaks, or stocks near market troughs, have more than overcome even relatively serious errors in individual stock selection." In other words, active asset allocation can be more important than security selection. Farrar divided managerial skill into six categories: market return, market-related risk, item-related risk, market forecasting, item selection, and luck. To this, we would like to add passive asset allocation, active asset allocation policy, timing, equity style characteristics, and for the global investor, country and currency selection.

Fama and Overall Performance

In 1972, Fama introduced the most comprehensive model for evaluating investment performance to date. His goal was to expand upon the works of Treynor, Sharpe, and Jensen in order to develop "finer breakdowns of performance." The basic idea behind his methods of performance evaluation was that "the returns on managed portfolios can be judged relative to those of *naively selected* portfolios with similar levels of risk." Fama defined the ex post market line as, $R_p = R_f + \left(\frac{R_m - R_f}{\sigma(R_m)}\right)\beta_p$. The element,

$\sigma(R_m)$, is a measure of the total risk in the return on the market portfolio. Chart 4–2 illustrates the ex post market line as well as a conceptual picture of the calculations of many of his components of investment return.

Fama postulated that, at its basic level, overall performance is composed of two components, selectivity and risk. Fama defined *selectivity* as "how well the portfolio did relative to a naively selected portfolio with the same level of risk." Thus, return from selectivity is the component of return due to the fund's active management decisions. Return from risk is the passive return that the portfolio earned due to the decision to take on positive amounts of risk. Thus, *overall performance* equals the return due to *selectivity* plus the return due to *risk*. The equations follow.

$$\text{Overall Performance} = R_a - R_f$$
$$\text{Selectivity} = R_a - R_x(B_a)$$
$$\text{Risk} = R_x(B_a) - R_f$$
$$\text{Overall Performance} = \text{Selectivity} + \text{Risk, since } R_a - R_f = [R_a - R_x(B_a)] + [R_x(B_a) - R_f]$$

In these equations, R_a is the actual return of the portfolio, R_f is the risk-free rate, $R_x(B_a)$ is the return that would be expected based on the portfolio's beta.

Here we begin to see some similarities to the BHB general framework. The return due to selectivity in Fama's framework is closely related to selection in the BHB framework. Both are measures of the portfolio manager's ability to select superior securities. The Fama framework does not account for asset allocation policy or timing. The return due to risk in Fama's framework is closely related to the passive, policy return in the BHB framework, although one measures the return based on a passive risk policy whereas the other is based on a passive asset allocation policy.

Fama dissected the two primary components of return even further. Specifically, he described the situation in which the portfolio manager deviated away from perfect diversification in an effort to overweight securities that he felt would outperform. The extent to which $\sigma(R_a)$ exceeds B_a is the amount by which the portfolio's overall level of risk was increased by this decision. According to Fama, we would not ordinarily expect this decision to take on unsystematic risk in addition to systematic risk to produce higher returns since the market does not compensate the investor for unsystematic risk. However, to the extent that the portfolio manager takes on this risk, we can fairly hold him responsible for obtaining an incrementally higher return. Thus, Fama divides selectivity into

CHART 4–2   Fama's Measure

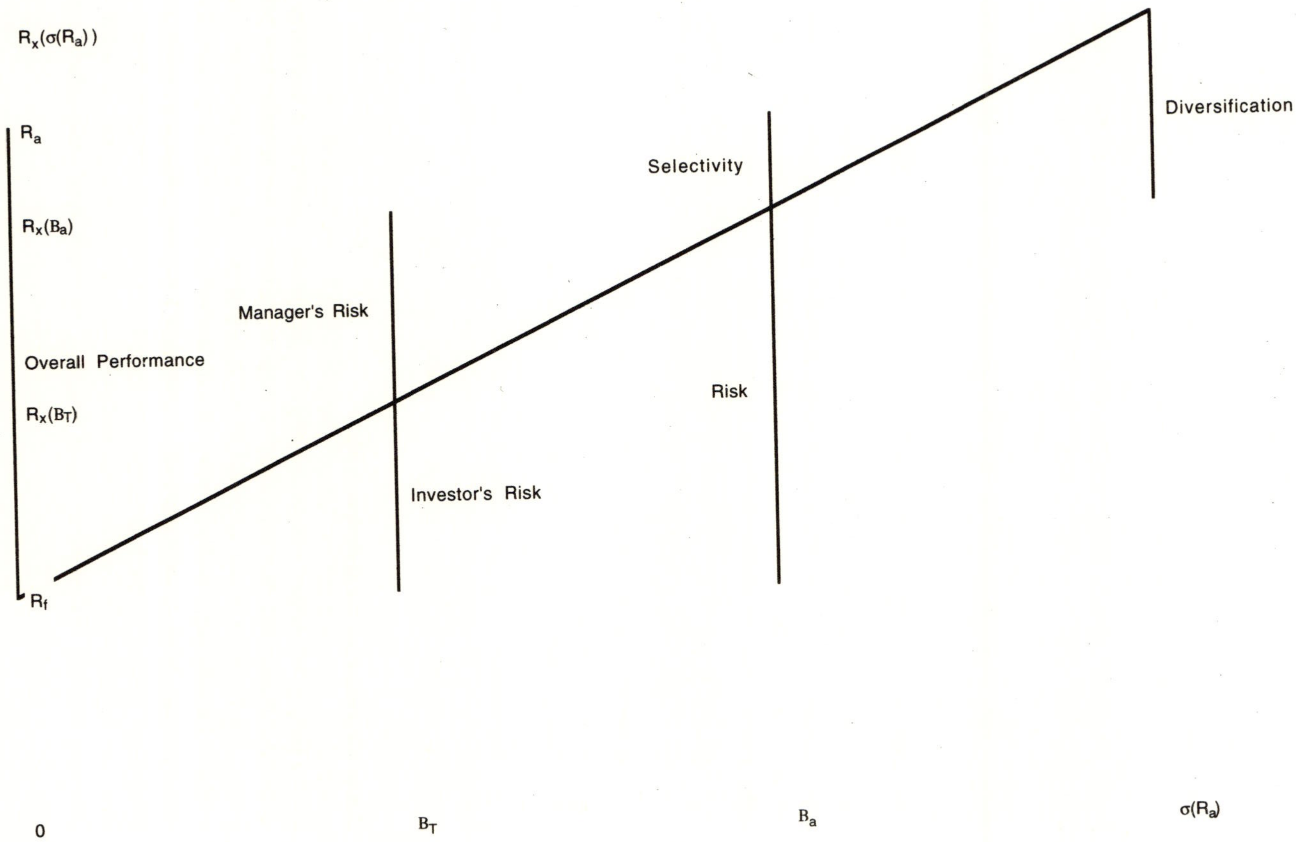

return due to *diversification* (or perhaps more accurately, we should call it lack of diversification) and *net selectivity*. The equations follow:

$$\text{Selectivity} = R_a - R_x(B_a)$$
$$\text{Net Selectivity} = R_a - R_x(\sigma(R_a))$$
$$\text{Diversification} = R_x(\sigma(R_a)) - R_x(B_a)$$
$$\text{Selectivity} = \text{Net Selectivity} + \text{Diversification since, } R_a - R_x(B_a) = [R_a - R_x(\sigma(R_a))] + [R_x(\sigma(R_a)) - R_x(B_a)]$$

In these equations, $R_x(\sigma(R_a))$ is the return on the combination of the riskless security and the market portfolio that has the same return dispersion as the actual portfolio. Net selectivity could be positive or negative depending on the portfolio manager's ability to produce sufficiently high returns through security selection to offset the additional risk due to lack of diversification.

Likewise, Fama divided risk into two subcomponents, *manager's risk* and *investor's risk*. The idea behind this division is that the actual portfolio beta, B_a, might differ from the investor's target beta, B_T. Fama defined the return due to the risk targeted by the investor as the investor's risk, and return due to the difference between actual and targeted risk as manager's risk. The equations follow:

$$\text{Risk} = R_x(B_a) - R_f$$
$$\text{Manager's Risk} = R_x(B_a) - R_x(B_T)$$
$$\text{Investor's Risk} = R_x(B_T) - R_f$$
$$\text{Risk} = \text{Manager's Risk} + \text{Investor's Risk since,}$$
$$R_x(B_a) - R_f = [R_x(B_a) - R_x(B_T)] + [R_x(B_T) - R_f]$$

This distinction is of primary interest because it introduces the idea of two levels of passive return, a concept similar to the distinction between passive allocation policy and active allocation policy.

The General Framework

Based upon this historical backdrop, we begin the process of creating our general framework for investment return analysis. As mentioned previously, the framework is a multi-level framework, ranging from the most passive benchmark index return up to the actual portfolio return. Thus, the bottom level of our general framework is the passive-passive asset allocation policy return. As discussed in the previous chapter, this is the passive benchmark index return based upon an estimate of what the average similar investment fund is using as their asset allocation policy mixes. This is the asset mix the investment fund might have if no active policy decisions were made.

The second level in our general framework is the passive asset allocation policy return, or the passive benchmark index return based upon the actual policy target asset class weights. This is the first level in the BHB framework. In the BHB framework, BHB determined the policy weights by taking the average of the observed asset class weights over the 10 year analysis period. This would be an acceptable way for an analyst evaluating fund performance to determine policy weights. However, actual policy target weights should be used when available. For an analysis covering an extended period of time, it is likely that policy will change during the measurement period. Those changes in policy should be reflected in the analysis.

We recommend careful consideration to the indices being used to represent the passive returns for each asset class. BHB used the Lehman Brothers Government / Corporate Bond index and the S&P 500 index to represent bonds and stocks, respectively. Frankly, these are not broad enough indices to represent an entire asset class. Two possible solutions present themselves. First, we can use a broader index. On the fixed income side, we can use the Lehman Brothers Aggregate Bond index or the Salomon Brothers Broad Investment Grade Bond (BIG) index. On the stock side, we can consider the Wilshire 5000 index. The second possible solution would be to use a weighted combination of a number of niche indices. In the fixed income arena, there is no shortage of available indices, subdividing fixed income securities by type, credit quality, maturity, etc.

On the stock side, we now have access to a plethora of indices subdivided by market capitalization, growth *versus* value, sector, etc. By creating a customized index, we can more closely approximate the particular investment fund's policy weights. Wherever possible, the passive benchmark index should be constructed to most accurately represent ex ante policy decisions.

Figures 4–1, 4–2, and 4–3 provide a visualization of three possible stock benchmark index setups. In Figure 4–1, the S&P 500, S&P 400 Midcap, and S&P 600 Smallcap indices are used to represent large-cap, midcap, and small-cap stocks, respectively, without regard to further breakdowns into value and growth style classifications.

Figure 4–2 shows how the S&P 500 can be replaced by the S&P/BARRA Value and S&P/BARRA Growth indices in order to allow for more flexibility in style classifications. Finally, Figure 4–3 uses the Frank Russell indices to allow for value and growth style classifications for both large- and small-cap stocks. Since we will be introducing a method of cal-

FIGURE 4–1 Stock Benchmark Composition: Example 1

	Value	Blend	Growth
Large-Cap Stocks		S&P 500	
Mid-Cap Stocks		S&P 400 Midcap	
Samll-Cap Stocks		S&P 600 Smallcap	

Indices

FIGURE 4–2 Stock Benchmark Composition: Example 2

<table>
<tr><th></th><th>Value</th><th>Blend</th><th>Growth</th></tr>
<tr><td>Large-Cap Stocks</td><td colspan="3">S&P/BARRA Value | S&P/BARRA Growth</td></tr>
<tr><td>Mid-Cap Stocks</td><td></td><td>S&P 400 Midcap</td><td></td></tr>
<tr><td>Samll-Cap Stocks</td><td></td><td>S&P 600 Smallcap</td><td></td></tr>
</table>

Indices

FIGURE 4–3 Stock Benchmark Composition: Example 3

<table>
<tr><th></th><th>Value</th><th>Blend</th><th>Growth</th></tr>
<tr><td>Large-Cap Stocks
Mid-Cap Stocks</td><td colspan="3">Frank Russell 1000 Value | Frank Russell 1000 Growth</td></tr>
<tr><td>Samll-Cap Stocks</td><td colspan="3">Frank Russell 2000 Value | Frank Russell 2000 Growth</td></tr>
</table>

Indices

culating the contribution to return from style selection, it makes sense to consider incorporating this concept in the passive benchmark index.

One can argue that rather than assign a new component of return to style selection we should simply modify our concept of asset classes to include these finer breakdowns of our main asset classes. In other words, the asset allocation decision is the decision to allocate among large-cap value stocks, large-cap growth stocks, mid-cap stocks, small-cap stocks, long-term government bonds, short-term government bonds, investment-grade corporate bonds, mortgage-backed securities, high yield bonds, etc. We believe that the framework provides more flexibility if we continue to view the basic asset classes as stocks, bonds, and cash. To the extent that the analyst feels the performance of other asset classes, such as real estate and precious metals, can be measured, they should be included as well.

The third level of our general framework combines the passive policy return with one active component of management, where the three active components are timing, style selection, and security selection, in that order. We can conceptualize the order as going from bigger to smaller. The biggest decision is the decision to deviate away from policy asset class weights. Within each asset class, the second decision is to deviate away from policy style weights. Within each style class, the final decision is to deviate away from the passive, benchmark index through active security selection. Unfortunately, the computations are not going to be as neat as under the BHB framework, where we simply had one passive axis and one actual axis.

Finally, the fourth level of our general framework is the actual portfolio return.

Mirroring the framework for returns is a similar framework for risk, which specifically measures variability (standard deviation) within each quadrant in the framework. Based on the returns and risk within each quadrant, we can calculate a separate Sharpe Ratio for each. Thus, we have a return- and risk-based framework for analyzing portfolio returns.

Figure 4–4 summarizes the general framework for return analysis. Figure 4–5 provides the method by which we will calculate each return. We will briefly explain the formulas and then work through an example.

Return Analysis

The lowest level, Passive Asset Allocation Policy, is the benchmark return, assuming the aggregate rest-of-the-world asset mix. Typically, this could best be represented using broad asset class indices such as the Wilshire

FIGURE 4–4 Return Analysis Framework

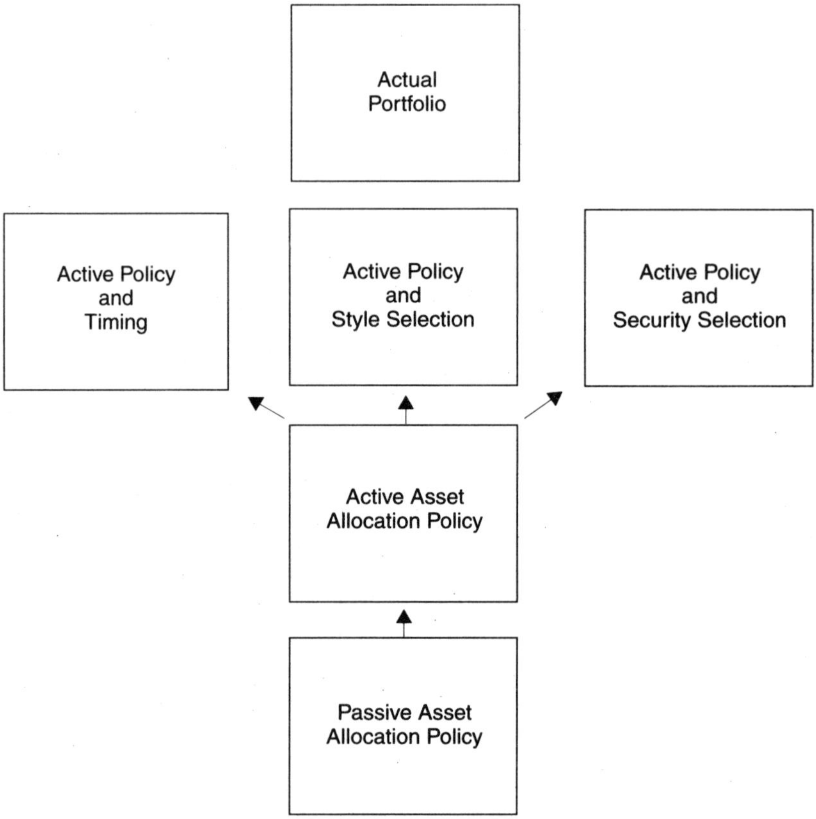

5000 and Lehman Brothers Aggregate Bond Index. In our example, we assume a constant passive asset allocation policy of 60% Wilshire 5000, 35% Lehman Brothers Aggregate Bond Index, and 5% Salomon Brothers 3-Month Treasury bills. The formula is:

$$\sum w(pp)_i \cdot [\sum w(pp)_j \cdot r(pp)_j],$$

where $w(pp)_i$ is the passive weighting of the *i*th asset class, $w(pp)_j$ is the passive style weighting of the *j*th style, within each asset class, and $r(pp)_j$ is the passive benchmark return of the *j*th style index. In our example, j never exceeds 1, so it works out to:

0.60 (Wilshire 5000) + 0.35 (LB Aggregate Bond) + 0.05 (3-Month T-Bills).

FIGURE 4–5 Return Calculations

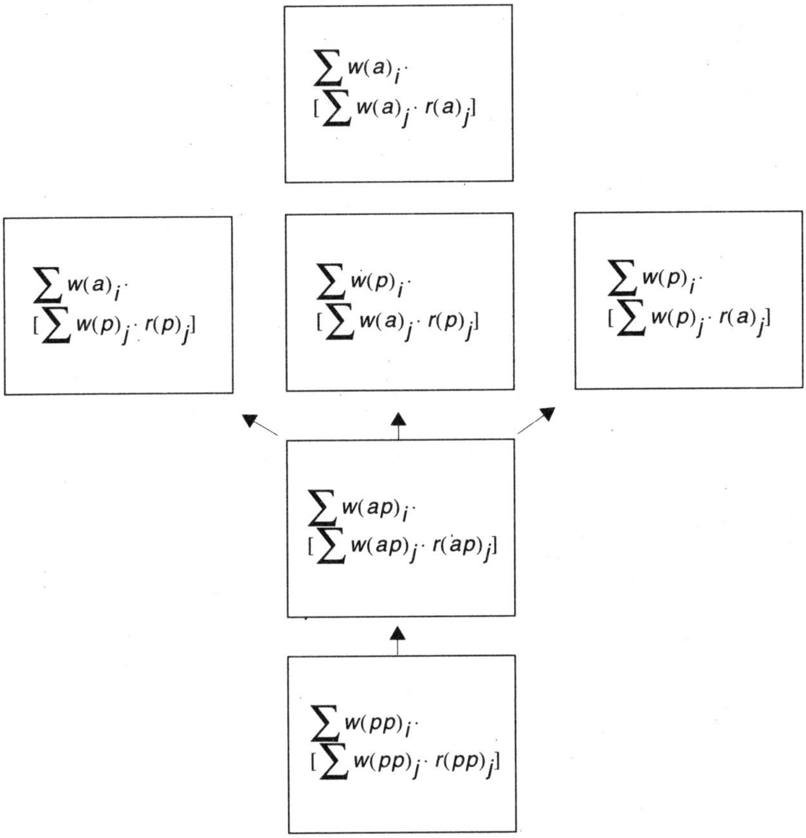

We have kept the formula general to allow for more flexibility in incorporating style-based indices in the passive benchmark.

Against the passive policy benchmark, the active policy decision is made. This will usually differ from the passive benchmark as a fund positions itself either more or less aggressively relative to the aggregate. In our example, we assume an active policy mix consisting of 70% stocks, 28% bonds, and 2% cash. Furthermore, within the stock category, we establish a policy mix of 55% S&P 500, 30% S&P 400 Midcap, and 15% S&P 600 Smallcap. Within the bond category, we substitute the Merrill Lynch 1-10 Year Government / Corporate Bond Index. In other words, our hypothetical fund has chosen to invest solely in short- to intermediate-Governments and Corporates. The formula is:

$$\sum w(ap)_i \cdot [\sum w(ap)_j \cdot r(ap)_j],$$

where $w(ap)_i$ is the active weighting of the *i*th asset class, $w(ap)_j$ is the active style weighting of the *j*th style, within each asset class, and $r(ap)_j$ is the passive benchmark return of the *j*th style index. In our example, j equals 3 for stocks, so it works out to:

0.70[0.55(S&P 500) + 0.30(S&P 400 Midcap) + 0.15(S&P 600 Smallcap)] + 0.28(Merrill Lynch 1-10 Year Gov't / Corp.) + 0.02(3-Month T-Bill).

In the next level, we have eliminated the differentiation between passive and active policy from our notation. From this level on, all references to policy are to active policy, not passive policy. Like the BHB framework, the third level formulas contain passive and actual elements. With three variables to consider, timing, style selection, and security selection, for each formula there are two passive components and one actual component. The formulas follow:

Policy and Timing:

$$\sum w(a)_i \cdot [\sum w(p)_j \cdot r(p)_j],$$

Policy and Style Selection:

$$\sum w(p)_i \cdot [\sum w(a)_j \cdot r(p)_j],$$

Policy and Security Selection:

$$\sum w(p)_i \cdot [\sum w(p)_j \cdot r(a)_j],$$

where w(p) and r(p) represent passive weights and returns, respectively, and w(a) and r(a) represent actual weights and returns, respectively. Finally, the actual portfolio return is:

$$\sum w(a)_i \cdot [\sum w(a)_j \cdot r(a)_j].$$

Return Analysis—An Example

To illustrate the framework, we will decompose the returns of a hypothetical fund over a three-year time period. As mentioned earlier, we assume the simplest case where the passive and active asset allocation remain constant over the entire three-year period, although in practice this probably would not happen.

For our example, we assume a passive benchmark consisting of 60% Wilshire 5000, 35% Lehman Brothers Aggregate Bond Index, and 5% Salomon 3-Month Treasury bills. Further, we assume that our fund chooses to increase its weighting in stocks and decrease its weighting in bonds and cash, relative to the passive benchmark. In this case, the active policy is 70% stocks, 28% bonds, and 2% cash. Furthermore, within the stock category, policy dictates a passive weighting of 55% large-cap, 30% mid-cap, and 15% small-cap. In actual usage, a variety of niche indices could be used including those that consider growth versus value, or industry indices.

Table 4–1 shows the quarter-by-quarter weightings in the various asset classes as well as style shifts. Table 4–2 shows the benchmark

TABLE 4–1 Asset Class Quarter-by-Quarter Weightings

	Stocks	Bonds	Cash	Large Cap	Mid Cap	Small Cap
Q1Y1	76.4%	22.4%	1.2%	60.4%	28.4%	11.2%
Q2Y1	73.8%	23.4%	2.8%	66.1%	24.7%	9.2%
Q3Y1	67.4%	28.5%	4.1%	69.3%	22.3%	8.4%
Q4Y1	64.1%	31.3%	4.6%	68.8%	21.7%	9.5%
Q1Y2	63.4%	32.8%	3.8%	62.0%	24.6%	13.4%
Q2Y2	63.8%	32.7%	3.5%	56.8%	26.8%	16.4%
Q3Y2	62.1%	34.7%	3.2%	54.1%	28.4%	17.5%
Q4Y2	72.1%	25.5%	2.4%	51.3%	30.6%	18.1%
Q1Y3	73.8%	24.1%	2.1%	49.7%	32.6%	17.7%
Q2Y3	76.1%	22.1%	1.8%	48.2%	33.4%	18.4%
Q3Y3	77.3%	21.3%	1.4%	51.8%	29.1%	19.1%
Q4Y3	75.7%	20.5%	3.8%	49.7%	28.6%	21.7%

TABLE 4–2 Benchmark Returns

	Stocks	Bonds	Cash	Large Cap	Mid Cap	Small Cap	Bonds
	Wilshire 5000	***LB Aggregate***	***3 Mo. T-Bill***	***S&P 500***	***S&P 400***	***S&P 600***	***ML 1-10 Yr.***
Q1Y1	3.6%	4.1%	0.7%	4.3%	3.3%	3.7%	4.0%
Q2Y1	1.0%	2.7%	0.7%	0.5%	2.3%	2.3%	2.1%
Q3Y1	3.4%	2.6%	0.7%	2.6%	5.0%	10.3%	2.4%
Q4Y1	1.2%	0.1%	0.7%	2.3%	2.6%	2.0%	0.2%
Q1Y2	-4.2%	-2.9%	0.7%	-3.8%	-3.8%	-5.1%	-1.9%
Q2Y2	-1.4%	-1.0%	0.9%	0.4%	-3.6%	-4.1%	-0.6%
Q3Y2	4.8%	0.6%	1.0%	4.9%	6.8%	7.6%	0.8%
Q4Y2	-1.4%	0.4%	1.2%	0.0%	-2.6%	-2.3%	-0.1%
Q1Y3	8.4%	5.0%	1.3%	9.7%	8.2%	4.8%	4.4%
Q2Y3	8.7%	6.1%	1.5%	9.5%	8.7%	9.6%	5.0%
Q3Y3	8.6%	2.0%	1.4%	8.0%	9.7%	12.9%	1.6%
Q4Y3	4.3%	4.3%	1.4%	6.0%	1.4%	0.6%	3.6%

TABLE 4–3 Actual Asset and Style Class Returns

	Cash	Bonds	Stocks		
			Large Cap	Mid Cap	Small Cap
Q1Y1	0.8%	4.3%	6.3%	1.7%	3.1%
Q2Y1	0.8%	2.6%	0.8%	2.1%	4.1%
Q3Y1	0.8%	4.5%	1.9%	5.8%	13.2%
Q4Y1	0.8%	2.1%	4.7%	0.5%	-1.6%
Q1Y2	0.8%	-1.0%	-4.1%	-0.9%	-6.3%
Q2Y2	0.9%	-6.0%	0.2%	-1.1%	-3.8%
Q3Y2	1.0%	-0.2%	3.9%	7.7%	6.2%
Q4Y2	1.2%	-1.2%	0.9%	-1.3%	-5.5%
Q1Y3	1.4%	4.6%	11.8%	7.7%	7.4%
Q2Y3	1.5%	8.9%	7.6%	8.4%	6.8%
Q3Y3	1.4%	0.9%	6.3%	9.2%	11.1%
Q4Y3	1.4%	3.7%	5.4%	2.9%	0.3%

TABLE 4–4 Overall Results

	Passive Asset Allocation Policy	Active Asset Allocation Policy	Policy + Timing	Policy + Style	Policy + Selection	Actual Portfolio
Q1Y1	3.63%	3.87%	3.89%	3.90%	4.33%	4.51%
Q2Y1	1.58%	1.52%	1.48%	1.38%	1.92%	1.68%
Q3Y1	2.99%	3.82%	3.73%	3.33%	4.61%	3.82%
Q4Y1	0.79%	1.71%	1.60%	1.71%	2.35%	2.74%
Q1Y2	-3.50%	-3.31%	-3.13%	-3.30%	-2.69%	-2.58%
Q2Y2	-1.15%	-1.18%	-1.11%	-1.14%	-2.22%	-2.44%
Q3Y2	3.14%	4.36%	3.96%	4.38%	3.73%	3.30%
Q4Y2	-0.64%	-0.79%	-0.81%	-0.85%	-0.82%	-0.95%
Q1Y3	6.86%	7.22%	7.37%	7.10%	8.25%	8.29%
Q2Y3	7.43%	7.92%	8.19%	7.91%	7.93%	7.87%
Q3Y3	5.93%	6.95%	7.51%	7.08%	5.80%	6.44%
Q4Y3	4.16%	3.70%	3.68%	3.49%	3.78%	3.52%
Annualized	10.60%	12.23%	12.43%	11.94%	12.66%	12.37%
Std. Deviation	6.67%	7.06%	7.19%	7.04%	7.16%	7.26%
Sharpe Ratio	0.97	1.15	1.15	1.11	1.19	1.13

returns for each of the indices used in the analysis. Table 4–3 shows the actual asset class and style class returns. Finally, Table 4–4 shows the overall results.

In order to clarify these concepts further, we will take the illustration one step further and calculate the returns for Quarter 1, Year 1 (abbreviated Q1Y1).

For Passive Asset Allocation Policy, we use the passive policy weightings and benchmark returns:

$$0.60\ (3.6\%) + 0.35\ (4.1\%) + 0.05\ (0.7\%) = 3.63\%.$$

For Active Asset Allocation Policy, we use the active policy weightings and benchmark returns:

$$0.70\ [\ (0.55)(4.3\%)+(0.30)(3.3\%)+(0.15)(3.7\%)\ ] + 0.28(4.0\%) + 0.02(0.7\%) = 3.87\%.$$

For Policy and Timing, we use the actual asset class weightings:

$$0.764\ [\ (0.55)(4.3\%)+(0.30)(3.3\%)+(0.15)(3.7\%)\ ] + 0.224(4.0\%) + 0.012(0.7\%) = 3.89\%.$$

For Policy and Style Selection, we use the actual style class weightings:

$$0.70\ [\ (0.604)(4.3\%)+(0.284)(3.3\%)+(0.112)(3.7\%)\ ] + 0.28(4.0\%) + 0.02(0.7\%) = 3.90\%.$$

For Policy and Security Selection, we use the actual asset class and style class returns:

$$0.70\ [\ (0.55)(6.3\%)+(0.30)(1.7\%)+(0.15)(3.1\%)\ ] + 0.28(4.3\%) + 0.02(0.8\%) = 4.33\%.$$

Finally, the Actual Portfolio return uses actual asset class and style class weights and returns:

$$0.764\ [\ (0.604)(6.3\%)+(0.284)(1.7\%)+(0.112)(3.1\%)\ ] + 0.224(4.3\%) + 0.012(0.8\%) = 4.51\%.$$

Unlike the BHB framework, our framework also considers risk, defined in this case by variability (standard deviation of returns). In addition, we use the Sharpe ratio to guide us in our analysis. Looking at Table 4–4, we see that return attributable to Active Asset Allocation Policy is 12.23%. The return attributable to Policy and Timing is 12.43%. Under the BHB framework, this would be all that we would consider and we would conclude that Timing added 0.20% to returns, which we would deem to be a positive. In considering risk as well, we see that Policy and Timing also added 0.13% to the standard deviation, resulting in a Sharpe ratio nearly identical to that of Policy.

We may conclude from this analysis that the incremental increase in risk was acceptable in exchange for the increase in return, depending on the guidelines under which the plan is to be managed. However, it should be clear that to look at return alone, without considering risk, could lead one to incorrect conclusions. Likewise, we can see that Policy and Style results in lower return but with slightly reduced risk. Policy and Security Selection results in higher returns, accompanied by higher risk. Overall, active management produces a 12.37% return, compared with 12.23% for the benchmark policy. Under the BHB framework, we would conclude that this is a success. Under our framework, it is not so conclusive. Return is higher but so is risk. The Sharpe ratio of the actual portfolio is 1.13 *versus* 1.15 for the benchmark. Granted, Sharpe ratio is not a perfect indicator and for a particular fund, a given increase in return may be worth a corresponding increase in variability, even if it results in a lower Sharpe ratio.

One important caveat is that determining style class weightings is not always easy. Christopherson addresses some of the issues involved with style class analysis. He compares a quantitative approach described by Sharpe and a more qualitative approach employed by his firm.

Sharpe advocates a method whereby asset class returns are regressed against various benchmark indices. Using the method of least-squares and constraining the sum of weightings to 100%, one obtains an average style class weighing over rolling time periods. The two primary drawback to this method are that the result is a rolling time period average, whereas our framework demands a period-specific weighting. Being a rolling time period average, it naturally reacts slowly to style changes and mutes the amplitude of style changes. Another drawback is that it is at best an estimate. Results are likely to be better, the closer the investments mimic the index. To the extent that security selection differs from the index, results will be increasingly unreliable. Christopherson clearly considers this to be the inferior methodology but to the analyst without access to better information, this may be the only method of determining style class weightings. In our opinion, an estimate of style class weightings, which the Sharpe method would provide, would lead to more useful results than ignoring style altogether.

Christopherson prefers determining the effective style mix through a direct analysis of the fund's holdings. Logically, we would agree that this method would work better but we do not always have access to this kind of information and processing that much information might prove unwieldy. If the analysis is to be used internally by the fund, a good compromise might be to classify the various fund managers according to a style (even if in practice fund managers do not always belong in the style class to which they profess). Again, we emphasize that a close approximation of style weightings is better than ignoring style altogether.

In this chapter, we have developed a general framework for return attribution. Our framework provides for the distinction between passive asset allocation policy and active asset allocation policy. It also provides for style classifications. Finally, the framework includes risk, which enables the analyst to make a more informed analysis than simply using return alone.

In the next chapter, we will look at a system that can be used to add value in the asset allocation process. We discuss a number of pitfalls and caveats of using such a system.

CHAPTER 5

A Disciplined Approach to Active Asset Allocation

We have seen that the relative importance of active asset allocation is largely determined by the range of freedom to shift asset class weights away from target weights as determined by investment policy. This chapter will explore a disciplined approach to active allocation that will improve returns. Any disciplined active asset allocation system we propose must share two important qualities: First, it must have demonstrated that it added value in the past and, second, it must have a logical reason behind it that leads us to believe it will continue to work in the future. If we simply search the data for relationships that have existed in the past without thinking about the causal relationships, we are likely to find the explanatory power of the system disappears as soon as we try to implement it for the future. As the old saying goes, if we torture a set of data long enough, sooner or later it will confess to something.

A classic example of a variable with tremendous explanatory power but without causal effect is the Super Bowl winner. It is well documented that the winner of this football championship has accurately predicted whether the U.S. stock market will post positive or negative returns in the ensuing year. By normal statistical methods, the null hypothesis that the Super Bowl winner does not determine future market direction can be rejected at even the most microscopic level of confidence. Logic tells us that the winner of a football game has no connection whatsoever with the financial markets.

The variables used in this discussion have all been reported as having predictive powers with regard to future asset class performance. In addition, they have enough connection with the financial markets that we can reasonably expect they will continue to have predictive powers. Unfortunately, despite any system's success in the past and even with theoretical groundwork to support why the system should work, a risk remains that it will not work in the future.

The goal in this chapter is to develop a systematic approach for active asset allocation, considering factors that logically seem would be good predictors of future asset class returns. Another goal is to simplify the model so inputs to the system are readily available from sources such as the *Wall Street Journal* or a Bloomberg terminal, and do not require a Ph.D. in mathematics. We will also look at some of the pitfalls of this kind of system.

The Klemkosky and Bharati Predictive Variables

In their article, "Time-Varying Expected Returns and Asset Allocation," (*Journal of Portfolio Management,* Summer 1995), Klemkosky and Bharati found eleven predictive variables over the January 1964 through December 1990 period that provided significant added value even when considering transaction costs. Specifically, they found that active allocation without transaction costs produced an arithmetic mean of annual returns of 16.06%, with standard deviation of 9.25%, and terminal wealth of $66.47 on an initial investment of $1.00. Active allocation with transaction costs produced an arithmetic mean of annual returns of 13.27%, with standard deviation of 9.12%, and terminal wealth of $31.60. Transaction costs reduced investment return by a full 2.79% a year, which is one of the hazards of a very active investment strategy. Even with the heavy drain due to transaction costs, the active asset allocation strategy far outdistanced a simple buy-and-hold strategy. A 60% stock/40% Treasury-bills mix over the same 27 year period resulted in an arithmetic mean of annual returns of only 9.08%, with a similar standard deviation of 9.15%, and terminal wealth of $10.29. The lowest risk mix of stocks and corporate bonds produced a higher standard deviation, 9.51%, than the active asset allocation strategy, while producing an arithmetic mean of annual returns of only 7.95%, and terminal wealth of $7.53.

Following is how Klemkosky and Bharati used the eleven predictive variables to create a successful active asset allocation system. Since all eleven of their variables were selected based upon research by other writers, reference to the original source in discussing their use will be made. In many cases, alternative variables are suggested that, for all practical purposes are equivalent, but are easier to obtain. Specifically, alternative variables seek to achieve our secondary goal: All information can be obtained from either the *Wall Street Journal* or a Bloomberg terminal.

Finally, we will look at the calculations developed by Klemkosky and Bharati and look for ways in which they might be simplified.

Following is a list of the eleven variables used by Klemkosky and Bharati in their analysis.

1. The yield of a one month T-bill.
2. The yield of a two month T-bill minus the yield on a one month T-bill.
3. The yield of a six month T-bill minus the yield on a one month T-bill.
4. One lag of the one month holding-period return on a two month T-bill less the return on a one month T-bill.
5. The yield on the Moody's Baa-rated bond minus the one-month T-bill yield.
6. The ratio of the real S&P Composite Index over its long-term average.
7. The negative logarithm of the share prices averaged across the last quintile of the NYSE.
8. The dividend yield on the S&P Composite Index.
9. The earnings yield on the S&P Composite Index.
10. The yield on long-term government bonds.
11. The yield on intermediate-term government bonds.

The Campbell Variables

Campbell identified the first four variables as having predictive value for the excess returns on two-month T-bills, six-month T-bills, five- to ten-year Treasury bonds, and the value-weighted index of New York Stock Exchange stocks over the period from May 1959 through November 1983. Data were obtained from the Center for Research in Security Prices (CRSP) tapes, augmented by Fama's term structure files on bills and bonds.

Campbell split the sample into two separate periods, May 1959 through August 1979 and September 1979 through November 1983 because of instability in data due to Federal Reserve operating procedure changes. For the first sample period, all asset returns, except bonds, were predictable at conventional significance levels. In the second sample period, all asset returns, including bonds, were predictable at conventional significance levels.

Campbell's methodology differed significantly from Klemkosky and Bharati's methodology in that Campbell regressed the predictive variables over the entire sample period while Klemkosky and Bharati used rolling five-year periods for their analysis. In order for these variables to have useful predictive value, coefficients for the predictive variables based on an analysis of past data that can be used to predict future asset class returns has to be determined. Unfortunately, the evidence in the Campbell study indicates that the coefficients in the second period were completely different from those in the first period, so that if one had obtained the results for the first period and tried to use them in the second period, the results would have been mediocre.

Applying the Campbell Variables

In order to simplify things, T-bill information will be from the *Wall Street Journal* rather than CRSP. For the one-month and the two-month bills, those with the shortest maturities, just over one and two months, respectively will be used. For the six-month bill, we will use the most recently auctioned six-month bill, meaning that its maturity might be slightly less than six months. The reason is straightforward. Variable four requires subtracting the return on the one-month bill from the return on the two-month bill. If we use a one month bill with a maturity just under a month, it will mature prior to the end of the following month, making a calculation of its return impossible. The most recently auctioned six-month bill is used because if we limit ourselves to those bills with maturities just over six months we will find that, since one-year bills are auctioned only once every four weeks, the available bills for measurement will range from six months to six months and four weeks. This would introduce unwanted error into our calculations. For purposes of valuing each bill, we will use the average of the bid and ask price as published in the *Wall Street Journal*, so that the widening spread that naturally occurs as the bill approaches maturity does not distort our valuations.

The Keim and Stambaugh Variables

Keim and Stambaugh identified variables five through seven as having predictive value for rates of return in excess of the short-term interest rate on a number of asset class returns over the period from January 1928 through November 1978. The seven bond and stock portfolios tested were long-term U.S. Government bonds, long-term high-grade corporate bonds, long-term BAA-rated corporate bonds, long-term under-BAA-rated corporate bonds, and common stocks making up the fifth, third, and first quintile of size on the New York Stock Exchange. Keim and Stambaugh concluded that the evidence "appears to support the hypothesis that expected risk premiums change over time and that levels of asset prices contain information about expected premiums, especially for the bond portfolios." Their basis for using these variables was a belief that the "levels of asset prices might be inversely related to expected future returns."

Keim and Stambaugh calculated a ratio of the current value of the S&P index relative to its recent average. For small stocks, they used the negative of the logarithm of the current value of small firms. It turns out that their primary reason for making this choice was a lack of earlier data for small firms. Either a ratio of current value relative to a recent average, the negative of the logarithm of the current value, or even a system of zones as described in Chapter 2, share the quality that they describe the current level of asset class prices, relative to other times.

Applying the Keim and Stambaugh Variables

For our purposes, we will use the current index level divided by the average of the previous five years of the S&P 500 to represent large stocks and the Frank Russell 2000 Index to represent small stocks. The index value of the S&P 500 is listed in the *Wall Street Journal,* while the values for the Frank Russell 2000 Index and the yield on the Moody's Baa corporate bond index is available from Bloomberg. The index names are SPX, RTY, and MCBAA, respectively.

Both the dividend yield (D/P) and the earnings yield (E/P) on the S&P 500 are available from Bloomberg. The index names are OYSPCSC and USEPSPEP. For their study, Klemkosky and Bharati used Ibbotson Associates data for yields on intermediate- and long-term Government Bonds. The Ibbotson Associates intermediate- and long-term Government Bond portfolios are generally made up of only one bond, which is changed infrequently. We feel that satisfactory results can be obtained by simply using the yield of the current ten-year Treasury Note and the thirty-year Treasury Bond. These can be found in the *Wall Street Journal* or on Bloomberg, as the generic ten-year note and the thirty-year bond index, named GT10 and GT30 in their system.

The Methodology

To summarize, the original list of eleven predictive variables was modified as indicated by the italicized in the following:

1. The yield of a one month T-bill.
2. The yield of a two month T-bill minus the yield on a one month T-bill.

3. The yield of a six month T-bill minus the yield on a one month T-bill.
4. One lag of the one month holding-period return on a two month T-bill less the return on a one month T-bill.
5. The yield on the Moody's Baa-rated bond minus the one-month T-bill yield.
6. *The index value of the S&P 500 Index divided by the monthly index values over the past sixty months.*
7. *The index value of the Frank Russell 2000 Index divided by the monthly index values over the past sixty months.*
8. The dividend yield on the S&P 500 Composite Index.
9. The earnings yield on the S&P 500 Composite Index.
10. The yield on the current ten-year Treasury Note.
11. *The yield on the current thirty-year Treasury Bond.*

In order to calculate the value for variable four, we had to compute the previous month's holding period return for the two month bill and the one month bill. To do this, we calculate the values of two month and one month bills, one month prior, and the current value of those bills when they have become the one and zero months bills, respectively. The formula for the value of a bill is, $Value = 100 - \frac{n \cdot Discount}{360}(100)$.

The asset classes whose returns we are trying to predict are U.S. stocks and bonds, as represented by the S&P 500 and the Lehman Brothers Government/Corporate Bond Index.

Klemkosky and Bharati hypothesized that "the monthly return on an asset class is a linear combination of the values of the eleven variables at the beginning of the month plus some random error." Mathematically, this can be stated as:

$$r_{it} = \alpha_i + \sum_{j=1}^{11} \beta_j z_{j,t-1} + \varepsilon_{it}$$

where r_{it} is the return on the *i*th asset class in time period *t*; α_i is the asset class-specific intercept term; β_j represents the coefficients on the predictive variables; $z_{j,t-1}$ refers to the eleven predictive variables; and ε_{it} is a zero mean random error term. Finding r_{it} requires performing a least-squares regression analysis using all eleven variables plus a constant, which in itself requires solving a system of twelve equations in twelve unknowns. This in itself seems like a lot of work but Klemkosky and Bharati go on to suggest that results can be further improved by finding Mallows' "criterion value" for all possible subsets of predictive variables and using the subset with the smallest criterion value. Unfortunately, that means performing 2^{11}, or 2048, separate regression analyses.

The criterion value is defined as:

$$C_p = \frac{(T - K_1)\sigma_1^2}{\sigma^2} + 2K_1 - T,$$

where σ^2 is the mean squared error estimate for the model using all explanatory variables, while σ_1^2 is the mean squared error for the model with only K_1 explanatory variables. T is the number of observations. The model with the lowest C_p (criterion value) is the model chosen. Interestingly, the work referenced by Klemkosky, *et al* in describing Mallows' criterion stated that "no rule such as minimizing C_p is advised in applied work."

With that caveat in mind, we will proceed.

Once the predictive models have been chosen and predictions for the ensuing month's stock and bond returns have been calculated, we must then make the asset allocation decision. Klemkosky and Bharati chose to use the mix that produced the highest Sharpe ratio among the two risky asset classes, stocks and bonds. They calculated this using the predicted values from the models as the expected return and using the historical variances and covariances from the previous five year period to determine portfolio variance. In many cases, the predicted value for the risky assets fell below the one-month Treasury-bill rate. In those cases, they invested in Treasury-bills.

For the remainder of this chapter we will examine whether over the five year period between 1991 and 1995 our modified strategy outperformed the Klemkosky-Bharati strategy. Following this review, we will look at some ways in which the strategy might be modified in order to improve its effectiveness.

Implementing the Methodology: Stock Returns, December 1985–November 1990

Our task has two parts. First, we must perform a least-squares regression analysis to find the eleven coefficients associated with each predictive variable plus the constant associated with subsequent stock and bond returns over the sixty-month period being examined. The calculation is not necessary for subsequent bill returns. Once the coefficients have been determined, they are applied to the data in the 61st month to produce the system's prediction for asset class returns. Second, we must do this same calculation for all possible combinations of predictive variables, 2048 in all, to determine which model is best. We determine the best model by calculating Mallows' Criterion for each model and choosing the model with the lowest value.

Table 5–1 shows the values of the eleven predictive variables from December 1985 through November 1990 as well as the ensuing one-month asset class returns. To complete the regression analysis, we must solve a set of twelve equations in twelve unknowns. The twelve equations are given by the following two formulas:

$$\text{Assuming, } y = \alpha + \sum_{i=1}^{11} B_i x_i + \varepsilon,$$

where α is the constant intercept term and each B_i is the coefficient for each dependent variable x_i, and ε is the zero expected mean error term,

$$\sum_{k=1}^{60} x_{ik} y_k = \alpha \sum_{k=1}^{60} x_{ik} + \sum_{j=1}^{11} \sum_{k=1}^{60} B_j x_{ik} x_{jk}, \text{ for i = 1 to 11, and}$$

$$\sum_{k=1}^{60} y_k = 60\alpha + \sum_{j=1}^{11} B_j \sum_{k=1}^{60} x_{jk}.$$

Table 5–2 shows the 12x12 matrix to be used to solve for the data in Table 5–1, based on the formulas given above.

To solve the 12x12 matrix we use a process called row reduction. Although row reducing one 12x12 matrix, let alone 2048 of them, is an extremely daunting task for most people, the process is well suited for a computer.

The process of row-reduction transforms the messy matrix in Table 5–2 to one which contains diagonal entries and zeroes everywhere else except in column 13. The numbers that remain in column 13 are the coefficients we are searching for. If we define the entries in the matrix as M(row #, column #), the generic code in Figure 5–1 will produce a row-reduced matrix.

Modifications to the code in Figure 5–1 must be made before solving for the other 2047 subsets of data to prevent division by zero errors. Excel users might also like to experiment with the built-in LINEST function, which solves systems of equations faster than the macro. This, however, presents problems when solving for systems of equations with zero entries, which will be the case when solving the 2047 subsets of data. We were unable to successfully incorporate the LINEST function.

TABLE 5–1 Eleven Predictive Variables: December 1985–November 1990

Month-end	TB1M	TB2MS	TB6MS	2M-1M HPR	Baa - TB1M	S&P 500 Ratio	FR 2000 Ratio	Div/P	E/P	TN10	TB30	Subsequent Month	Subsequent Returns: Stocks	Bonds	Bills
Dec-85	6.392%	0.524%	0.890%	0.140%	5.188%	1.405	1.360	3.88%	7.42%	8.99%	9.27%	Jan-86	0.447%	0.590%	0.56%
Jan-86	6.763%	0.292%	0.535%	0.047%	4.677%	1.397	1.367	3.90%	7.10%	9.05%	9.32%	Feb-86	7.609%	4.200%	0.53%
Feb-86	6.864%	0.252%	0.391%	0.029%	4.246%	1.483	1.448	3.72%	7.01%	8.14%	8.28%	Mar-86	5.519%	3.540%	0.60%
Mar-86	6.203%	0.273%	0.257%	0.092%	4.297%	1.545	1.499	3.50%	6.51%	7.35%	7.44%	Apr-86	-1.283%	0.450%	0.52%
Apr-86	5.834%	0.241%	0.504%	0.080%	4.356%	1.507	1.502	3.43%	6.28%	7.34%	7.45%	May-86	5.348%	-1.980%	0.49%
May-86	6.085%	0.261%	0.497%	0.009%	4.205%	1.565	1.535	3.42%	6.12%	8.05%	7.75%	Jun-86	1.639%	2.900%	0.52%
Jun-86	6.018%	0.028%	0.092%	0.053%	4.322%	1.568	1.513	3.36%	5.97%	7.32%	7.23%	Jul-86	-5.699%	0.650%	0.52%
Jul-86	5.570%	0.259%	0.384%	0.040%	4.590%	1.458	1.354	3.43%	6.07%	7.28%	7.42%	Aug-86	7.517%	2.640%	0.46%
Aug-86	5.064%	0.086%	0.233%	0.078%	5.116%	1.545	1.382	3.36%	5.89%	6.92%	7.20%	Sep-86	-8.227%	-1.250%	0.45%
Sep-86	5.137%	0.133%	0.379%	0.008%	5.063%	1.395	1.280	3.43%	6.08%	7.42%	7.60%	Oct-86	5.638%	1.450%	0.46%
Oct-86	5.064%	-0.010%	0.360%	0.006%	5.176%	1.454	1.316	3.49%	6.20%	7.32%	7.61%	Nov-86	2.509%	1.220%	0.39%
Nov-86	5.014%	0.360%	0.547%	0.005%	5.056%	1.468	1.296	3.40%	6.01%	7.14%	7.41%	Dec-86	-2.684%	0.360%	0.49%
Dec-86	5.055%	0.621%	0.713%	0.062%	4.915%	1.409	1.244	3.38%	5.96%	7.23%	7.49%	Jan-87	13.387%	1.370%	0.42%
Jan-87	5.519%	0.095%	0.222%	0.070%	4.201%	1.577	1.373	3.17%	5.59%	7.18%	7.48%	Feb-87	4.138%	0.660%	0.43%
Feb-87	5.306%	0.211%	0.287%	0.032%	4.344%	1.611	1.468	3.02%	5.28%	7.16%	7.46%	Mar-87	2.739%	-0.550%	0.47%
Mar-87	5.238%	0.174%	0.665%	0.043%	4.372%	1.627	1.483	2.93%	5.07%	7.54%	7.92%	Apr-87	-0.886%	-2.660%	0.44%
Apr-87	4.802%	0.466%	1.322%	0.064%	5.238%	1.582	1.417	2.99%	5.01%	8.18%	8.44%	May-87	1.048%	-0.440%	0.38%
May-87	5.327%	0.390%	1.021%	0.041%	5.183%	1.567	1.392	3.02%	5.25%	8.47%	8.64%	Jun-87	4.995%	1.240%	0.48%
Jun-87	5.390%	0.278%	0.729%	0.057%	5.130%	1.616	1.405	2.92%	5.03%	8.37%	8.50%	Jul-87	4.986%	-0.220%	0.46%
Jul-87	5.503%	0.279%	0.790%	0.044%	5.107%	1.665	1.424	2.83%	4.89%	8.65%	8.90%	Aug-87	3.814%	-0.560%	0.47%
Aug-87	5.471%	0.642%	1.000%	0.051%	5.329%	1.693	1.444	2.69%	4.48%	8.97%	9.16%	Sep-87	-2.187%	-2.150%	0.45%
Sep-87	6.416%	0.165%	0.768%	0.024%	4.894%	1.622	1.395	2.78%	4.52%	9.59%	9.75%	Oct-87	-21.563%	3.750%	0.60%
Oct-87	3.935%	0.793%	2.156%	0.207%	7.685%	1.248	0.953	3.25%	5.17%	8.88%	9.04%	Nov-87	-8.181%	0.630%	0.35%
Nov-87	3.906%	1.135%	2.341%	0.147%	7.324%	1.131	0.895	3.66%	6.33%	8.97%	9.10%	Dec-87	7.381%	1.370%	0.39%
Dec-87	3.774%	1.627%	2.595%	0.165%	7.516%	1.204	0.962	3.71%	6.49%	8.86%	8.98%	Jan-88	4.222%	3.430%	0.29%
Jan-88	5.200%	0.455%	1.007%	0.158%	5.870%	1.242	0.997	3.66%	6.37%	8.26%	8.42%	Feb-88	4.689%	1.150%	0.46%
Feb-88	5.214%	0.388%	0.839%	0.075%	5.406%	1.282	1.079	3.56%	6.31%	8.15%	8.34%	Mar-88	-3.075%	-0.990%	0.44%
Mar-88	5.787%	0.098%	0.613%	0.002%	4.783%	1.228	1.121	3.48%	6.57%	8.54%	8.76%	Apr-88	1.029%	-0.580%	0.46%
Apr-88	5.685%	0.328%	0.886%	0.020%	5.215%	1.229	1.138	3.57%	6.62%	8.89%	9.10%	May-88	0.772%	-0.670%	0.51%
May-88	6.214%	0.306%	0.854%	0.005%	4.826%	1.224	1.105	3.80%	7.08%	9.15%	9.24%	Jun-88	4.646%	2.260%	0.49%
Jun-88	6.425%	0.160%	0.510%	0.023%	4.575%	1.267	1.179	3.59%	6.84%	8.88%	8.92%	Jul-88	-0.394%	-0.570%	0.51%

TABLE 5–1 *(Continued)*

Month-end	TB1M	TB2MS	TB6MS	2M-1M HPR	Baa - TB1M	S&P 500 Ratio	FR 2000 Ratio	Div/P	E/P	TN10	TB30	Subsequent Returns: Subsequent Month	Subsequent Returns: Stocks	Subsequent Returns: Bonds	Subsequent Returns: Bills
Jul-88	6.302%	0.577%	1.093%	0.047%	4.808%	1.250	1.164	3.65%	6.93%	9.11%	9.21%	Aug-88	-3.329%	0.260%	0.59%
Aug-88	7.090%	0.198%	0.685%	0.032%	4.120%	1.192	1.127	3.75%	7.26%	9.24%	9.30%	Sep-88	4.234%	2.190%	0.62%
Sep-88	7.042%	0.213%	0.698%	0.010%	3.858%	1.230	1.149	3.69%	8.08%	8.94%	9.05%	Oct-88	2.689%	1.770%	0.61%
Oct-88	6.688%	0.582%	1.079%	0.060%	3.732%	1.252	1.130	3.61%	7.85%	8.65%	8.74%	Nov-88	-1.420%	-1.130%	0.57%
Nov-88	6.760%	1.108%	1.535%	0.088%	3.720%	1.218	1.085	3.70%	8.29%	9.06%	9.07%	Dec-88	1.770%	0.340%	0.63%
Dec-88	6.287%	1.542%	2.265%	0.166%	4.363%	1.226	1.121	3.68%	8.20%	9.14%	8.99%	Jan-89	7.222%	1.330%	0.55%
Jan-89	7.841%	0.421%	0.877%	0.139%	2.809%	1.302	1.166	3.64%	7.65%	8.98%	8.82%	Feb-89	-2.486%	-0.760%	0.61%
Feb-89	7.726%	1.061%	1.357%	0.079%	2.884%	1.252	1.165	3.59%	7.70%	9.30%	9.12%	Mar-89	2.359%	0.540%	0.67%
Mar-89	8.635%	0.167%	0.742%	0.094%	2.035%	1.266	1.182	3.68%	8.14%	9.28%	9.10%	Apr-89	5.140%	2.122%	0.67%
Apr-89	8.477%	0.153%	0.419%	0.035%	2.133%	1.317	1.225	3.59%	7.86%	9.06%	8.93%	May-89	4.044%	2.459%	0.79%
May-89	8.502%	0.201%	0.246%	0.010%	1.958%	1.343	1.266	3.52%	7.78%	8.60%	8.60%	Jun-89	-0.545%	3.260%	0.71%
Jun-89	8.137%	-0.074%	-0.105%	0.063%	1.893%	1.322	1.225	3.44%	7.69%	8.08%	8.04%	Jul-89	8.982%	2.076%	0.70%
Jul-89	7.829%	0.043%	-0.094%	0.012%	2.041%	1.423	1.266	3.38%	7.54%	7.81%	7.92%	Aug-89	1.917%	-1.549%	0.74%
Aug-89	7.657%	0.272%	0.453%	-0.046%	2.223%	1.426	1.281	3.28%	7.27%	8.25%	8.21%	Sep-89	-0.378%	0.439%	0.65%
Sep-89	7.604%	0.345%	0.601%	0.010%	2.306%	1.399	1.270	3.29%	7.28%	8.29%	8.24%	Oct-89	-2.355%	2.529%	0.68%
Oct-89	7.873%	-0.029%	1.445%	0.032%	1.937%	1.348	1.183	3.29%	7.22%	7.91%	7.91%	Nov-89	2.064%	0.907%	0.69%
Nov-89	7.129%	0.579%	0.553%	0.032%	2.681%	1.354	1.179	3.39%	7.04%	7.83%	7.89%	Dec-89	2.363%	0.147%	0.61%
Dec-89	6.196%	1.346%	1.560%	0.152%	3.624%	1.367	1.171	3.32%	6.80%	7.94%	7.98%	Jan-90	-6.714%	-1.369%	0.57%
Jan-90	7.313%	0.504%	0.672%	0.139%	2.627%	1.258	1.058	3.41%	6.96%	8.42%	8.45%	Feb-90	1.277%	0.219%	0.57%
Feb-90	7.653%	0.262%	0.371%	0.052%	2.487%	1.257	1.084	3.54%	7.04%	8.52%	8.55%	Mar-90	2.608%	0.007%	0.64%
Mar-90	7.949%	0.021%	0.169%	0.007%	2.261%	1.275	1.119	3.49%	6.77%	8.63%	8.63%	Apr-90	-2.472%	-0.922%	0.69%
Apr-90	7.707%	0.170%	0.601%	0.021%	2.583%	1.228	1.075	3.51%	6.75%	9.02%	9.00%	May-90	9.746%	2.905%	0.68%
May-90	7.586%	0.256%	0.459%	0.024%	2.824%	1.329	1.143	3.44%	6.31%	8.60%	8.58%	Jun-90	-0.686%	1.614%	0.63%
Jun-90	7.635%	0.191%	0.273%	0.022%	2.585%	1.304	1.138	3.36%	6.00%	8.41%	8.40%	Jul-90	-0.326%	1.241%	0.68%
Jul-90	7.457%	0.146%	0.148%	0.051%	2.743%	1.284	1.081	3.37%	6.01%	8.34%	8.41%	Aug-90	-9.039%	-1.447%	0.66%
Aug-90	7.412%	0.074%	0.221%	0.011%	2.998%	1.151	0.929	3.65%	6.42%	8.85%	8.99%	Sep-90	-4.924%	0.831%	0.60%
Sep-90	6.945%	0.304%	0.482%	0.031%	3.695%	1.084	0.842	3.85%	6.71%	8.80%	8.95%	Oct-90	-0.349%	1.325%	0.68%
Oct-90	6.674%	0.496%	0.660%	0.079%	4.066%	1.069	0.789	4.01%	6.96%	8.62%	8.76%	Nov-90	6.415%	2.176%	0.57%
Nov-90	6.581%	0.443%	0.675%	0.084%	4.039%	1.125	0.846	3.91%	6.85%	8.25%	8.49%	Dec-90	2.771%	1.511%	0.60%
Dec-90	5.937%	0.498%	0.693%	0.116%	4.493%	1.145	0.877	3.74%	6.58%	8.07%	8.25%	Jan-91	4.431%	1.123%	0.52%

TABLE 5–2 Row-Reduction Matrix

	1	2	3	4	5	6	7	8	9	10	11	12	13
1	2.5533E-01	1.3807E-02	2.6799E-02	2.0681E-03	1.4753E-01	5.2053E+00	4.6501E+00	1.3355E-01	2.5756E-01	3.2369E-01	3.2678E-01	3.8486E+00	4.4595E-02
2	1.3807E-02	1.6558E-03	2.7340E-03	2.0346E-04	1.0482E-02	3.0210E-01	2.6473E-01	8.0140E-03	1.5365E-02	1.9596E-02	1.9781E-02	2.2883E-01	3.7180E-03
3	2.6799E-02	2.7340E-03	5.2004E-03	3.6477E-04	2.0588E-02	5.9180E-01	5.1919E-01	1.5459E-02	2.9409E-02	3.8202E-02	3.8608E-02	4.4526E-01	6.1239E-03
4	2.0681E-03	2.0346E-04	3.6477E-04	3.4696E-05	1.5592E-03	4.5462E-02	3.9825E-02	1.1938E-03	2.2580E-03	2.8849E-03	2.9167E-03	3.4121E-02	4.3395E-04
5	1.4753E-01	1.0482E-02	2.0588E-02	1.5592E-03	1.1070E-01	3.3422E+00	2.9665E+00	8.4212E-02	1.5667E-01	2.0419E-01	2.0718E-01	2.4424E+00	2.8175E-02
6	5.2053E+00	3.0210E-01	5.9180E-01	4.5462E-02	3.3422E+00	1.1262E+02	1.0063E+02	2.8013E+00	5.3192E+00	6.8029E+00	6.8851E+00	8.1664E+01	8.7536E-01
7	4.6501E+00	2.6473E-01	5.1919E-01	3.9825E-02	2.9665E+00	1.0063E+02	9.0244E+01	2.4973E+00	4.7514E+00	6.0578E+00	6.1297E+00	7.2782E+01	8.1882E-01
8	1.3355E-01	8.0140E-03	1.5459E-02	1.1938E-03	8.4212E-02	2.8013E+00	2.4973E+00	7.2143E-02	1.3763E-01	1.7389E-01	1.7584E-01	2.0736E+00	2.7200E-02
9	2.5756E-01	1.5365E-02	2.9409E-02	2.2580E-03	1.5667E-01	5.3192E+00	4.7514E+00	1.3763E-01	2.6510E-01	3.3176E-01	3.3513E-01	3.9486E+00	5.4867E-02
10	3.2369E-01	1.9596E-02	3.8202E-02	2.8849E-03	2.0419E-01	6.8029E+00	6.0578E+00	1.7389E-01	3.3176E-01	4.2304E-01	4.2768E-01	5.0217E+00	5.7118E-02
11	3.2678E-01	1.9781E-02	3.8608E-02	2.9167E-03	2.0718E-01	6.8851E+00	6.1297E+00	1.7584E-01	3.3513E-01	4.2768E-01	4.3248E-01	5.0795E+00	5.7710E-02
12	3.8486E+00	2.2883E-01	4.4526E-01	3.4121E-02	2.4424E+00	8.1664E+01	7.2782E+01	2.0736E+00	3.9486E+00	5.0217E+00	5.0795E+00	6.0000E+01	7.0471E-01

FIGURE 5–1 Generating a Row-Reduced Matrix

```
FOR I = 1 TO 12
    FOR J = 1 TO 12
        IF I <> J
            RATIO = - M(I,I)/M(J,I)
            FOR K = 1 TO 13
                M(J,K) = M(J,K) + RATIO * M(J,K)
            NEXT
        END IF
    NEXT
NEXT
FOR I = 1 TO 12
    M(I,13) = M(I,13) / M(I,I)
NEXT
```

Table 5–3 shows the results from solving for the data in Table 5–2. Beta 1 through Beta 11 refer to the coefficients associated with each of the eleven predictive variables, respectively. Alpha is the remaining constant.

As with all regression models, the coefficients and variables result in predicted values. Table 5–4 compares the predicted values with the ensuing month's actual values. From these data, we can make two important observations. First, there is a clear positive correlation between the predicted values and the actual values. In forty-one out of sixty months, the sign of the predicted value and actual value was the same. Furthermore, immediately before market collapses in the fall of 1987 and summer of 1990, the predicted values turned decidedly negative. Despite these positives, our second observation is that, in most cases, there is a wide discrepancy between the predicted and actual values. In statistic jargon, the standard error is high. Standard error is a measure of dispersion similar to standard deviation except that it measures the dispersion of actual values away from predicted values. Standard error is calculated as the square root of the sum of the squared errors divided by the number of observations. Squared error is the difference between the predicted and actual values squared. A standard error of 4.625% implies that 68.3% of actual values will fall within 4.625% of their predicted values and 95.4% of actual values will fall within 9.250%, or twice the standard error, of their predicted values. A standard error of 4.625% on a variable whose arithmetic mean is 1.175% is very high.

The most important thing to understand, however, is that we are using the information from the regression analyses to derive a useful predicted return for the 61st month. *We must take a leap of faith that a regression model, optimized for the preceding sixty month period, will also closely fit the data for the 61st month as well.* There is no guarantee that this will be the case. In the case of the data in Table 5–4, we can see that the predicted

TABLE 5–3 Regression Analysis: Stock Returns

Coefficient	Regression Result
Beta1	-1.0780E+01
Beta2	-3.5302E+00
Beta3	1.3159E+00
Beta4	2.8287E+00
Beta5	-8.1170E+00
Beta6	8.6286E-02
Beta7	5.5054E-02
Beta8	1.4882E+01
Beta9	1.3430E+00
Beta10	3.4599E+00
Beta11	7.5637E-01
Alpha	-1.0485E-01

TABLE 5–4 Predicted *versus* Subsequent Month's Actual Return: Stocks

Month-end	Predicted Return	Subsequent Month	Actual Return	Squared Error
Dec-85	3.658%	Jan-86	0.447%	1.031E-03
Jan-86	3.964%	Feb-86	7.609%	1.328E-03
Feb-86	0.732%	Mar-86	5.519%	2.292E-03
Mar-86	0.880%	Apr-86	-1.283%	4.679E-04
Apr-86	3.085%	May-86	5.348%	5.119E-04
May-86	4.337%	Jun-86	1.639%	7.277E-04
Jun-86	0.414%	Jul-86	-5.699%	3.737E-03
Jul-86	1.954%	Aug-86	7.517%	3.094E-03
Aug-86	1.860%	Sep-86	-8.227%	1.018E-02
Sep-86	2.815%	Oct-86	5.638%	7.971E-04
Oct-86	4.583%	Nov-86	2.509%	4.302E-04
Nov-86	2.666%	Dec-86	-2.684%	2.862E-03
Dec-86	2.045%	Jan-87	13.387%	1.286E-02
Jan-87	2.427%	Feb-87	4.138%	2.929E-04
Feb-87	1.214%	Mar-87	2.739%	2.324E-04
Mar-87	2.644%	Apr-87	-0.886%	1.246E-03
Apr-87	2.872%	May-87	1.048%	3.327E-04
May-87	-0.884%	Jun-87	4.995%	3.456E-03
Jun-87	-2.803%	Jul-87	4.986%	6.068E-03
Jul-87	-3.531%	Aug-87	3.814%	5.395E-03
Aug-87	-6.959%	Sep-87	-2.187%	2.277E-03
Sep-87	-9.194%	Oct-87	-21.563%	1.530E-02
Oct-87	-5.769%	Nov-87	-8.181%	5.818E-04
Nov-87	3.015%	Dec-87	7.381%	1.906E-03
Dec-87	3.026%	Jan-88	4.222%	1.431E-04
Jan-88	0.144%	Feb-88	4.689%	2.066E-03
Feb-88	2.334%	Mar-88	-3.075%	2.926E-03
Mar-88	2.332%	Apr-88	1.029%	1.698E-04
Apr-88	2.502%	May-88	0.772%	2.993E-04
May-88	4.758%	Jun-88	4.646%	1.261E-06
Jun-88	0.802%	Jul-88	-0.394%	1.431E-04
Jul-88	1.384%	Aug-88	-3.329%	2.221E-03
Aug-88	0.982%	Sep-88	4.234%	1.057E-03
Sep-88	2.962%	Oct-88	2.689%	7.445E-06
Oct-88	4.487%	Nov-88	-1.420%	3.489E-03
Nov-88	5.680%	Dec-88	1.770%	1.528E-03
Dec-88	5.294%	Jan-89	7.222%	3.718E-04
Jan-89	2.095%	Feb-89	-2.486%	2.099E-03
Feb-89	1.142%	Mar-89	2.359%	1.481E-04
Mar-89	2.699%	Apr-89	5.140%	5.960E-04
Apr-89	1.113%	May-89	4.044%	8.589E-04
May-89	-0.732%	Jun-89	-0.545%	3.485E-06
Jun-89	0.447%	Jul-89	8.982%	7.285E-03
Jul-89	0.998%	Aug-89	1.917%	8.445E-05
Aug-89	1.129%	Sep-89	-0.378%	2.273E-04
Sep-89	1.152%	Oct-89	-2.355%	1.230E-03
Oct-89	1.161%	Nov-89	2.064%	8.157E-05
Nov-89	0.818%	Dec-89	2.363%	2.388E-04
Dec-89	1.334%	Jan-90	-6.714%	6.477E-03
Jan-90	1.152%	Feb-90	1.277%	1.572E-06
Feb-90	1.431%	Mar-90	2.608%	1.385E-04
Mar-90	0.226%	Apr-90	-2.472%	7.282E-04
Apr-90	1.554%	May-90	9.746%	6.711E-03
May-90	-1.731%	Jun-90	-0.686%	1.091E-04
Jun-90	-2.992%	Jul-90	-0.326%	7.108E-04
Jul-90	-2.849%	Aug-90	-9.039%	3.832E-03
Aug-90	0.759%	Sep-90	-4.924%	3.229E-03
Sep-90	1.820%	Oct-90	-0.349%	4.704E-04
Oct-90	2.951%	Nov-90	6.415%	1.200E-03
Nov-90	2.079%	Dec-90	2.771%	4.782E-05
Dec-90	1.899%	Jan-91	4.431%	
Standard Error			4.625%	

value of 1.899%, which we consider to be a favorable prediction, is followed by an actual return of 4.431%.

Applying Mallow's Criterion

The next step is to perform regression analyses for the other 2047 possible combinations of predictive variables and select the model possessing the lowest Mallows' Criterion. The idea behind selecting the lowest Mallows' Criterion is that we want to use the model that has the most explanatory power per variable used, based on the belief that some of the variables have more explanatory power than others. By using all eleven variables, we minimize the standard error. However, an acceptably close standard error can be produced by using fewer variables. As shown in Table 5–5, for the January 1991 predicted return, Mallows' Criterion was minimized using five variables, as follows:

1. The yield of a one month T-bill.
5. The yield on the Moody's Baa-rated bond minus the one-month T-bill yield.
7. The index value of the Frank Russell 2000 Index divided by the average of the monthly index values over the past sixty months.
8. The dividend yield on the S&P 500 Composite Index.
10. The yield on the current ten year Treasury Note.

The coefficients for the other variables are set to zero.

It is interesting to note the signs of the coefficients in the model. The yield on the one month Treasury-bill is inversely related to ensuing stock

TABLE 5–5 Regression Results Applying Five Variables*

Coefficient	Regression Result
Beta1	-9.7075E+00
Beta2	0.0000E+00
Beta3	0.0000E+00
Beta4	0.0000E+00
Beta5	-7.6102E+00
Beta6	0.0000E+00
Beta7	1.0906E-01
Beta8	1.5172E+01
Beta9	0.0000E+00
Beta10	3.7382E+00
Beta11	0.0000E+00
Alpha	-2.5292E-02

*Coefficients for variables 2, 3, 4, 6, 9, and 11 are set at 0.

returns. Furthermore, a tightening of the spread between the Moody's Baa-rated bonds and one month Treasury-bills is also positively correlated with ensuing stock returns. Ironically, the Frank Russell 2000 Index ratio has a positive coefficient, meaning that the higher the index is relative to its past average, the higher ensuing stock returns are likely to be. This flies in the face of the original descriptions of Keim and Stambaugh who expected that the opposite would be true. Higher dividend yields are associated with higher ensuing stock returns.

Finally, the yield on the ten-year Treasury Note is directly related to ensuing stock returns. This is somewhat interesting considering that the opposite is true for the short end of the yield curve. It is also interesting that three of the five variables in the model are measurements of the bond market, while only two measure valuation levels in the stock market. Glaringly absent are variable six, the ratio of the real S&P 500 Composite Index over its long-term average, and variable nine, the earnings to price ratio.

Table 5–6 shows the predicted and actual values using the five variable model. The data in Table 5–6 are remarkably similar to those in Table 5–4. The standard error is only slightly higher, 4.676% *versus* 4.625%. The Mallows' Criterion is 6.2342. By definition, the Mallows' Criterion for the model with all explanatory variables is equal to the number of variables, or 11. Thus, the Mallows' Criterion in this case in nearly half as much as in the model using all eleven variables. More importantly, the predicted value for January 1991 is 2.117%, a better estimate than the one produced using the eleven variable model—1.899%.

Implementing the Methodology: Bond Returns, December 1985–November 1990

Table 5–7 shows the results of the regression analysis using all eleven predictive variables for predicting bond returns. Table 5–8 shows the corresponding predicted and actual values associated with the model. Again, we see a positive correlation between predicted and actual values. In 14 out of the 15 months with actual returns greater than 2%, the predicted value was positive. The one month that was incorrect was the fourth of four consecutive month with greater than 2% returns, indicating that something unusual was happening at that time in the bond market. Furthermore, the biggest down month, March 1987, had the largest negative prediction. We should, however, note that the predicted values still deviate from the actual values by quite a bit. The standard error is 1.216%, much lower than for stocks (4.625%), due to a generally lower level of variability in bond returns.

TABLE 5–6 Predicted *versus* Subsequent Month's Actual Return: Five Variable Model

Month-end	Predicted Return	Subsequent Month	Actual Return	Squared Error
Dec-85	3.241%	Jan-86	0.447%	7.806E-04
Jan-86	4.130%	Feb-86	7.609%	1.210E-03
Feb-86	1.183%	Mar-86	5.519%	1.881E-03
Mar-86	1.477%	Apr-86	-1.283%	7.618E-04
Apr-86	3.549%	May-86	5.348%	3.236E-04
May-86	5.117%	Jun-86	1.639%	1.210E-03
Jun-86	1.006%	Jul-86	-5.699%	4.495E-03
Jul-86	2.494%	Aug-86	7.517%	2.523E-03
Aug-86	1.293%	Sep-86	-8.227%	9.063E-03
Sep-86	2.809%	Oct-86	5.638%	8.001E-04
Oct-86	3.582%	Nov-86	2.509%	1.152E-04
Nov-86	2.723%	Dec-86	-2.684%	2.924E-03
Dec-86	2.864%	Jan-87	13.387%	1.107E-02
Jan-87	1.837%	Feb-87	4.138%	5.297E-04
Feb-87	1.500%	Mar-87	2.739%	1.535E-04
Mar-87	2.159%	Apr-87	-0.886%	9.273E-04
Apr-87	2.391%	May-87	1.048%	1.804E-04
May-87	-1.027%	Jun-87	4.995%	3.626E-03
Jun-87	-2.981%	Jul-87	4.986%	6.347E-03
Jul-87	-4.010%	Aug-87	3.814%	6.121E-03
Aug-87	-6.105%	Sep-87	-2.187%	1.535E-03
Sep-87	-8.819%	Oct-87	-21.563%	1.624E-02
Oct-87	-6.319%	Nov-87	-8.181%	3.469E-04
Nov-87	2.641%	Dec-87	7.381%	2.247E-03
Dec-87	3.538%	Jan-88	4.222%	4.682E-05
Jan-88	-0.407%	Feb-88	4.689%	2.597E-03
Feb-88	1.958%	Mar-88	-3.075%	2.533E-03
Mar-88	1.845%	Apr-88	1.029%	6.663E-05
Apr-88	2.405%	May-88	0.772%	2.667E-04
May-88	4.327%	Jun-88	4.646%	1.020E-05
Jun-88	0.803%	Jul-88	-0.394%	1.433E-04
Jul-88	1.828%	Aug-88	-3.329%	2.659E-03
Aug-88	1.020%	Sep-88	4.234%	1.033E-03
Sep-88	1.683%	Oct-88	2.689%	1.011E-04
Oct-88	3.574%	Nov-88	-1.420%	2.494E-03
Nov-88	5.369%	Dec-88	1.770%	1.295E-03
Dec-88	5.466%	Jan-89	7.222%	3.083E-04
Jan-89	1.484%	Feb-89	-2.486%	1.576E-03
Feb-89	2.456%	Mar-89	2.359%	9.492E-07
Mar-89	1.576%	Apr-89	5.140%	1.270E-03
Apr-89	0.639%	May-89	4.044%	1.159E-03
May-89	-0.601%	Jun-89	-0.545%	3.158E-07
Jun-89	-0.173%	Jul-89	8.982%	8.381E-03
Jul-89	0.222%	Aug-89	1.917%	2.874E-04
Aug-89	0.793%	Sep-89	-0.378%	1.372E-04
Sep-89	0.858%	Oct-89	-2.355%	1.033E-03
Oct-89	-1.312%	Nov-89	2.064%	1.140E-03
Nov-89	1.424%	Dec-89	2.363%	8.814E-05
Dec-89	2.563%	Jan-90	-6.714%	8.605E-03
Jan-90	1.236%	Feb-90	1.277%	1.694E-07
Feb-90	1.630%	Mar-90	2.608%	9.573E-05
Mar-90	0.516%	Apr-90	-2.472%	8.928E-04
Apr-90	1.697%	May-90	9.746%	6.479E-03
May-90	-0.854%	Jun-90	-0.686%	2.812E-06
Jun-90	-1.492%	Jul-90	-0.326%	1.359E-04
Jul-90	-1.702%	Aug-90	-9.039%	5.384E-03
Aug-90	1.299%	Sep-90	-4.924%	3.873E-03
Sep-90	2.427%	Oct-90	-0.349%	7.704E-04
Oct-90	3.402%	Nov-90	6.415%	9.080E-04
Nov-90	2.237%	Dec-90	2.771%	2.852E-05
Dec-90	2.117%	Jan-91	4.431%	
Standard Error			4.676%	
Mallows' Criterion			6.2342	

TABLE 5–7 Regression Analysis: Bond Returns

Coefficient	Regression Result
Beta1	2.4677E+00
Beta2	-1.6000E-01
Beta3	1.4733E+00
Beta4	-1.4666E+01
Beta5	1.8115E+00
Beta6	1.0990E-01
Beta7	-5.9856E-02
Beta8	4.3588E+00
Beta9	-4.9107E-01
Beta10	2.4052E+00
Beta11	-3.3532E+00
Alpha	-3.3903E-01

We should also emphasize again, the data should fit well for the sixty months because the regression model is based on those sixty month's data. The real question is how well will the model work for the 61st month.

Applying Mallow's Criterion

As we did for stocks, we must find the model for bonds that minimizes Mallows' Criterion. Table 5–9 shows the results of this search. For bonds, it turns out to be nine variable model that minimizes Mallows' Criterion. The nine predictive variables in this case are:

1. The yield of a one month T-bill.
3. The yield of a six month T-bill minus the yield on a one month T-bill.
4. One lag of the one month holding-period return on a two month T-bill less the return on a one month T-bill.
5. The yield on the Moody's Baa-rated bond minus the one-month T-bill yield.
6. The index value of the S&P 500 Index divided by the monthly index values over the past sixty months.
7. The index value of the Frank Russell 2000 Index divided by the monthly index values over the past sixty months.
8. The dividend yield on the S&P 500 Index.
10. The yield on the current ten year Treasury Note.
11. The yield on the current thirty year Treasury Bond.

TABLE 5–8 Predicted *versus* Subsequent Month's Actual Return: Bonds

Month-end	Predicted Return	Subsequent Month	Actual Return	Squared Error
Dec-85	1.553%	Jan-86	0.590%	9.269E-05
Jan-86	2.514%	Feb-86	4.200%	2.843E-04
Feb-86	3.064%	Mar-86	3.540%	2.263E-05
Mar-86	0.970%	Apr-86	0.450%	2.699E-05
Apr-86	0.029%	May-86	-1.980%	4.037E-04
May-86	2.579%	Jun-86	2.900%	1.028E-05
Jun-86	1.388%	Jul-86	0.650%	5.445E-05
Jul-86	0.613%	Aug-86	2.640%	4.109E-04
Aug-86	0.019%	Sep-86	-1.250%	1.610E-04
Sep-86	0.352%	Oct-86	1.450%	1.205E-04
Oct-86	0.769%	Nov-86	1.220%	2.036E-05
Nov-86	0.877%	Dec-86	0.360%	2.670E-05
Dec-86	-0.367%	Jan-87	1.370%	3.017E-04
Jan-87	-1.026%	Feb-87	0.660%	2.844E-04
Feb-87	-1.333%	Mar-87	-0.550%	6.125E-05
Mar-87	-1.869%	Apr-87	-2.660%	6.256E-05
Apr-87	-0.775%	May-87	-0.440%	1.125E-05
May-87	0.356%	Jun-87	1.240%	7.823E-05
Jun-87	0.126%	Jul-87	-0.220%	1.199E-05
Jul-87	0.084%	Aug-87	-0.560%	4.150E-05
Aug-87	0.218%	Sep-87	-2.150%	5.607E-04
Sep-87	1.300%	Oct-87	3.750%	6.003E-04
Oct-87	0.431%	Nov-87	0.630%	3.946E-06
Nov-87	1.096%	Dec-87	1.370%	7.502E-06
Dec-87	1.818%	Jan-88	3.430%	2.599E-04
Jan-88	0.810%	Feb-88	1.150%	1.159E-05
Feb-88	0.522%	Mar-88	-0.990%	2.287E-04
Mar-88	-0.207%	Apr-88	-0.580%	1.394E-05
Apr-88	0.408%	May-88	-0.670%	1.162E-04
May-88	2.257%	Jun-88	2.260%	6.310E-10
Jun-88	1.234%	Jul-88	-0.570%	3.256E-04
Jul-88	1.500%	Aug-88	0.260%	1.537E-04
Aug-88	1.737%	Sep-88	2.190%	2.048E-05
Sep-88	1.228%	Oct-88	1.770%	2.940E-05
Oct-88	0.358%	Nov-88	-1.130%	2.214E-04
Nov-88	0.643%	Dec-88	0.340%	9.184E-06
Dec-88	0.777%	Jan-89	1.330%	3.053E-05
Jan-89	1.188%	Feb-89	-0.760%	3.794E-04
Feb-89	1.504%	Mar-89	0.540%	9.301E-05
Mar-89	1.464%	Apr-89	2.122%	4.334E-05
Apr-89	1.742%	May-89	2.459%	5.140E-05
May-89	1.355%	Jun-89	3.260%	3.629E-04
Jun-89	-0.568%	Jul-89	2.076%	6.990E-04
Jul-89	0.108%	Aug-89	-1.549%	2.747E-04
Aug-89	1.357%	Sep-89	0.439%	8.420E-05
Sep-89	0.572%	Oct-89	2.529%	3.831E-04
Oct-89	1.723%	Nov-89	0.907%	6.665E-05
Nov-89	0.326%	Dec-89	0.147%	3.208E-06
Dec-89	-0.712%	Jan-90	-1.369%	4.313E-05
Jan-90	-1.365%	Feb-90	0.219%	2.509E-04
Feb-90	0.354%	Mar-90	0.007%	1.202E-05
Mar-90	0.965%	Apr-90	-0.922%	3.562E-04
Apr-90	0.912%	May-90	2.905%	3.973E-04
May-90	1.782%	Jun-90	1.614%	2.833E-06
Jun-90	0.938%	Jul-90	1.241%	9.208E-06
Jul-90	0.155%	Aug-90	-1.447%	2.567E-04
Aug-90	0.959%	Sep-90	0.831%	1.630E-06
Sep-90	1.650%	Oct-90	1.325%	1.055E-05
Oct-90	2.102%	Nov-90	2.176%	5.452E-07
Nov-90	1.697%	Dec-90	1.511%	3.447E-06
Dec-90	0.279%	Jan-91	1.123%	
Standard Error			1.216%	

TABLE 5–9 Regression Results Applying Nine Variables*

Coefficient	Regression Result
Beta1	2.4602E+00
Beta2	0.0000E+00
Beta3	1.0571E+00
Beta4	-1.5084E+01
Beta5	2.0326E+00
Beta6	1.2791E-01
Beta7	-7.7238E-02
Beta8	3.4067E+00
Beta9	0.0000E+00
Beta10	2.5752E+00
Beta11	-3.5050E+00
Alpha	-3.4904E-01

*Coefficients for variables 2 and 9 are set at 0.

Unlike stocks, the one-month Treasury-bill yield is directly related to ensuing bond returns. The yield on the ten-year Treasury Note is directly related to ensuing bond returns, while the yield on the thirty-year Treasury Bond is indirectly related. The most interesting variable is variable four, which purports to measure changes in bond yields. Specifically, a low value would generally indicate rising interest rates, while a high value would indicate falling interest rates. Of course, a shift in the shape of the yield curve would distort this variable. Unfortunately, variable four only measures what is happening on the short end of the yield curve. There is no similar measure for the intermediate- to long-end of the curve.

As indicated in Table 5–9, the coefficient for variable four is negative, from which we would conclude, albeit counter-intuitively, that rising interest rates were favorable for ensuing bond returns. While this seems perplexing, a look ahead to Table 5–13 indicates that in every model where variable four is included, the coefficient is negative. There are two feasible explanations for this. First, there could be significant twisting in the yield curve at extremely short maturities. Second, changes in interest rates might not trend. A rise in rates one month might be followed by a decline in the next, and vice versa.

Similar to Table 5–6, Table 5–10 shows the predicted and actual returns for the sixty-month period used for the regression, a predicted value for the 61st month, the standard error and Mallows' Criterion. As before, the standard error is only slightly higher than in the eleven variable model, 1.226% versus 1.216%. Mallows' Criterion is 9.8599. The predicted value for January 1991 was 0.298%, whereas in the eleven variable model it was 0.279%, a very slight difference. In light of the actual return of 1.123%, it appears that the model based on Mallows' Criterion did a

TABLE 5–10 Predicted *versus* Subsequent Month's Actual Return: Nine Variable Model

Month-end	Predicted Return	Subsequent Month	Actual Return	Squared Error
Dec-85	1.544%	Jan-86	0.590%	1.2948E-04
Jan-86	2.335%	Feb-86	4.200%	3.8819E-04
Feb-86	2.996%	Mar-86	3.540%	2.8011E-05
Mar-86	0.932%	Apr-86	0.450%	5.6866E-05
Apr-86	-0.222%	May-86	-1.980%	6.2892E-04
May-86	2.387%	Jun-86	2.900%	2.3343E-04
Jun-86	1.314%	Jul-86	0.650%	3.4062E-05
Jul-86	0.546%	Aug-86	2.640%	3.9905E-04
Aug-86	0.150%	Sep-86	-1.250%	1.6606E-04
Sep-86	0.407%	Oct-86	1.450%	7.9992E-05
Oct-86	0.864%	Nov-86	1.220%	3.8406E-05
Nov-86	0.979%	Dec-86	0.360%	8.1067E-06
Dec-86	-0.365%	Jan-87	1.370%	2.5410E-04
Jan-87	-0.983%	Feb-87	0.660%	3.6818E-04
Feb-87	-1.362%	Mar-87	-0.550%	2.3297E-05
Mar-87	-2.075%	Apr-87	-2.660%	1.2067E-04
Apr-87	-1.050%	May-87	-0.440%	2.4258E-05
May-87	0.313%	Jun-87	1.240%	7.9938E-05
Jun-87	0.228%	Jul-87	-0.220%	9.2890E-06
Jul-87	0.215%	Aug-87	-0.560%	3.6117E-05
Aug-87	0.330%	Sep-87	-2.150%	6.0493E-04
Sep-87	1.252%	Oct-87	3.750%	4.9073E-04
Oct-87	0.416%	Nov-87	0.630%	2.9546E-05
Nov-87	1.075%	Dec-87	1.370%	1.8338E-05
Dec-87	1.854%	Jan-88	3.430%	4.6576E-04
Jan-88	0.926%	Feb-88	1.150%	2.0019E-05
Feb-88	0.619%	Mar-88	-0.990%	1.9009E-04
Mar-88	-0.138%	Apr-88	-0.580%	1.4769E-04
Apr-88	0.410%	May-88	-0.670%	3.0231E-04
May-88	2.261%	Jun-88	2.260%	2.5710E-05
Jun-88	1.330%	Jul-88	-0.570%	4.9210E-04
Jul-88	1.435%	Aug-88	0.260%	2.4798E-04
Aug-88	1.665%	Sep-88	2.190%	6.7290E-08
Sep-88	1.583%	Oct-88	1.770%	4.7459E-06
Oct-88	0.602%	Nov-88	-1.130%	3.4972E-04
Nov-88	0.931%	Dec-88	0.340%	1.0313E-05
Dec-88	0.899%	Jan-89	1.330%	2.3698E-05
Jan-89	1.190%	Feb-89	-0.760%	2.6006E-04
Feb-89	1.444%	Mar-89	0.540%	9.4295E-05
Mar-89	1.442%	Apr-89	2.122%	4.9381E-05
Apr-89	1.850%	May-89	2.459%	5.2355E-05
May-89	1.492%	Jun-89	3.260%	1.7642E-04
Jun-89	-0.302%	Jul-89	2.076%	3.2600E-04
Jul-89	0.510%	Aug-89	-1.549%	3.9041E-04
Aug-89	1.610%	Sep-89	0.439%	6.6213E-05
Sep-89	0.739%	Oct-89	2.529%	3.1409E-04
Oct-89	1.396%	Nov-89	0.907%	1.0077E-04
Nov-89	0.464%	Dec-89	0.147%	4.4865E-06
Dec-89	-0.712%	Jan-90	-1.369%	5.0703E-05
Jan-90	-1.352%	Feb-90	0.219%	1.8877E-04
Feb-90	0.325%	Mar-90	0.007%	2.8261E-06
Mar-90	0.843%	Apr-90	-0.922%	2.7966E-04
Apr-90	0.674%	May-90	2.905%	5.3375E-04
May-90	1.579%	Jun-90	1.614%	1.2250E-05
Jun-90	0.630%	Jul-90	1.241%	1.5399E-05
Jul-90	-0.040%	Aug-90	-1.447%	2.5768E-04
Aug-90	0.756%	Sep-90	0.831%	1.8513E-05
Sep-90	1.503%	Oct-90	1.325%	2.3171E-05
Oct-90	2.012%	Nov-90	2.176%	1.7897E-04
Nov-90	1.606%	Dec-90	1.511%	4.8887E-05
Dec-90	0.298%	Jan-91	1.123%	
Standard Error			1.226%	
Mallows' Criterion			9.8599	

better job. However, both models predicted a return below the risk-free rate, 0.495%. Since the selection methodology uses the Sharpe Ratio, a predicted value below the risk-free rate ensures a negative contribution to the Sharpe Ratio. As a result, under both models, we would not include bonds in the portfolio.

Table 5–11 shows the values for the eleven predictive variables and subsequent asset class returns for the December 1990 through November 1995 period. The format is the same as in Table 5–1. This information will in following the calculations in Tables 5–12 through 5–14. These data can also be used by the interested reader who wants to develop his own active asset allocation system based on these variables.

Implementing the Methodology: Stock and Bond Returns, December 1990–November 1995

Tables 5–12 and 5–13 show the coefficients for the eleven variables as well as the constant, alpha, for stocks and bonds, respectively. In addition, we have included the values of K (the number of variables included in the optimal model), mean squared error, and Mallows' Criterion (C_p). From Table 5–12 we can make three key observations:

1. Generally, between three and eight variables are used for each model.
2. Generally, the signs of the coefficients for each variable are consistently the same over time. Notable exceptions are variables five, seven, and eight.
3. All of the variables are used at some time or another but some variables are used much more than others. Variables one, two, five, and six appear the most (more than 40 times), while variables three and four appear rarely (7 and 2 times, respectively).

From Table 5–13 we can make four observations:

1. The model on many occasions uses very few variables, sometimes even just two.
2. Again, the signs of the coefficients for each variable are consistently the same over time, with a modest number of exceptions.
3. Variables six, seven, ten, and eleven are used most, while variables two and three are used very little.
4. Variable ten, the intermediate term Treasury Note yield, appears in only 37 out of 60 months. Klemkosky and Bharati found that this variable occurred in 318 out of 324 models, or 98.1% of them.

TABLE 5–11 Eleven Predictive Variables: December 1990–November 1995

	Eleven Predictive Variables											Subsequent Returns			
Month-end	TB1M	TB2MS	TB6MS	2M-1M HPR	Baa - TB1M	S&P 500 Ratio	FR 2000 Ratio	Div/P	E/P	TN10	TB30	Subsequent Month	Stocks	Bonds	Bills
Dec-90	5.937%	0.498%	0.693%	0.116%	4.493%	1.145	0.877	3.74%	6.58%	8.07%	8.25%	Jan-91	4.431%	1.123%	0.52%
Jan-91	5.813%	0.374%	0.577%	0.093%	4.637%	1.184	0.956	3.82%	6.69%	8.01%	8.20%	Feb-91	7.162%	0.859%	0.48%
Feb-91	5.651%	0.443%	0.569%	0.055%	4.419%	1.255	1.060	3.35%	5.95%	8.04%	8.21%	Mar-91	2.371%	0.690%	0.44%
Mar-91	5.809%	0.053%	0.120%	0.063%	4.281%	1.272	1.130	3.26%	5.72%	8.06%	8.25%	Apr-91	0.280%	1.151%	0.53%
Apr-91	5.481%	0.045%	0.242%	0.041%	4.459%	1.263	1.125	3.19%	5.60%	8.02%	8.19%	May-91	4.277%	0.464%	0.47%
May-91	5.327%	0.174%	0.510%	0.020%	4.533%	1.302	1.173	3.23%	5.58%	8.06%	8.27%	Jun-91	-4.569%	-0.108%	0.42%
Jun-91	5.125%	0.383%	0.712%	0.044%	4.835%	1.229	1.099	3.23%	5.57%	8.23%	8.41%	Jul-91	4.666%	1.254%	0.49%
Jul-91	5.480%	0.074%	0.337%	0.036%	4.410%	1.276	1.132	3.22%	5.53%	8.15%	8.34%	Aug-91	2.361%	2.304%	0.46%
Aug-91	5.246%	0.109%	0.252%	0.029%	4.404%	1.291	1.169	3.10%	5.07%	7.82%	8.06%	Sep-91	-1.644%	2.089%	0.46%
Sep-91	5.057%	0.112%	0.186%	0.034%	4.453%	1.256	1.171	3.15%	5.03%	7.45%	7.81%	Oct-91	1.332%	0.894%	0.42%
Oct-91	4.732%	0.048%	0.209%	0.013%	4.758%	1.260	1.197	3.14%	5.02%	7.46%	7.92%	Nov-91	-4.032%	0.997%	0.39%
Nov-91	4.015%	0.351%	0.474%	0.064%	5.435%	1.195	1.135	3.15%	4.76%	7.38%	7.95%	Dec-91	11.433%	3.373%	0.38%
Dec-91	3.885%	-0.009%	0.008%	0.075%	5.375%	1.320	1.218	3.11%	4.58%	6.70%	7.40%	Jan-92	-1.850%	-1.483%	0.34%
Jan-92	3.683%	0.102%	0.306%	0.012%	5.447%	1.282	1.308	2.90%	4.28%	7.28%	7.76%	Feb-92	1.282%	0.531%	0.28%
Feb-92	3.804%	0.136%	0.258%	0.009%	5.426%	1.285	1.338	2.94%	4.20%	7.25%	7.79%	Mar-92	-1.974%	-0.546%	0.34%
Mar-92	3.976%	0.063%	0.274%	0.007%	5.274%	1.249	1.284	3.01%	3.93%	7.53%	7.96%	Apr-92	2.921%	0.596%	0.32%
Apr-92	3.462%	0.202%	0.444%	0.049%	5.748%	1.276	1.233	3.02%	3.92%	7.59%	8.04%	May-92	0.533%	1.941%	0.28%
May-92	3.592%	0.094%	0.303%	0.025%	5.538%	1.269	1.243	2.99%	3.89%	7.32%	7.84%	Jun-92	-1.453%	1.465%	0.32%
Jun-92	3.472%	0.060%	0.237%	0.028%	5.578%	1.239	1.176	3.06%	3.99%	7.12%	7.78%	Jul-92	4.035%	2.558%	0.31%
Jul-92	3.039%	0.078%	0.286%	0.042%	5.801%	1.281	1.211	3.00%	3.90%	6.71%	7.46%	Aug-92	-2.023%	0.893%	0.26%
Aug-92	2.988%	0.150%	0.295%	0.018%	5.662%	1.244	1.171	2.97%	3.92%	6.61%	7.41%	Sep-92	1.150%	1.365%	0.26%
Sep-92	2.657%	0.056%	0.214%	0.056%	5.963%	1.250	1.195	3.00%	4.10%	6.36%	7.38%	Oct-92	0.361%	-1.526%	0.23%
Oct-92	2.737%	0.149%	0.495%	-0.005%	6.103%	1.247	1.229	3.07%	4.18%	6.79%	7.63%	Nov-92	3.377%	-0.092%	0.23%
Nov-92	2.999%	0.250%	0.531%	0.001%	5.961%	1.274	1.310	2.98%	4.15%	6.94%	7.60%	Dec-92	1.313%	1.723%	0.28%
Dec-92	2.888%	0.168%	0.437%	0.032%	5.922%	1.274	1.340	2.90%	4.16%	6.69%	7.40%	Jan-93	0.733%	2.175%	0.23%
Jan-93	2.828%	0.037%	0.280%	0.034%	5.842%	1.271	1.370	2.88%	4.13%	6.36%	7.20%	Feb-93	1.351%	2.076%	0.22%
Feb-93	2.687%	0.260%	0.400%	0.018%	5.703%	1.274	1.322	2.81%	4.12%	6.02%	6.90%	Mar-93	2.172%	0.339%	0.25%
Mar-93	2.828%	0.057%	0.208%	0.035%	5.322%	1.287	1.351	2.76%	4.13%	6.03%	6.93%	Apr-93	-2.456%	0.769%	0.24%
Apr-93	2.817%	0.047%	0.198%	0.009%	5.323%	1.242	1.301	2.82%	4.31%	6.01%	6.94%	May-93	2.688%	-0.053%	0.22%
May-93	2.917%	0.089%	0.345%	0.000%	5.293%	1.260	1.346	2.80%	4.31%	6.15%	6.98%	Jun-93	0.326%	2.270%	0.25%

TABLE 5–11 *(Continued)*

	Eleven Predictive Variables											Subsequent Returns			
Month-end	TB1M	TB2MS	TB6MS	2M-1M HPR	Baa - TB1M	S&P 500 Ratio	FR 2000 Ratio	Div/P	E/P	TN10	TB30	Subsequent Month	Stocks	Bonds	Bills
Jun-93	2.828%	0.158%	0.342%	0.024%	5.242%	1.250	1.341	2.81%	4.43%	5.78%	6.68%	Jul-93	-0.472%	0.639%	0.24%
Jul-93	2.828%	0.190%	0.394%	0.023%	5.102%	1.233	1.349	2.81%	4.44%	5.81%	6.57%	Aug-93	3.811%	2.296%	0.25%
Aug-93	2.969%	0.027%	0.189%	0.022%	4.631%	1.266	1.393	2.76%	4.34%	5.45%	6.10%	Sep-93	-0.732%	0.348%	0.26%
Sep-93	2.747%	0.167%	0.330%	0.017%	4.593%	1.242	1.418	2.73%	4.21%	5.38%	6.03%	Oct-93	2.039%	0.409%	0.22%
Oct-93	2.797%	0.149%	0.424%	0.024%	4.513%	1.255	1.438	2.72%	4.17%	5.43%	5.97%	Nov-93	-0.953%	-1.130%	0.25%
Nov-93	2.969%	0.138%	0.365%	0.011%	4.691%	1.228	1.376	2.73%	4.43%	5.82%	6.30%	Dec-93	1.232%	0.437%	0.23%
Dec-93	2.908%	0.067%	0.334%	0.020%	4.782%	1.231	1.407	2.72%	4.25%	5.80%	6.35%	Jan-94	3.363%	1.505%	0.25%
Jan-94	2.757%	0.210%	0.423%	0.024%	4.893%	1.260	1.435	2.69%	4.35%	5.64%	6.24%	Feb-94	-2.716%	-2.175%	0.21%
Feb-94	3.100%	0.220%	0.534%	0.004%	4.660%	1.213	1.416	2.70%	4.72%	6.13%	6.66%	Mar-94	-4.339%	-2.446%	0.27%
Mar-94	3.351%	0.110%	0.503%	0.012%	4.779%	1.148	1.325	2.78%	4.92%	6.74%	7.10%	Apr-94	1.290%	-0.828%	0.27%
Apr-94	3.572%	0.205%	0.802%	-0.004%	4.948%	1.154	1.322	2.90%	4.98%	7.04%	7.31%	May-94	1.634%	-0.185%	0.32%
May-94	3.765%	0.285%	0.995%	0.021%	4.855%	1.161	1.295	2.89%	4.96%	7.15%	7.43%	Jun-94	-2.482%	-0.235%	0.31%
Jun-94	3.482%	0.486%	1.270%	0.067%	5.168%	1.124	1.240	2.84%	5.06%	7.32%	7.61%	Jul-94	3.309%	1.999%	0.28%
Jul-94	3.904%	0.299%	0.878%	0.049%	4.896%	1.153	1.252	2.87%	5.36%	7.11%	7.40%	Aug-94	4.071%	0.041%	0.37%
Aug-94	4.339%	0.116%	0.556%	0.013%	4.401%	1.191	1.312	2.78%	5.29%	7.18%	7.45%	Sep-94	-2.417%	-1.514%	0.37%
Sep-94	4.439%	0.178%	0.912%	0.005%	4.541%	1.153	1.297	2.80%	5.48%	7.61%	7.82%	Oct-94	2.313%	-0.111%	0.38%
Oct-94	4.286%	0.557%	1.305%	0.040%	4.924%	1.171	1.283	2.82%	5.70%	7.81%	7.97%	Nov-94	-3.668%	-0.179%	0.37%
Nov-94	4.894%	0.528%	1.242%	0.040%	4.316%	1.119	1.220	2.86%	6.03%	7.91%	8.00%	Dec-94	1.472%	0.659%	0.44%
Dec-94	4.681%	0.709%	1.730%	0.077%	4.419%	1.128	1.243	2.91%	5.89%	7.82%	7.88%	Jan-95	2.592%	1.920%	0.42%
Jan-95	5.122%	0.627%	1.177%	0.084%	3.958%	1.150	1.217	2.87%	6.16%	7.58%	7.70%	Feb-95	3.878%	2.319%	0.40%
Feb-95	5.430%	0.329%	0.653%	0.079%	3.420%	1.185	1.255	2.81%	6.17%	7.20%	7.45%	Mar-95	2.965%	0.671%	0.46%
Mar-95	5.711%	0.056%	0.306%	0.036%	2.989%	1.209	1.266	2.76%	6.06%	7.20%	7.43%	Apr-95	2.948%	1.395%	0.44%
Apr-95	5.670%	0.021%	0.304%	0.010%	2.930%	1.235	1.282	2.68%	6.24%	7.06%	7.34%	May-95	3.955%	4.191%	0.54%
May-95	5.581%	0.045%	0.141%	0.010%	2.379%	1.271	1.290	2.60%	6.09%	6.29%	6.65%	Jun-95	2.347%	0.799%	0.47%
Jun-95	5.266%	0.201%	0.221%	0.029%	2.634%	1.289	1.343	2.55%	5.95%	6.21%	6.62%	Jul-95	3.356%	-0.385%	0.45%
Jul-95	5.401%	0.064%	0.105%	0.023%	2.639%	1.320	1.407	2.50%	6.04%	6.43%	6.85%	Aug-95	0.271%	1.279%	0.47%
Aug-95	5.307%	0.022%	0.118%	0.017%	2.883%	1.309	1.418	2.49%	6.18%	6.29%	6.65%	Sep-95	4.201%	1.016%	0.43%
Sep-95	5.296%	0.068%	0.170%	-0.001%	2.634%	1.349	1.423	2.42%	5.93%	6.18%	6.50%	Oct-95	-0.364%	1.469%	0.47%
Oct-95	5.076%	0.234%	0.355%	0.032%	2.674%	1.328	1.339	2.41%	6.18%	6.02%	6.33%	Nov-95	4.401%	1.646%	0.42%
Nov-95	5.358%	0.012%	0.004%	0.016%	2.322%	1.368	1.377	2.28%	5.83%	5.74%	6.13%	Dec-95	1.847%	1.473%	0.49%

TABLE 5-12 Predicted Stock Returns: December 1990–November 1995

Month-end	Beta1	Beta2	Beta3	Beta4	Beta5	Beta6	Beta7	Beta8	Beta9	Beta10	Beta11	Alpha	K	Mean Sq. Error	C_P
Dec-90	-9.7075	0.0000	0.0000	0.0000	-7.6102	0.0000	0.1091	15.1716	0.0000	3.7382	0.0000	-0.0253	5	0.002187	6.23
Jan-91	-9.3193	0.0000	0.0000	0.0000	-7.4502	0.0000	0.1180	15.9683	0.0000	0.0000	3.8646	-0.1083	5	0.002176	6.40
Feb-91	-9.6188	0.0000	0.0000	0.0000	-7.5188	0.0000	0.0953	14.9608	0.0000	3.4587	0.0000	0.0132	5	0.002174	6.48
Apr-91	-10.8251	0.0000	0.0000	0.0000	-8.5227	0.0000	0.0799	14.3917	0.0000	3.9404	0.0000	0.1279	5	0.002128	7.32
Apr-91	-10.4089	0.0000	0.0000	0.0000	-8.1771	0.0000	0.0856	14.5912	0.0000	3.7189	0.0000	0.0925	5	0.002123	7.09
May-91	-11.4696	-3.1249	0.0000	0.0000	-7.9914	0.0000	0.0000	6.2979	2.5401	3.8136	0.0000	0.3768	6	0.002071	7.35
Jun-91	-5.1449	0.0000	0.0000	0.0000	-3.4111	0.0000	0.0000	4.7393	2.1104	0.0000	0.0000	0.1759	4	0.002249	7.56
Jul-91	-13.5471	-4.5297	0.0000	0.0000	-9.1511	0.1749	0.0000	19.7091	0.0000	26.3901	-22.3611	0.0384	7	0.002003	7.57
Aug-91	-13.4453	-4.2587	0.0000	0.0000	-9.2029	0.1701	0.0000	19.4180	0.0000	24.9542	-20.7003	0.0280	7	0.001987	7.94
Sep-91	-11.8113	-4.6113	0.0000	0.0000	-7.5666	0.2177	0.0000	21.3665	0.0000	25.8579	-23.3801	-0.1169	7	0.001757	8.27
Oct-91	-11.8339	-4.6424	0.0000	0.0000	-7.5849	0.2085	0.0000	20.9863	0.0000	25.5100	-23.1421	-0.0800	7	0.001763	8.14
Nov-91	-12.1843	-5.5737	0.0000	0.0000	-7.5023	0.2487	0.0000	23.3389	0.0000	28.5563	-26.4768	-0.1625	7	0.001728	7.98
Dec-91	-6.0895	0.0000	0.0000	0.0000	-4.2149	0.0000	0.1732	18.1924	0.0000	0.0000	0.0000	-0.2518	4	0.001938	7.52
Jan-92	-12.3944	-4.6661	0.0000	0.0000	-8.1332	0.2066	0.0000	21.6756	0.0000	21.3358	-18.6065	-0.0771	7	0.001772	8.33
Feb-92	-12.2734	-4.6548	0.0000	0.0000	-8.0325	0.2117	0.0000	21.9000	0.0000	21.2219	-18.6020	-0.0940	7	0.001772	8.30
Mar-92	-12.1536	-4.6989	0.0000	0.0000	-7.9040	0.2187	0.0000	22.2209	0.0000	21.5362	-19.0516	-0.1148	7	0.001779	8.30
Apr-92	-12.6282	-4.7815	0.0000	0.0000	-8.2851	0.2477	0.0000	23.5151	0.0000	21.1411	-18.5019	-0.1644	7	0.001765	8.31
May-92	-11.7615	-4.4563	0.0000	0.0000	-7.6466	0.2573	0.0000	23.4450	0.0000	19.9289	-17.8285	-0.2116	7	0.001791	8.36
Jun-92	-10.2637	-4.7588	0.0000	0.0000	-6.1398	0.1673	0.0000	15.9842	1.8019	16.0104	-14.4127	-0.0733	8	0.001733	8.39
Jul-92	-5.0185	0.0000	0.0000	0.0000	-3.4127	0.0000	0.0000	7.1850	2.0541	0.0000	0.0000	0.0840	4	0.001748	7.41
Aug-92	-9.1849	-3.9812	0.0000	0.0000	-5.6853	0.0000	0.0000	11.1483	2.1314	14.8276	-13.6440	0.2271	7	0.001462	7.73
Sep-92	-1.9388	-2.7766	0.0000	0.0000	0.0000	-0.5354	0.1661	0.0000	2.5545	12.7184	-17.3143	0.8758	7	0.001041	7.81
Oct-92	-2.3892	-3.3074	0.0000	0.0000	0.0000	-0.7205	0.2209	0.0000	3.2648	16.6707	-23.6781	1.2417	7	0.000988	7.63
Nov-92	-2.4639	-3.2933	0.0000	0.0000	0.0000	-0.6499	0.1914	0.0000	3.1642	15.4567	-21.6698	1.1285	7	0.000986	7.51
Dec-92	-2.1916	-3.2174	0.0000	0.0000	0.0000	-0.6528	0.1975	0.0000	3.0867	14.4996	-20.7883	1.1172	7	0.000972	7.48
Jan-93	-1.8145	-3.8563	0.0000	0.0000	0.0000	-0.6842	0.2102	0.0000	3.0166	13.8649	-20.4354	1.1472	7	0.000954	8.20
Feb-93	-5.8857	-4.9737	0.0000	0.0000	-3.6383	-0.6273	0.1524	0.0000	3.6614	15.8510	-19.2064	1.2302	8	0.000908	8.79
Mar-93	-5.7908	-5.1874	0.0000	0.0000	-3.3086	-0.5870	0.1335	0.0000	3.6925	16.2416	-19.5850	1.1808	8	0.000902	8.89
Apr-93	-5.4117	-5.3360	0.0000	0.0000	-2.7308	-0.5355	0.1103	0.0000	3.5117	16.7834	-19.8731	1.0878	8	0.000950	8.91
May-93	-5.2481	-5.2613	0.0000	0.0000	-2.5647	-0.5198	0.1046	0.0000	3.4016	16.8807	-19.9350	1.0616	8	0.000955	9.05
Jun-93	-2.0743	-4.0095	0.0000	0.0000	0.0000	-0.5221	0.1281	0.0000	2.5719	14.6118	-19.5296	0.9419	7	0.000985	8.71
Jul-93	-2.5272	-4.7152	0.0000	0.0000	0.0000	-0.4397	0.0970	0.0000	2.6965	14.7829	-18.5195	0.7979	7	0.001006	8.34

TABLE 5–12 *(Continued)*

Month-end	Beta1	Beta2	Beta3	Beta4	Beta5	Beta6	Beta7	Beta8	Beta9	Beta10	Beta11	Alpha	K	Mean Sq. Error	C_P
Aug-93	-2.5874	-4.5590	0.0000	0.0000	0.0000	-0.3736	0.0828	0.0000	2.7189	12.5619	-14.9257	0.6146	7	0.000987	7.53
Sep-93	-2.7423	-4.4655	0.0000	0.0000	0.0000	-0.1977	0.0000	0.0000	2.8439	8.2845	-8.9086	0.3354	6	0.001057	6.66
Oct-93	-3.0928	-5.2402	0.0000	0.0000	0.0000	-0.1822	0.0000	0.0000	3.3367	7.6629	-7.6587	0.2565	6	0.001042	6.76
Nov-93	0.0000	-4.5725	0.0000	0.0000	2.5686	-0.2666	0.0000	-8.1066	4.7124	0.0000	0.0000	0.2486	5	0.000990	6.41
Dec-93	0.0000	-4.4404	0.0000	0.0000	2.9250	-0.2759	0.0000	-8.9548	5.2798	0.0000	0.0000	0.2410	5	0.000955	6.28
Jan-94	0.0000	-4.6165	0.0000	0.0000	2.7953	-0.2831	0.0000	-9.0319	5.1660	0.0000	0.0000	0.2648	5	0.000956	6.32
Feb-94	0.0000	-4.3531	0.0000	0.0000	2.7660	-0.2701	0.1215	0.0000	4.0707	0.0000	0.0000	-0.1247	5	0.000935	6.72
Mar-94	0.0000	-4.7900	0.0000	0.0000	2.8284	-0.2056	0.0846	0.0000	3.9241	0.0000	0.0000	-0.1570	5	0.001014	6.10
Apr-94	0.0000	-4.7403	0.0000	0.0000	2.7939	-0.1767	0.0706	0.0000	3.7857	0.0000	0.0000	-0.1682	5	0.001026	6.15
May-94	0.0000	-4.6833	0.0000	0.0000	2.7056	-0.1577	0.0584	0.0000	3.5933	0.0000	0.0000	-0.1639	5	0.001032	6.12
Jun-94	-2.3965	-5.2983	0.0000	0.0000	0.0000	0.0000	0.0000	6.5870	2.8400	0.0000	0.0000	-0.2227	4	0.001074	6.33
Jul-94	0.0000	-3.2243	0.0000	0.0000	2.2036	-0.1017	0.0000	0.0000	2.4281	0.0000	0.0000	-0.0841	4	0.000996	5.04
Aug-94	0.0000	-2.7226	0.0000	0.0000	2.1110	-0.1217	0.0000	0.0000	2.2450	0.0000	0.0000	-0.0465	4	0.000989	4.93
Sep-94	0.0000	0.0000	0.0000	0.0000	1.7294	-0.1337	0.0000	0.0000	1.6228	0.0000	0.0000	0.0115	3	0.001029	5.42
Oct-94	0.0000	0.0000	0.0000	0.0000	1.7390	-0.1281	0.0000	0.0000	1.6538	0.0000	0.0000	0.0025	3	0.001029	5.42
Nov-94	-1.0254	0.0000	0.0000	0.0000	0.0000	-0.1341	0.0000	5.8383	0.0000	0.0000	0.0000	0.0390	3	0.001044	4.81
Dec-94	0.0000	0.0000	0.0000	0.0000	1.2574	-0.1774	0.0000	3.2752	0.0000	0.0000	0.0000	0.0668	3	0.001010	5.15
Jan-95	-1.2881	0.0000	3.0731	0.0000	0.0000	0.0000	0.0000	7.5713	0.0000	0.0000	0.0000	-0.1817	3	0.000944	5.07
Feb-95	-1.2387	0.0000	3.3540	0.0000	0.0000	0.0000	0.0000	7.2461	0.0000	0.0000	0.0000	-0.1748	3	0.000959	5.93
Mar-95	0.0000	0.0000	0.0000	27.0678	1.0448	-0.1525	0.0000	1.6723	0.0000	0.0000	0.0000	0.0872	4	0.000944	5.60
Apr-95	0.0000	0.0000	0.0000	34.2170	0.6594	-0.1545	0.0000	0.0000	0.0000	0.0000	0.0000	0.1571	3	0.000977	5.24
May-95	6.8281	0.0000	0.0000	0.0000	8.2588	-0.2211	-0.1863	-10.7863	0.0000	0.0000	-7.1259	0.6922	6	0.000761	7.64
Jun-95	7.0853	0.0000	0.0000	0.0000	8.6529	-0.2249	-0.2714	-14.1804	0.0000	0.0000	-7.8744	0.9307	6	0.000736	8.54
Jul-95	0.0000	11.8734	-11.8156	0.0000	5.2356	-0.2426	-0.2850	-15.7294	3.4579	6.6345	-9.1358	0.9603	9	0.000649	9.16
Aug-95	6.4915	9.6697	-6.5773	0.0000	7.7727	-0.3102	-0.2239	-15.8700	0.0000	0.0000	-6.1857	0.9807	8	0.000621	9.29
Sep-95	5.2016	9.1923	-6.9139	0.0000	6.0504	-0.3105	-0.1923	-13.6336	0.0000	0.0000	-4.7000	0.9030	8	0.000600	8.58
Oct-95	0.0000	10.0399	-7.5554	0.0000	0.0000	-0.2818	-0.1395	-5.8669	0.0000	0.0000	0.0000	0.7250	5	0.000570	6.61
Nov-95	0.0000	11.3356	-8.2370	0.0000	0.0000	-0.2878	-0.1591	-6.7415	0.0000	0.0000	0.0000	0.7841	5	0.000574	6.47

TABLE 5-13 Predicted Bond Returns: December 1990–November 1995

Month-end	Beta1	Beta2	Beta3	Beta4	Beta5	Beta6	Beta7	Beta8	Beta9	Beta10	Beta11	Alpha	K	Mean Sq. Error	C_P
Dec-90	2.4602	0.0000	1.0571	-15.0836	2.0326	0.1279	-0.0772	3.4067	0.0000	2.5752	-3.5050	-0.3490	9	0.0001503	9.86
Jan-91	2.9871	0.0000	1.6428	-12.6780	2.0338	0.0956	-0.0453	4.4107	-0.5610	0.0000	-1.1213	-0.3670	9	0.0001485	9.74
Feb-91	2.4343	0.0000	0.9599	-14.3791	2.0589	0.1191	-0.0815	2.7736	0.0000	3.1605	-4.2383	-0.2962	9	0.0001428	9.46
Apr-91	1.8380	0.0000	0.6668	-13.8211	1.6950	0.0940	-0.0777	1.8489	0.0000	4.2599	-5.1686	-0.1935	9	0.0001425	9.26
Apr-91	1.2472	0.0000	0.0000	-9.6310	1.3951	0.0000	-0.0248	0.0000	0.0000	4.5135	-5.1535	-0.0359	6	0.0001533	7.60
May-91	1.5016	0.0000	0.0000	-8.4243	1.5854	0.0000	-0.0202	0.0000	0.0000	4.2421	-5.0577	-0.0509	6	0.0001458	7.24
Jun-91	1.5668	0.0000	0.0000	-7.7263	1.5938	0.0000	-0.0202	0.0000	0.0000	3.6303	-4.4246	-0.0584	6	0.0001452	7.11
Jul-91	1.4358	0.0000	0.0000	-8.9961	1.5855	0.0000	-0.0204	0.0000	0.0000	4.8490	-5.7454	-0.0384	6	0.0001454	7.30
Aug-91	0.8779	0.0000	0.0000	-8.9595	1.0826	0.0000	-0.0242	0.0000	0.0000	4.5142	-4.9827	-0.0148	6	0.0001477	6.91
Sep-91	0.0000	-0.7764	0.0000	-7.0100	0.5049	0.0000	-0.0266	0.0000	0.0000	6.2938	-6.4388	0.0439	6	0.0001513	7.13
Oct-91	0.0000	-0.7375	0.0000	-6.5562	0.4533	0.0000	-0.0269	0.0000	0.0000	5.6061	-5.7081	0.0415	6	0.0001530	7.37
Nov-91	0.0000	0.0000	0.0000	0.0000	0.0000	-0.0253	0.0000	0.0000	0.0000	0.4422	0.0000	0.0034	2	0.0001618	6.68
Dec-91	0.8307	0.0000	0.0000	0.0000	0.5954	-0.0819	0.0424	0.0000	-0.4529	0.0000	0.0000	0.0191	5	0.0001647	5.95
Jan-92	0.0000	0.0000	0.0000	0.0000	0.0000	-0.0470	0.0000	-1.1724	0.0000	0.6621	0.0000	0.0533	3	0.0001707	5.75
Feb-92	0.0000	0.0000	0.0000	0.0000	0.0000	-0.0569	0.0000	-1.5989	0.0000	0.8294	0.0000	0.0663	3	0.0001648	6.00
Mar-92	0.0000	0.0000	0.0000	0.0000	0.0000	-0.0591	0.0000	-1.6151	0.0000	0.9456	0.0000	0.0596	3	0.0001651	5.33
Apr-92	0.0000	0.0000	0.0000	0.0000	0.0000	-0.0487	0.0000	-1.2809	0.0000	0.8246	0.0000	0.0451	3	0.0001612	5.02
May-92	0.0000	0.0000	0.0000	0.0000	0.0000	-0.0514	0.0000	-1.4565	0.0000	0.8170	0.0000	0.0554	3	0.0001635	4.90
Jun-92	0.0000	0.0000	0.0000	0.0000	0.0000	-0.0587	0.0000	-1.6389	0.0000	0.8194	0.0000	0.0708	3	0.0001618	4.82
Jul-92	0.0000	0.0000	0.0000	0.0000	0.0000	-0.0629	0.0000	-1.7965	0.0000	0.7610	0.0000	0.0867	3	0.0001674	4.91
Aug-92	0.0000	0.0000	0.0000	0.0000	0.0000	-0.0609	0.0000	-1.7832	0.0000	0.7272	0.0000	0.0867	3	0.0001677	5.00
Sep-92	0.0000	0.0000	0.0000	0.0000	0.0000	0.0000	0.0000	0.0000	-0.3012	0.0000	0.9483	-0.0518	2	0.0001536	3.78
Oct-92	0.0000	0.0000	0.0000	0.0000	0.0000	-0.1185	0.0376	0.0000	-0.3265	3.1135	-3.3797	0.1641	5	0.0001440	6.35
Nov-92	0.0000	0.0000	0.0000	0.0000	0.0000	-0.1191	0.0376	0.0000	-0.3349	3.2228	-3.5027	0.1668	5	0.0001442	6.24
Dec-92	0.0000	0.0000	0.0000	0.0000	0.0000	-0.1265	0.0419	0.0000	-0.3302	3.2477	-3.5767	0.1752	5	0.0001455	6.51
Jan-93	0.0000	0.0000	0.0000	-6.8026	0.0000	-0.1988	0.0681	0.0000	0.0000	3.9999	-5.4070	0.3107	5	0.0001290	6.39
Feb-93	0.0000	0.0000	0.0000	-8.7774	0.0000	-0.2240	0.0800	0.0000	0.0000	4.5193	-6.1442	0.3489	5	0.0001246	7.11
Mar-93	0.0000	0.0000	0.0000	-8.2439	0.0000	-0.2046	0.0716	0.0000	0.0000	4.1575	-5.5685	0.3151	5	0.0001258	7.35
Apr-93	0.0000	0.0000	0.0000	-9.0899	0.0000	-0.2014	0.0695	0.0000	0.0000	3.9912	-5.2760	0.3032	5	0.0001207	6.78
May-93	0.0000	0.0000	0.0000	-8.6116	0.0000	-0.1744	0.0616	0.0000	0.0000	3.2242	-4.0341	0.2370	5	0.0001205	6.66
Jun-93	0.0000	0.0000	0.0000	-8.4404	0.0000	-0.1861	0.0655	0.0000	0.0000	3.6201	-4.6713	0.2679	5	0.0001193	6.45
Jul-93	0.0000	0.0000	0.0000	-8.7482	0.0000	-0.1709	0.0625	0.0000	0.0000	3.1471	-3.8497	0.2226	5	0.0001152	6.93

TABLE 5–13 *(Continued)*

Month-end	Beta1	Beta2	Beta3	Beta4	Beta5	Beta6	Beta7	Beta8	Beta9	Beta10	Beta11	Alpha	K	Mean Sq. Error	C_P
Aug-93	0.0000	0.0000	0.0000	-8.5525	0.0000	-0.1665	0.0631	0.0000	0.0000	2.8929	-3.4312	0.2023	5	0.0001142	6.92
Sep-93	0.0000	0.0000	0.0000	-7.9123	0.0000	-0.1355	0.0538	0.0000	0.0000	1.8033	-1.8087	0.1270	5	0.0001192	6.77
Oct-93	0.0000	0.0000	0.0000	-7.0714	0.0000	-0.1059	0.0471	0.0000	0.0000	0.5595	0.0000	0.0477	4	0.0001233	6.75
Nov-93	1.0893	0.0000	0.0000	-8.2893	1.1572	-0.1166	0.0655	0.0000	0.0000	0.0000	0.0000	-0.0241	5	0.0001175	7.55
Dec-93	1.1650	0.0000	0.0000	-7.9341	1.2456	-0.1200	0.0687	0.0000	0.0000	0.0000	0.0000	-0.0314	5	0.0001156	7.89
Jan-94	1.4559	0.0000	0.0000	-9.4687	1.7803	-0.1488	0.0487	-3.5216	0.7149	0.0000	0.0000	0.0653	7	0.0001116	7.86
Feb-94	0.0000	-1.3759	0.7462	0.0000	0.0000	-0.0938	0.0530	0.0000	0.0000	0.0000	1.1506	-0.0262	5	0.0001232	7.59
Mar-94	0.0000	0.0000	0.0000	0.0000	0.0000	-0.0873	0.0548	0.0000	0.0000	0.0000	1.3011	-0.0484	3	0.0001431	6.28
Apr-94	1.4709	0.0000	0.0000	0.0000	1.6927	-0.0841	0.0695	0.0000	0.0000	0.0000	0.0000	-0.1161	4	0.0001477	6.69
May-94	0.0000	0.0000	0.0000	0.0000	0.0000	0.0000	0.0000	0.0000	0.0000	-1.1596	2.0156	-0.0631	2	0.0001542	6.19
Jun-94	0.0000	-0.7896	0.0000	0.0000	0.2806	0.0000	0.0000	0.0000	0.0000	0.0000	0.7453	-0.0613	3	0.0001426	4.41
Jul-94	0.0000	0.0000	0.8917	-7.7146	0.0000	0.0000	-0.0308	0.0000	-0.5357	0.0000	0.5620	0.0277	5	0.0001335	5.69
Aug-94	0.0000	0.0000	0.0000	0.0000	0.3066	0.0000	0.0000	0.0000	0.0000	0.0000	0.7101	-0.0613	2	0.0001372	4.76
Sep-94	0.0000	0.0000	0.0000	0.0000	0.3199	0.0000	0.0000	0.0000	0.0000	0.0000	0.7320	-0.0639	2	0.0001439	5.40
Oct-94	0.0000	-1.2234	1.3248	0.0000	0.0000	0.0000	0.0000	2.7096	-0.9579	0.0000	0.4171	-0.0640	5	0.0001243	5.80
Nov-94	0.0000	0.0000	0.0000	0.0000	0.0000	0.0000	-0.0415	0.0000	-0.7300	0.0000	0.4677	0.0581	3	0.0001269	4.93
Dec-94	0.0000	0.0000	0.0000	0.0000	0.0000	-0.0367	0.0000	1.6526	-0.8835	0.0000	0.6704	-0.0056	4	0.0001245	5.57
Jan-95	0.4191	0.0000	2.0233	0.0000	0.0000	0.0000	0.0000	3.0777	-1.6015	0.0000	0.0000	-0.0346	4	0.0001197	5.08
Feb-95	0.0000	2.8973	0.0000	0.0000	0.0000	0.0000	0.0000	1.2568	-0.8348	0.0000	0.6681	-0.0461	4	0.0001253	5.78
Mar-95	0.0000	2.4588	0.0000	0.0000	0.0000	0.0000	-0.0259	0.0000	-0.7106	0.0000	0.6014	0.0239	4	0.0001260	6.02
Apr-95	0.0000	1.6098	0.0000	0.0000	0.0000	0.0000	0.0000	0.0000	0.0000	-1.3196	2.1542	-0.0648	3	0.0001300	6.08
May-95	0.0000	0.0000	0.0000	0.0000	0.0000	0.0000	-0.0774	-2.5771	0.0000	0.0000	0.0000	0.1808	2	0.0001510	5.31
Jun-95	0.0000	0.0000	0.0000	0.0000	0.0000	0.0000	-0.1030	-3.3028	-0.2567	0.0000	0.0000	0.2469	3	0.0001464	5.01
Jul-95	0.0000	0.0000	0.0000	0.0000	0.3200	0.0000	-0.1034	-3.5562	0.0000	0.0000	0.0000	0.2266	3	0.0001458	4.17
Aug-95	0.6050	1.4629	0.0000	0.0000	0.0000	0.0000	-0.0787	-2.8741	-0.9704	0.0000	0.0000	0.2119	5	0.0001344	7.20
Sep-95	1.9184	0.0000	2.2559	0.0000	0.0000	0.0000	0.0000	0.0000	-1.5082	-3.6321	3.3794	-0.0043	5	0.0001308	6.63
Oct-95	2.0462	0.0000	2.3320	0.0000	0.0000	0.0000	0.0000	0.0000	-1.5693	-3.8349	3.5326	-0.0038	5	0.0001304	6.44
Nov-95	1.7117	0.0000	1.8682	0.0000	0.0000	0.0000	-0.0535	-2.2965	-1.4703	-3.0639	2.8323	0.1403	7	0.0001275	7.11

Determining Monthly Asset Mixes

The final step is to use the predicted values garnered in the earlier steps to arrive at our monthly asset mixes. Using Table 5–14 we will work through the calculations required to derive the monthly asset mixes.

The two columns on the left, labeled "Stock Exp. Return" and "Bond Exp. Return" are equivalent to the predicted values generated by the model coefficients presented in Tables 5–12 (for stocks) and 5–13 (for bonds). The predicted values are calculated by multiplying each coefficient by its corresponding actual variable value, as given in Table 5–11, plus the constant coefficient, alpha.

The next three columns, labeled "Stock Variance," "Bond Variance," and "Covariance" are calculated using the actual asset class returns over the prior sixty month period. For example, the value of 0.00294 listed under "Stock Variance" for December 1990 is the variance of actual stock returns for the sixty month period, January 1986 through December 1990. The next figure below, 0.00295, is calculated using February 1986 through January 1991.

In determining the weights to be assigned to stocks and bonds, we must calculate the portfolio's expected return and variance, from which we can calculate the portfolio's standard deviation and Sharpe Ratio. The formula for the portfolio's expected return is:

$$w_s E(r_s) + w_b E(r_b).$$

The formula for the portfolio's variance is:

$$w_s^2 \text{ var}_s + w_b^2 \text{ var}_b + 2 w_s w_b \text{ cov}_{s,b}.$$

The portfolio's standard deviation is the square root of its variance. Given the risk-free rate, we can calculate the portfolio's Sharpe Ratio, as:

$$\frac{E(r_p) - r_f}{\sigma_p}.$$

In seventeen of sixty months, the portfolio held 100% stocks. In seven months, the portfolio held 100% bonds. In six months the portfolio held 100% cash. In the other 30 months, the portfolio held some combination of stocks and bonds.

These results differ dramatically from those obtained by Klemkosky and Bharati. They found that 30% of the time the portfolio was invested 100% in Treasury-bills. Furthermore, the portfolio held 100% stocks, 26% of the time and 100% bonds, 19% of the time. Only 25% of the time was there a combination of stocks and bonds.

TABLE 5-14 Monthly Asset Mixes: December 1990–November 1995

Month-end	Stock Exp. Return	Bond Exp. Return	Stock Variance	Bond Variance	Covariance	Stock%	Bond%	Exp. Return	Variance	Std. Dev.	Risk-Free Rate	Sharpe Ratio	Subsequent Month	Actual Portfolio Return
Dec-90	2.12%	0.30%	0.00294	0.00025	0.00023	100.0%	0.0%	2.12%	0.00294	0.05420	0.495%	0.299	Jan-91	4.43%
Jan-91	4.42%	0.75%	0.00295	0.00025	0.00023	73.7%	26.3%	3.46%	0.00167	0.04083	0.484%	0.728	Feb-91	5.51%
Feb-91	1.76%	-0.80%	0.00294	0.00023	0.00020	100.0%	0.0%	1.76%	0.00294	0.05426	0.471%	0.238	Mar-91	2.37%
Mar-91	1.13%	-1.31%	0.00292	0.00022	0.00018	100.0%	0.0%	1.13%	0.00292	0.05399	0.484%	0.120	Apr-91	0.28%
Apr-91	1.73%	0.27%	0.00291	0.00022	0.00017	100.0%	0.0%	1.73%	0.00291	0.05391	0.457%	0.236	May-91	4.28%
May-91	5.07%	-0.09%	0.00289	0.00020	0.00019	100.0%	0.0%	5.07%	0.00289	0.05379	0.444%	0.859	Jun-91	-4.57%
Jun-91	1.79%	0.01%	0.00295	0.00020	0.00020	100.0%	0.0%	1.79%	0.00295	0.05429	0.427%	0.252	Jul-91	4.67%
Jul-91	3.28%	-0.01%	0.00289	0.00020	0.00020	100.0%	0.0%	3.28%	0.00289	0.05375	0.457%	0.526	Aug-91	2.36%
Aug-91	1.73%	-0.05%	0.00282	0.00020	0.00018	100.0%	0.0%	1.73%	0.00282	0.05314	0.437%	0.242	Sep-91	-1.64%
Sep-91	-0.93%	-0.21%	0.00269	0.00019	0.00014	0.0%	0.0%	0.00%	0.00000	0.00000	0.421%		Oct-91	0.42%
Oct-91	-1.11%	-0.42%	0.00265	0.00019	0.00014	0.0%	0.0%	0.00%	0.00000	0.00000	0.394%		Nov-91	0.39%
Nov-91	-4.40%	0.58%	0.00270	0.00019	0.00014	0.0%	100.0%	0.58%	0.00019	0.01383	0.335%	0.179	Dec-91	3.37%
Dec-91	6.18%	0.61%	0.00285	0.00020	0.00018	79.9%	20.1%	5.06%	0.00185	0.04304	0.324%	1.101	Jan-92	-1.78%
Jan-92	2.15%	0.72%	0.00261	0.00021	0.00018	27.7%	72.3%	1.12%	0.00035	0.01861	0.307%	0.436	Feb-92	0.74%
Feb-92	0.24%	0.63%	0.00260	0.00021	0.00018	0.0%	100.0%	0.63%	0.00021	0.01451	0.317%	0.217	Mar-92	-0.55%
Mar-92	2.92%	0.84%	0.00261	0.00021	0.00019	31.4%	68.6%	1.49%	0.00040	0.01989	0.331%	0.584	Apr-92	1.32%
Apr-92	5.60%	0.69%	0.00261	0.00019	0.00018	62.7%	37.3%	3.77%	0.00109	0.03306	0.288%	1.052	May-92	1.06%
May-92	2.69%	0.65%	0.00261	0.00019	0.00018	37.6%	62.4%	1.42%	0.00048	0.02198	0.299%	0.508	Jun-92	0.37%
Jun-92	1.19%	0.62%	0.00259	0.00019	0.00017	15.4%	84.6%	0.71%	0.00022	0.01483	0.289%	0.285	Jul-92	2.78%
Jul-92	2.93%	0.33%	0.00258	0.00019	0.00019	100.0%	0.0%	2.93%	0.00258	0.05076	0.253%	0.527	Aug-92	-2.02%
Aug-92	0.85%	0.60%	0.00258	0.00019	0.00019	8.7%	91.3%	0.62%	0.00019	0.01391	0.249%	0.270	Sep-92	1.35%
Sep-92	-1.22%	0.58%	0.00256	0.00017	0.00018	0.0%	100.0%	0.58%	0.00017	0.01321	0.221%	0.273	Oct-92	-1.53%
Oct-92	0.63%	0.25%	0.00170	0.00017	0.00029	100.0%	0.0%	0.63%	0.00170	0.04118	0.228%	0.096	Nov-92	3.38%
Nov-92	2.65%	0.78%	0.00155	0.00017	0.00028	41.1%	58.9%	1.55%	0.00039	0.01973	0.250%	0.659	Dec-92	1.55%
Dec-92	4.18%	0.91%	0.00149	0.00017	0.00028	57.0%	43.0%	2.77%	0.00058	0.02414	0.241%	1.049	Jan-93	1.35%
Jan-93	4.75%	1.40%	0.00147	0.00016	0.00026	34.5%	65.5%	2.56%	0.00031	0.01748	0.236%	1.327	Feb-93	1.83%
Feb-93	3.41%	1.59%	0.00145	0.00017	0.00026	18.5%	81.5%	1.93%	0.00020	0.01415	0.224%	1.202	Mar-93	0.68%
Mar-93	3.77%	1.05%	0.00142	0.00016	0.00025	39.3%	60.7%	2.12%	0.00034	0.01839	0.236%	1.024	Apr-93	-0.50%
Apr-93	4.64%	1.64%	0.00145	0.00016	0.00025	26.1%	73.9%	2.42%	0.00023	0.01525	0.235%	1.434	May-93	0.66%
May-93	4.72%	1.68%	0.00145	0.00016	0.00024	25.2%	74.8%	2.45%	0.00023	0.01500	0.243%	1.470	Jun-93	1.78%
Jun-93	5.00%	1.84%	0.00143	0.00016	0.00023	24.2%	75.8%	2.60%	0.00022	0.01471	0.236%	1.609	Jul-93	0.37%

TABLE 5–14 *(Continued)*

Month-end	Stock Exp. Return	Bond Exp. Return	Stock Variance	Bond Variance	Covari-ance	Stock%	Bond%	Exp. Return	Variance	Std. Dev.	Risk-Free Rate	Sharpe Ratio	Subse-quent Month	Actual Portfolio Return
Jul-93	6.78%	2.41%	0.00143	0.00015	0.00023	24.0%	76.0%	3.46%	0.00021	0.01457	0.236%	2.213	Aug-93	2.66%
Aug-93	7.13%	2.60%	0.00141	0.00015	0.00023	23.9%	76.1%	3.68%	0.00021	0.01456	0.247%	2.360	Sep-93	0.09%
Sep-93	3.55%	2.17%	0.00140	0.00015	0.00023	10.9%	89.1%	2.32%	0.00016	0.01264	0.229%	1.654	Oct-93	0.59%
Oct-93	3.15%	1.11%	0.00140	0.00015	0.00022	27.6%	72.4%	1.68%	0.00023	0.01518	0.233%	0.951	Nov-93	-1.08%
Nov-93	2.29%	0.84%	0.00139	0.00015	0.00022	28.7%	71.3%	1.26%	0.00024	0.01541	0.247%	0.656	Dec-93	0.67%
Dec-93	1.90%	0.94%	0.00139	0.00015	0.00022	18.0%	82.0%	1.12%	0.00018	0.01341	0.242%	0.651	Jan-94	1.84%
Jan-94	1.71%	0.90%	0.00134	0.00015	0.00022	17.1%	82.9%	1.04%	0.00017	0.01322	0.230%	0.611	Feb-94	-2.27%
Feb-94	3.14%	1.27%	0.00134	0.00016	0.00023	25.6%	74.4%	1.75%	0.00022	0.01491	0.258%	0.999	Mar-94	-2.93%
Mar-94	4.20%	1.64%	0.00139	0.00018	0.00026	27.9%	72.1%	2.35%	0.00025	0.01597	0.279%	1.300	Apr-94	-0.24%
Apr-94	3.82%	1.51%	0.00136	0.00018	0.00025	28.9%	71.1%	2.18%	0.00026	0.01606	0.298%	1.171	May-94	0.34%
May-94	2.50%	0.37%	0.00134	0.00018	0.00024	100.0%	0.0%	2.50%	0.00134	0.03667	0.314%	0.597	Jun-94	-2.48%
Jun-94	-0.11%	0.61%	0.00136	0.00017	0.00025	0.0%	100.0%	0.61%	0.00017	0.01306	0.290%	0.243	Jul-94	2.00%
Jul-94	2.72%	0.60%	0.00126	0.00017	0.00024	85.9%	14.1%	2.42%	0.00096	0.03099	0.325%	0.676	Aug-94	3.50%
Aug-94	1.71%	0.51%	0.00127	0.00016	0.00024	85.9%	14.1%	1.54%	0.00097	0.03119	0.362%	0.379	Sep-94	-2.29%
Sep-94	2.48%	0.79%	0.00129	0.00017	0.00025	52.7%	47.3%	1.68%	0.00046	0.02143	0.370%	0.611	Oct-94	1.17%
Oct-94	3.24%	0.16%	0.00128	0.00017	0.00026	100.0%	0.0%	3.24%	0.00128	0.03572	0.357%	0.807	Nov-94	-3.67%
Nov-94	0.58%	0.08%	0.00131	0.00017	0.00026	100.0%	0.0%	0.58%	0.00131	0.03616	0.408%	0.049	Dec-94	1.47%
Dec-94	1.76%	0.18%	0.00130	0.00017	0.00027	100.0%	0.0%	1.76%	0.00130	0.03611	0.390%	0.378	Jan-95	2.59%
Jan-95	0.58%	0.03%	0.00121	0.00016	0.00024	100.0%	0.0%	0.58%	0.00121	0.03482	0.427%	0.045	Feb-95	3.88%
Feb-95	-1.66%	-0.30%	0.00123	0.00017	0.00025	0.0%	0.0%	0.00%	0.00000	0.00000	0.453%		Mar-95	0.46%
Mar-95	-1.01%	-0.59%	0.00123	0.00017	0.00025	0.0%	0.0%	0.00%	0.00000	0.00000	0.476%		Apr-95	0.44%
Apr-95	-1.09%	0.04%	0.00122	0.00016	0.00025	0.0%	0.0%	0.00%	0.00000	0.00000	0.473%		May-95	0.54%
May-95	-0.59%	1.40%	0.00110	0.00017	0.00023	0.0%	100.0%	1.40%	0.00017	0.01316	0.465%	0.708	Jun-95	0.80%
Jun-95	-0.57%	0.90%	0.00110	0.00017	0.00023	0.0%	100.0%	0.90%	0.00017	0.01312	0.439%	0.351	Jul-95	-0.39%
Jul-95	-1.11%	0.06%	0.00110	0.00017	0.00023	0.0%	0.0%	0.00%	0.00000	0.00000	0.450%		Aug-95	0.47%
Aug-95	1.37%	0.12%	0.00093	0.00017	0.00019	100.0%	0.0%	1.37%	0.00093	0.03050	0.442%	0.303	Sep-95	4.20%
Sep-95	0.44%	0.69%	0.00088	0.00017	0.00019	0.0%	100.0%	0.69%	0.00017	0.01289	0.441%	0.194	Oct-95	1.47%
Oct-95	1.92%	0.41%	0.00088	0.00017	0.00019	100.0%	0.0%	1.92%	0.00088	0.02965	0.423%	0.505	Nov-95	4.40%
Nov-95	1.87%	1.80%	0.00085	0.00016	0.00019	9.5%	90.5%	1.81%	0.00016	0.01258	0.446%	1.083	Dec-95	1.51%

The column on the right hand side, labeled "Actual Portfolio Return," is based on the asset class weightings given in Table 5–14 and the actual ensuing returns given in Table 5–11.

Reviewing the Results

Our final table, Table 5–15 (graphically shown in Chart 5–1), shows the results achieved by our active strategy *versus* a buy-and-hold strategy invested 100% in stocks, bonds, and T-bills, and 50% stocks/50% bonds. Each depicts a hypothetical one dollar investment in each strategy. At the end of five years, one dollar invested in the active strategy was worth about $1.70. The active strategy trailed the 100% stock and the 50/50 stock and bond combination strategies. The active strategy beat the 100% bond and 100% Treasury-bills strategies. One dollar invested in stocks resulted in a terminal value of $2.15. One dollar invested in bonds produced $1.60. The 50/50 combination of stocks and bonds ended with a terminal value of $1.86. Lagging the other strategies by a wide margin, was the ultra-conservative Treasury-bills strategy with a $1.23 terminal value.

The active strategy failed to decisively beat all the other strategies for the five year period, January 1991 through December 1995. The reader should consider the following three possibilities for this:

1. There is nothing wrong with the strategy. This particular time period by chance happened to produce unsatisfactory results but, in general, the strategy works well.
2. There was an error in the strategy's implementation.
3. The strategy is flawed. The fact that it worked for Klemkosky and Bharati may have been either a happy coincidence or the strategy itself may have been developed as a result of data mining. We should also consider that the strategy may not contain all the variables necessary for a complete analysis.

Klemkosky and Bharati divided their results for their twenty-five year study into five, five year periods. They compared the results of their active asset allocation strategy to 100% investment in stocks, bonds, and Treasury-bills. In addition, they looked at 70% stock/30% bond, 50% stock/50% bond, and 30% stock/70% bond combinations. They found that in one of the five periods their strategy underperformed the 50/50 combination, which means that it outperformed in four periods. This being the case, there is precedence for the system failing to add value over a five-year period. If we were to state that our

TABLE 5-15 Strategy Results

Month-end	Active Strategy	Stocks	Bonds	T-Bills	50%Stocks/ 50%Bonds
Dec-90	1.000	1.000	1.000	1.000	1.000
Jan-91	1.044	1.044	1.011	1.005	1.028
Feb-91	1.102	1.119	1.020	1.010	1.069
Mar-91	1.128	1.146	1.027	1.014	1.085
Apr-91	1.131	1.149	1.039	1.020	1.093
May-91	1.179	1.198	1.044	1.025	1.119
Jun-91	1.126	1.143	1.042	1.029	1.093
Jul-91	1.178	1.197	1.056	1.034	1.125
Aug-91	1.206	1.225	1.080	1.039	1.151
Sep-91	1.186	1.205	1.102	1.044	1.154
Oct-91	1.191	1.221	1.112	1.048	1.167
Nov-91	1.196	1.172	1.123	1.052	1.149
Dec-91	1.236	1.305	1.161	1.056	1.234
Jan-92	1.214	1.281	1.144	1.060	1.214
Feb-92	1.223	1.298	1.150	1.063	1.225
Mar-92	1.216	1.272	1.144	1.066	1.209
Apr-92	1.232	1.309	1.151	1.070	1.230
May-92	1.246	1.316	1.173	1.073	1.246
Jun-92	1.250	1.297	1.190	1.076	1.246
Jul-92	1.285	1.349	1.221	1.079	1.287
Aug-92	1.259	1.322	1.232	1.082	1.280
Sep-92	1.276	1.337	1.248	1.085	1.296
Oct-92	1.256	1.342	1.229	1.087	1.288
Nov-92	1.299	1.388	1.228	1.090	1.309
Dec-92	1.319	1.406	1.249	1.093	1.329
Jan-93	1.337	1.416	1.276	1.096	1.348
Feb-93	1.361	1.435	1.303	1.098	1.372
Mar-93	1.371	1.466	1.307	1.101	1.389
Apr-93	1.364	1.430	1.317	1.103	1.377
May-93	1.373	1.469	1.317	1.106	1.395
Jun-93	1.397	1.474	1.347	1.109	1.413

Month-end	Active Strategy	Stocks	Bonds	T-Bills	50%Stocks/ 50%Bonds
Jul-93	1.402	1.467	1.355	1.111	1.415
Aug-93	1.440	1.523	1.386	1.114	1.458
Sep-93	1.441	1.511	1.391	1.117	1.455
Oct-93	1.449	1.542	1.397	1.119	1.473
Nov-93	1.434	1.528	1.381	1.122	1.457
Dec-93	1.443	1.546	1.387	1.125	1.470
Jan-94	1.470	1.598	1.408	1.127	1.505
Feb-94	1.437	1.555	1.377	1.130	1.469
Mar-94	1.394	1.487	1.344	1.133	1.419
Apr-94	1.391	1.507	1.333	1.136	1.422
May-94	1.396	1.531	1.330	1.140	1.432
Jun-94	1.361	1.493	1.327	1.143	1.413
Jul-94	1.388	1.543	1.353	1.146	1.450
Aug-94	1.437	1.605	1.354	1.151	1.480
Sep-94	1.404	1.567	1.334	1.155	1.451
Oct-94	1.421	1.603	1.332	1.159	1.467
Nov-94	1.368	1.544	1.330	1.164	1.439
Dec-94	1.389	1.567	1.338	1.169	1.454
Jan-95	1.425	1.607	1.364	1.174	1.487
Feb-95	1.480	1.670	1.396	1.178	1.533
Mar-95	1.487	1.719	1.405	1.184	1.561
Apr-95	1.493	1.770	1.425	1.189	1.595
May-95	1.501	1.840	1.484	1.195	1.660
Jun-95	1.513	1.883	1.496	1.201	1.686
Jul-95	1.507	1.946	1.491	1.206	1.711
Aug-95	1.514	1.952	1.510	1.212	1.724
Sep-95	1.578	2.034	1.525	1.217	1.769
Oct-95	1.601	2.026	1.547	1.223	1.779
Nov-95	1.672	2.115	1.573	1.228	1.833
Dec-95	1.697	2.154	1.596	1.234	1.863

CHART 5–1 Strategy Results

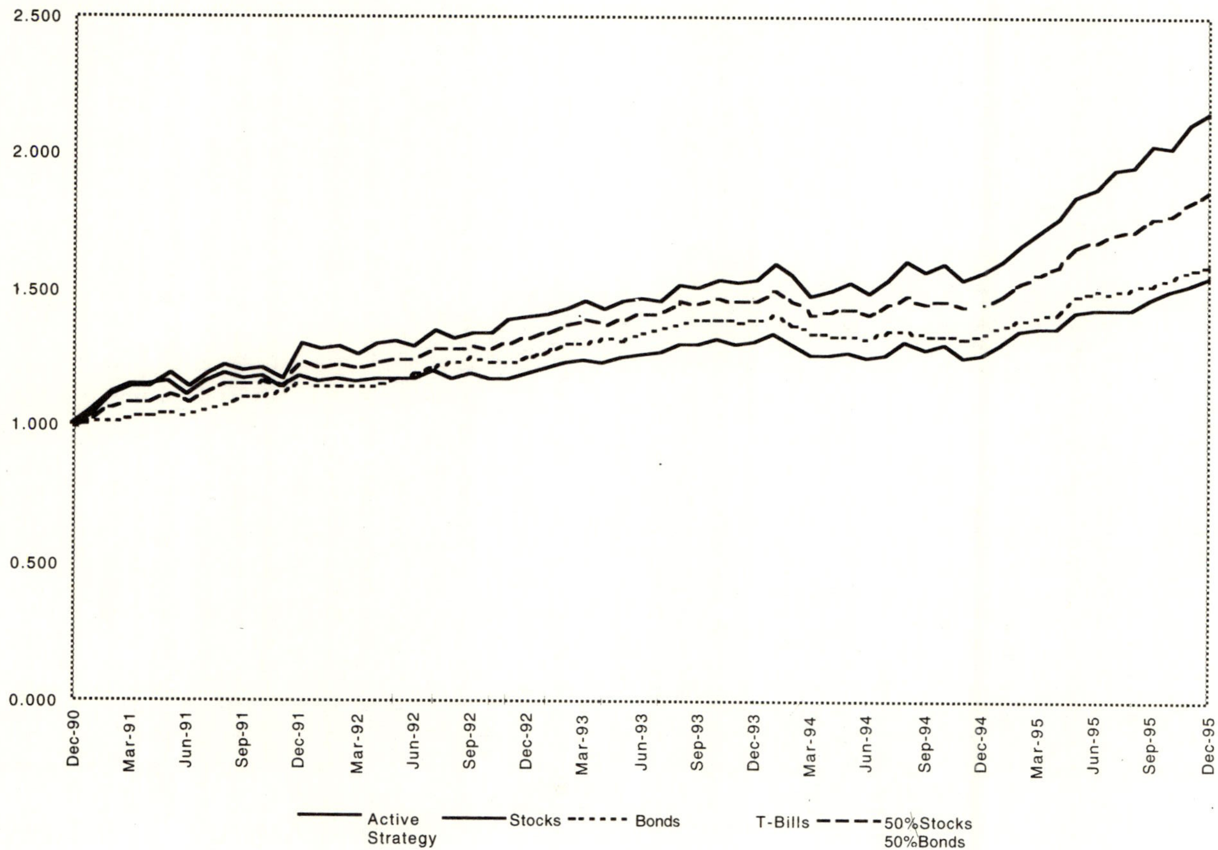

five-year period was simply the second period of underperformance out of six, five-year periods, we would still find that, overall, the strategy added value. If we combine the terminal value of the active strategy (without transaction costs) calculated by Klemkosky and Bharati, with our results, we obtain an overall terminal value of $112.80. The terminal value of a 100% stocks buy-and-hold strategy would have been $27.55. The terminal value of a 50% stocks/50% bonds buy-and-hold strategy would have been even lower, $17.87. Furthermore, Klemkosky and Bharati found that standard deviations of monthly return were lower using the active strategy than any of the buy-and-hold strategies. Unfortunately, we cannot combine their data with our data to arrive at an overall standard deviation figure. When we review the standard deviations of monthly returns for the active strategy, the 100% stocks strategy, and the 50% stocks/50% bonds strategy, we see that the standard deviations for the active strategy is lower than for 100% stocks, 2.14% *versus* 2.25%, but higher than for the 50% stocks/50% bonds strategy, 1.37%.

There is a possibility that either we or Klemkosky and Bharati made an error in the implementation or measurement of the results of the system. We have tried to be careful in following the descriptions given by Klemkosky and Bharati. We have double-checked our results. However, we are particularly disturbed by two glaring discrepancies in our results. First, there was a large discrepancy in the average number of variables in the bond models. Klemkosky and Bharati reported that their bond model averaged 6.7 variables. From Table 5–13, we see that our model often used three or fewer variables and, on average, used 4.5 variables. It is also difficult to believe that a variable, the intermediate term Treasury Note yield, could appear in 98.1% of their models and only a little more than 60% of ours. The second major discrepancy lies in the number of times the portfolio invested solely in Treasury-bills. Klemkosky and Bharati found that this happened 30% of the time. We had only six instances out of sixty, or 10%, where the active strategy called for 100% investment in Treasury-bills. On the other hand, they found only 25% of their portfolios held combinations of stocks and bonds, while we experienced this result in 30 of 60 models, or 50% of the time.

With regard to the first issue, as principal volatility increases in the bond market, the percentage of total return attributable to yield decreases. Thus, the yield on the ten-year Treasury Note would have a decreased influence on ensuing bond market returns. For the first half of the Klemkosky and Bharati study period, the late fifties through the early seventies, bond market price volatility was relatively low. However, the latter half of their study period was one of tremendous bond market price volatility. The period 1991 through 1995 actually experienced a reduction in volatility, relative to the eighties.

With regard to the second issue, a lower Treasury-bill yield could result in the model selecting an all cash position on fewer occasions. The way the model is designed, the portfolio holds cash only on those occasions where both of the other asset classes are expected to underperform cash. A lower Treasury-bill yield means that this would happen less often. Since the period from 1991 through 1995 was one in which Treasury-bill yields fell as low as 2.7% annualized, it is conceivable that this could have been the case. However, even assuming a 6% annualized Treasury-bill yield, or 0.50% monthly, a look back at Table 5–14 reveals that there was not even a single month in which both predicted returns for stocks and bonds fell below this level, except for the six cases in which the model chose cash. Thus, it is possible that changes within the financial markets, undetected by us, could have caused these departures from the Klemkosky and Bharati's results, but we remain suspicious.

Another source of error into the strategy could have been unintentional misinterpretation of the predictive variables as well as inappropriate intentional changes of the variables. In particular, variables two, three, and four are extremely sensitive to errors in their determination. It is also unknown what, if any, effect changing the method used to measure the relative level of small cap stocks (variable seven) has on overall results.

Even though Klemkosky and Bharati's results were quite convincing, we still must consider the possibility that it was a coincidence. Klemkosky and Bharati found that their active strategy, without transaction costs, outperformed the buy and hold large stock portfolio with a t-statistic of 2.16, meaning that the null hypothesis that there was no difference between the means of the two strategies can be rejected with 5% confidence. Likewise, they found that their active strategy, with transaction costs, outperformed the buy and hold strategies for portfolios with less than 69% stocks, with the null hypothesis of no difference rejected at the 5% confidence level. Another way to look at it is to consider how the results would look if just one key month, such as October 1987, were removed. We do not know for certain, but it is likely that the active strategy selected bonds instead of stocks for October 1987. If the strategy had chosen stocks instead of bonds, the terminal wealth of the active strategy would have been $50.25, not $66.47. This is a significant reduction in terminal wealth but it is still much higher than terminal wealth under the buy and hold stocks strategy, which ended with a terminal wealth of $12.79.

In short, we believe that a disciplined system of asset allocation can add value, but the use of such a system must be tempered with a degree of caution and human judgment. Computers cannot solve all of our problems! We hope that the interested reader might use the system described above as a base and perhaps modify the system as appropriate.

Areas of Possible Improvement

A review of our results for the five year period, 1991 through 1995, reveals two important areas of possible improvement. First, the system predicted an abysmal return in stocks for December 1991, -4.40%. The actual return in stocks for December 1991 was 11.433%, by far the single best one month return of any asset class in our study period. Why did the system so completely underestimate stock returns that month? The system was not equipped to know that the Fed would cut the Discount Rate by a full 1.0% on December 20, sending the stock market into a dizzying year-end rally. This result suggests the inclusion of a variable for Fed action. We can choose to use either (or both) the Discount Rate (index symbol DISCRATE on Bloomberg) or the Fed Funds Target Rate (FDTR on Bloomberg).

We must also decide whether to use the actual value or change in value. The decision centers on whether the prevailing level of interest rates is a predictor of ensuing asset class returns or whether the act of changing interest rates introduces something new into the financial markets, unpredicted by our other variables. Our preference would be to use a change in value of the Fed Funds Target Rate variable. One caveat is that, unlike all the other variables, this variable would be unknown at the beginning of the month. We would have to use an estimate of what Fed action might be during the month. This reduces the "systematicness" of the system, in favor of, we believe, greater usefulness.

The second area where the system failed was in excluding stocks from the portfolio for the majority of 1995, a year where stocks produced a 37.5% return. The key variable in this case, was variable eight, the earnings to price ratio. In this analysis, we have used twelve-month trailing earnings, as opposed to forecast earnings. Trailing earnings did not adequately sense the tremendous increase in earnings that occurred during 1995, fueling the market's rapid rise. Thus, the model incorrectly assumed a lower earnings to price ratio than actually existed during this time. Furthermore, the period 1990 and 1991 was a period of recession, which included some unusual earnings to price ratios. Given that the model uses rolling five year periods, these figures were picked up in the calculations.

A closer look back at Table 5–12 reveals that in late 1994 and early 1995, variable nine was included in the model with a positive coefficient, as we would expect. However, in mid-1995 to late 1995, the sign of this coefficient had reversed and became significantly negative. We believe this problem could be remedied, and the model as a whole enhanced, by using forecast future earnings instead of trailing earnings. Again, this requires that we use an estimated variable, instead of a known variable, possibly subjecting the model to the risk of faulty estimates. We believe that the model will be better using new, albeit possibly slightly incorrect, information rather than using old, absolutely correct, information.

We have considered many other ways the model might be modified for improvement, none of which has been adequately tested. We encourage the reader to experiment with some of these ideas.

1. Increase or decrease the length of the rolling time period, i.e., ten- or three-years.
2. Adjust the time interval between rebalancing the portfolio. Currently, we are using one month. This could be changed to quarterly or weekly.
3. Eliminate some of the variables that are used in very few of the models.
4. Make mandatory the use of some of the variables that appeared in most of the models.
5. Instead of selecting the model with the lowest Mallows' Criterion, select the portfolio with the lowest Mallows' Criterion using a predetermined minimum number of variables, such as four, to eliminate models based on only two or three variables.
6. Eliminate the use of Mallows' Criterion altogether and use all the variables.
7. Invest entirely in the asset class with the highest expected return instead of the mix with the highest Sharpe Ratio.
8. Use forecast earnings instead of trailing earnings for variable eight, earnings to price ratio.
9. Use forecast dividends instead of trailing dividends for variable nine, dividend to price ratio.
10. Include a variable for Fed action, as discussed above.
11. Replace variable four with a more straightforward measure, such as yield on the one month Treasury-bill minus yield on the one month Treasury-bill one month ago.
12. Augment variables ten and eleven in a manner similar to number ten above. Consider adding, change in yield in the ten year Treasury Note and change in yield in the thirty year Treasury Bond.

In short, we believe that Klemkosky and Bharati have developed an effective base model for a disciplined, quantitative approach to asset allocation. We have tested their system and found it to be full of potential but not without problems. With proper modifications, we believe that this model can be used to enhance human judgment in the asset allocation process.

CHAPTER 6

Optimization

In the previous chapter we focused on the first part of the asset allocation problem, obtaining suitable predictions of future asset class returns. Specifically, we looked at a systematic method of processing relevant information to arrive at asset class return estimates. Past research has shown that such variables do exist and that they can assist in predicting future asset class returns. However, we found in our five year test period that the results were imperfect, leading us to conclude that a systematic approach is not a guaranteed way to arrive at superior returns. Results from a systematic method probably should be tempered with the judgment that a human analyst can add to the thought process. Intuitively, we believe that a thoughtful approach to estimating asset class returns, variances, and covariances is an integral part of the asset allocation process.

In this chapter we look at the second part of the asset allocation problem, constructing a suitable portfolio based on our asset class return, variance, and covariance inputs. We call this process portfolio optimization. A tremendous amount of thoughtful research exists on the subject of portfolio optimization. Our goal is to provide a brief review of some of these works and then to expand upon them in a new direction.

Discussion on portfolio optimization will be from two different viewpoints. First, we look at Markowitz's mean-variance optimization method. Researchers have noted that Markowitz's optimization method requires accurate inputs to produce accurate output. Errors in inputs tend to be exaggerated, resulting in suboptimal portfolios. We consider the possibility that inputs are likely to be incorrect and present a method of modifying Markowitz's theory to account for these errors in inputs. Second, we consider the research of behavioral psychologists who have found that human decision-making processes contradict expected utility theory. In *Portfolio Selection,* Markowitz alluded to some of these contradictions but concluded that expected utility theory should be used in portfolio selection anyway. We explore ways in which the behavioral psychologists' findings can be incorporated into Markowitz's theory.

The Markowitz Mean-Variance Optimization Model

In this first section on optimization we present a model that addresses one important problem with Markowitz's mean-variance optimization model, its tendency to magnify errors in inputs. We call our model "three-dimensional portfolio optimization."

Markowitz's theory of portfolio selection, for which he received the Nobel Prize in Economic Science in 1990, was a major step forward in the science of investment management. It is fair to call Markowitz the father of modern portfolio theory. This having been said, it is fair to say as well that his theory is not without shortfalls. However, it provides a crucially important starting point.

In *Portfolio Selection,* Markowitz says,

> "The process of selecting a portfolio may be divided into two stages. The first stage starts with observation and experience and ends with beliefs about the future performances of available securities. The second stage starts with the relevant beliefs about future performances and ends with the choice of portfolio. This paper is concerned with the second stage."

Markowitz provides the mathematics necessary to create "efficient" portfolios given a set of inputs but he only offers suggestions as to how those inputs are to be determined. Techniques available to security analysts have improved greatly in the forty-four years since Markowitz wrote *Portfolio Selection,* but inputs in the optimizer remain, at best, estimates, and, at worst, outright guesses.

Michaud summarized the problem best when he said, "The fundamental problem is that the level of mathematical sophistication of the optimization algorithm is far greater than the level of information in the input forecasts." Another adage that applies is: Garbage In, Garbage Out.

In Douglas Adams's book *The Hitchhiker's Guide to the Galaxy* there is a scene where the most powerful computer in the known universe is asked to answer the "ultimate question of life, the universe, and everything." After pondering this question for $7^1/_2$ million years the computer finally answered, "42." Why such an implausible answer? Bad inputs. The answer was not incorrect. The question was simply not the right question. The solution, of course, was to build a more powerful computer to determine what the question should have been.

The idea behind three-dimensional portfolio optimization is that the Markowitz theory is a valuable starting point but needs to be taken to another level, or dimension, to account for the fact that the inputs are likely to be incorrect. Our fundamental belief is that the inputs used in the Markowitz optimization process will be incorrect, despite the best efforts of the analysts. We seek a way to identify the optimal portfolio that both reduces the effect of errors in the inputs and produces a result that is close to being efficient under the Markowitz optimization technique, to within a user-defined level of tolerance.

According to Markowitz, the expected return of a portfolio is a function of the weights of the securities in the portfolio and their individual expected returns, or

$$E(r_p) = \Sigma\, w_i\, E(r_i),$$

where $E(r_p)$ is the expected return of the portfolio, w_i is the weight of the *i*th security in the portfolio and $E(r_i)$ is the expected return of the *i*th security. The variance of a portfolio is a function of the weights of the securities in the portfolio, their individual variances, and the covariances between every possible combination of two securities, or

$$Var_p = \Sigma\, w_i^2\, Var_i + 2\, \Sigma\, \Sigma\, w_i\, w_j\, Cov_{ij},$$

where Var_p is the variance of the portfolio, w_i and w_j are the weights of the *i*th and *j*th securities in the portfolio, Var_i is the variance of the *i*th security and Cov_{ij} is the covariance between the *i*th and *j*th securities.

It is important to note that the expected return of the portfolio is not a function of the variances or covariances. Likewise, the variance of the portfolio is not a function of expected return. The only variables shared by the two formulas are the weights of the securities. These weights are the unknowns sought. This distinction is important. It will be helpful to be able to address expected return and variance separately as we discuss the three-dimensional concept further.

The Impact of Errors in the Estimation of Inputs

As we have seen, Markowitz's optimization requires inputs for expected means, variances, and covariances, all of which will likely be incorrect. Chopra and Ziemba studied the relative impact of errors in the estimation of the inputs. They found, for average risk levels, errors in means are about eleven times as important as errors in variance. Furthermore, errors in variance are about twice as important as errors in covariance. The relative importance of errors in means, variance, and covariance also depends upon the investor's risk tolerance. The higher the level of risk tolerance, the more important errors in estimates of mean were relative to errors in estimates of variance and covariance. Chopra and Ziemba reached these conclusions on the basis of observations made while assuming that all errors were proportional to the inputs being estimated. That is, the error term associated with an asset with expected return of 12% was twice as large as that associated with an asset with expected return of 6%. We believe that errors in estimates for high risk securities will likely be even greater than proportional to low risk securities. If this proved to be true, it would mean that errors in means could be even more important than Chopra and Ziemba reported, especially in high risk-tolerance portfolios. It is beyond the scope of this book to analyze the methodology used by Chopra and Ziemba in more detail. It is sufficient to note that we can safely say that at all risk levels, errors in means are substantially more important than errors in variance and covariance. This result is important because as an intermediate step in developing three-dimensional optimization we allow for errors in means and assume that there are no errors in variance and covariance. The mathematics of this intermediate step is much simpler than the general solution.

Mean-Variance Optimization Model: Example 1

Before describing three-dimensional optimization, we will look at an example of Markowitz's mean-variance optimization. Table 6–1 provides the inputs in our hypothetical example. As with all other such tables in this chapter, these inputs are for illustrative purposes only and do not represent any attempt to forecast returns, variance, or covariance over any particular time period. We are assuming asset class returns will be normally distributed over our particular time frame, although we do not specify what that time frame is. Whatever the time frame, there exists a Treasury-bill with a maturity exactly coinciding with the end of the time frame so that its return is known with certainty—its variance is zero and covariance with all other asset classes is zero. We assume a U.S. investor but we ignore the currency issue in this illustration. For now, it is irrelevant if the investments in Pacific stocks and European stocks are hedged or unhedged. Finally, we have specifically included the case where European stocks are expected to produce a lower return than U.S. stocks but with a higher variance. Obviously, we would generally prefer U.S. stocks to European stocks under these circumstances, but Markowitz theory forces us to consider that these asset classes behave with less than perfect

TABLE 6–1 Expected Returns and Covariance Matrix: Example 1

Asset Class Information				***Covariance***			
Asset Class	**E(r)**	**Std. Dev.**	**Variance**	**Pacific Stocks**	**Europe Stocks**	**Long Bonds**	**Intermediate Bonds**
US Stocks	12.0%	0.16	0.0256	0.0115	0.0128	0.0040	0.0019
Pacific Stocks	13.0%	0.24	0.0576		0.0240	0.0012	0.0010
Europe Stocks	11.0%	0.20	0.0400			0.0010	0.0008
Long Bonds	7.0%	0.05	0.0025				0.0016
Intermediate Bonds	6.5%	0.04	0.0016				
Treasury Bills	5.0%	0.00	0.0000				

positive correlation. This means that a combination of these two asset classes would produce risk-return characteristics more favorable than would be predicted based on their expected returns and variances alone. To the extent that this diversification benefit is sufficient to offset the initial risk-return disadvantage of European stocks, the efficient portfolio will contain a small percentage of European stocks.

Chart 6–1 shows the resulting efficient frontier, based upon the inputs in Table 6–1. By definition, these portfolios provide the highest possible return for any given level of risk. Stated differently, these portfolios provide the lowest risk for a given level of risk. The range of possibilities extends from a portfolio of 100% Treasury-bills, which would be expected to produce a return of 5% with no risk, to a portfolio of 100% Pacific stocks, which would be expected to produce a return of 13% with a standard deviation of 24%. The checked line below the efficient frontier is the "inefficient frontier," those portfolios that provide the worst possible return for a given level of risk, or the highest risk for a given level of return. All possible portfolios fall somewhere on or between these two frontiers.

The inefficient frontier exhibits an interesting feature. It turns sharply at the point (20%, 11%). In fact, from the point (0%, 5%) it is a straight line corresponding with all possible linear combinations of Treasury-bills and the least efficient asset class, European stocks. The inefficient frontier continues from point (20%, 11.67%) to (24%, 13%), as a linear combination of Treasury-bills and the only other asset class with a higher variance than European stocks, Pacific stocks. The reason the inefficient frontier possesses this characteristic is that linear combinations of risky assets with the risk-free asset do not benefit from the risk reduction element that exists in all combinations of non-perfectly positively correlated risky assets. Otherwise, the curve from point (20%, 11%) to (24%, 13%)

CHART 6–1 Efficient Frontier: Example 1

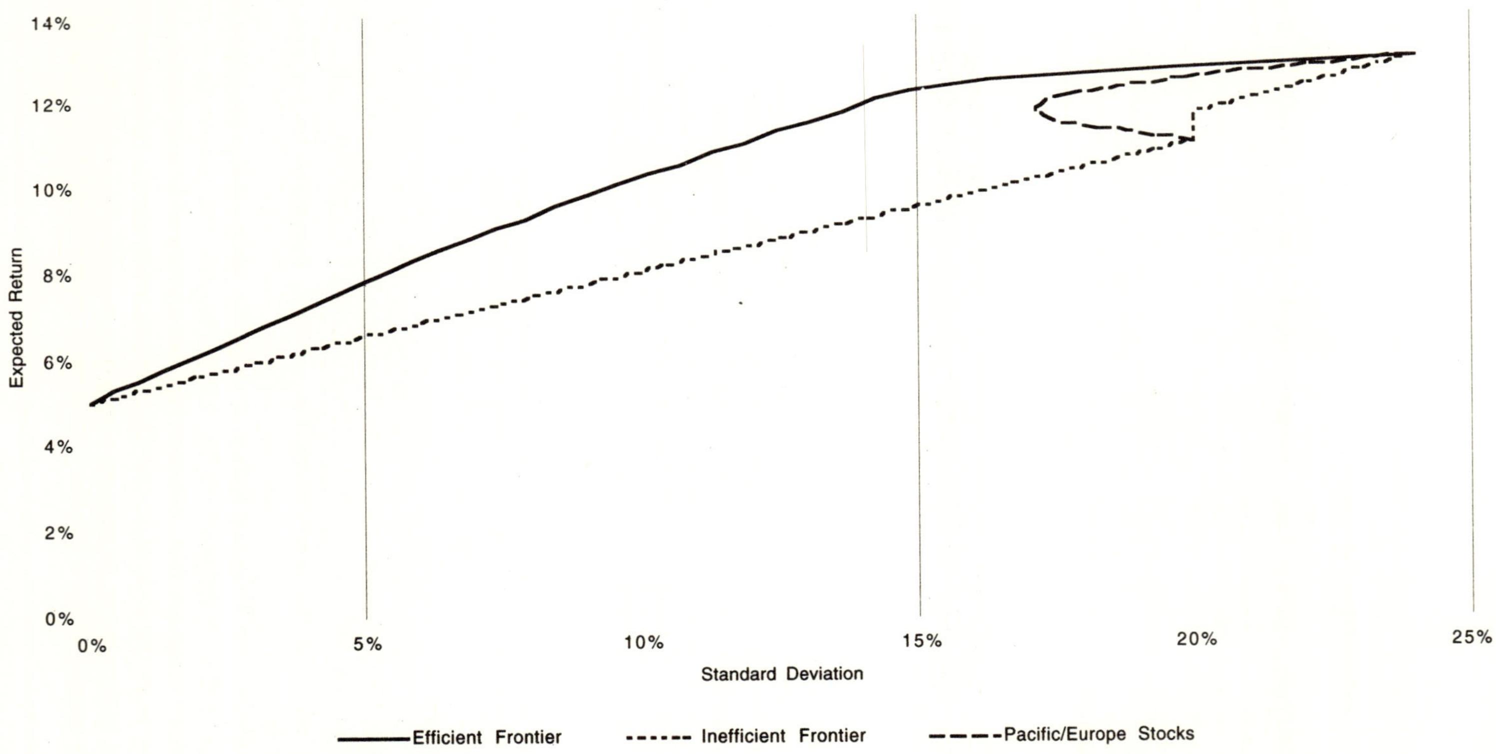

would consist of linear combinations of European stocks and Pacific stocks. Instead, as the inwardly bowed curve on Chart 6–1 shows, linear combinations of these asset classes are far from the inefficient frontier. Why is the inefficient frontier important? We use the inefficient frontier as a reference point to gauge the relative distance between a particular non-efficient portfolio from its efficient counterpart.

Chart 6–2 graphically shows the asset class weights assigned to each of the asset classes for efficient portfolios at a number of expected return levels. At low risk levels, Treasury-bills tend to be the dominant asset class. At high risk levels, U.S. stocks and Pacific stocks tend to dominate. More subtly, at low risk levels, intermediate bonds carry more weight than long bonds, but at higher risk levels, this trend reverses and long bonds carry more weight than intermediate bonds. At nearly all risk levels, especially so in the intermediate risk range, European stocks carry a small weight. This is a typical result of the Markowitz mean-variance optimization process.

Mean-Variance Optimization Model: Example 2

Now, let us assume that our estimates for asset class expected returns shown in Table 6–1 were erroneous and that they should have been as shown in Table 6–2. Before continuing, we must make a very important distinction. In using mean-variance optimization, we establish estimates for the expected returns, variances, and covariances of each possible asset, knowing that the actual returns that occur will differ from our estimated expected return by some amount, as governed by the parameters of a normal distribution. When we say that the original estimates were erroneous, we are not referring to the difference between the return that will actually be observed and what had been estimated. We are referring to an unknowable quantity; that amount by which our estimates differ from what they should have been had we possessed better information. Keep in mind that for every model there is one and only one actual observation and there is no way to attribute the differences in the observed returns relative to the estimated returns to what could normally be expected based upon the variances of the distributions versus errors in the original inputs.

Having made that clarification, we can now ask two questions:

1. What does the efficient frontier look like using the correct inputs?
2. How do the risk-return profiles of what we originally believed were efficient asset class mixes compare with the actual efficient portfolios?

CHART 6–2 Asset Class Weights and Expected Returns: Example 1

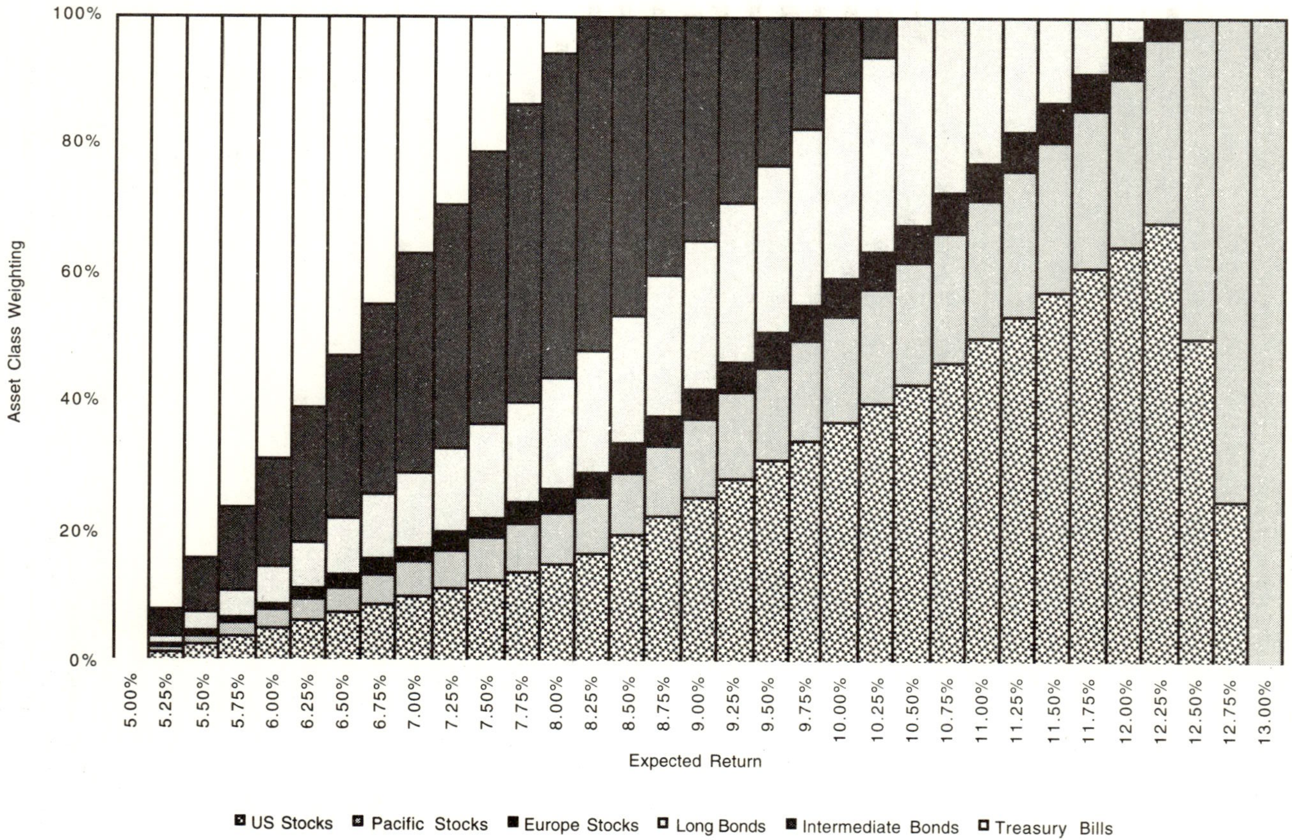

TABLE 6–2 Expected Returns: Example 2

Asset Class	E(r)
US Stocks	13.0%
Pacific Stocks	11.0%
Europe Stocks	12.0%
Long Bonds	8.0%
Intermediate Bonds	7.0%
Treasury Bills	5.0%

Chart 6–3 graphically shows the answer to both questions. In Chart 6–3, we have plotted the risk-return profiles of the efficient portfolios as well as the risk-return profiles for those asset class mixes that were determined earlier to have been efficient under the set of input assumptions in Table 6–1. Up to a standard deviation of 16% there is a small loss of efficiency between the correct efficient frontier and what we previously thought was the efficient frontier. However, at higher risk levels there is a large problem. Under the new assumptions, U.S. stocks are the highest expected return asset, not Pacific stocks. Thus, the new efficient frontier does not extend beyond a standard deviation of 16%. All of the previously efficient portfolios with standard deviations above 16% turn out to produce increasingly lower returns with higher levels of risk. Furthermore, the incorrect efficient frontier fails to reach the return level of the highest return portfolio.

Mean-Variance Optimization Model: Example 3

Now, instead of assuming that our asset class expected returns were incorrect, we will assume that the asset class variances and covariances shown in Table 6–1 were erroneous and should have been as shown in Table 6–3. When the efficient portfolios are plotted against the formerly efficient portfolios in Chart 6–4, we again see the loss of efficiency associated with the errors in inputs.

Unfortunately, Charts 6–3 and 6–4, despite their technical correctness, fail to slap us in the face and convince us of the tremendous importance that errors in our inputs have in the formation of efficient portfolios. It is difficult to conceptualize the importance of the information presented in those charts. As skeptics, we should want to ask,

1. When does the efficient frontier based on our incorrect inputs fall sufficiently below the correct efficient frontier to be important?
2. When does the efficient frontier based on our incorrect inputs extend sufficiently into non-efficient risk levels to be important?

CHART 6–3 Efficient Frontier: Example 2

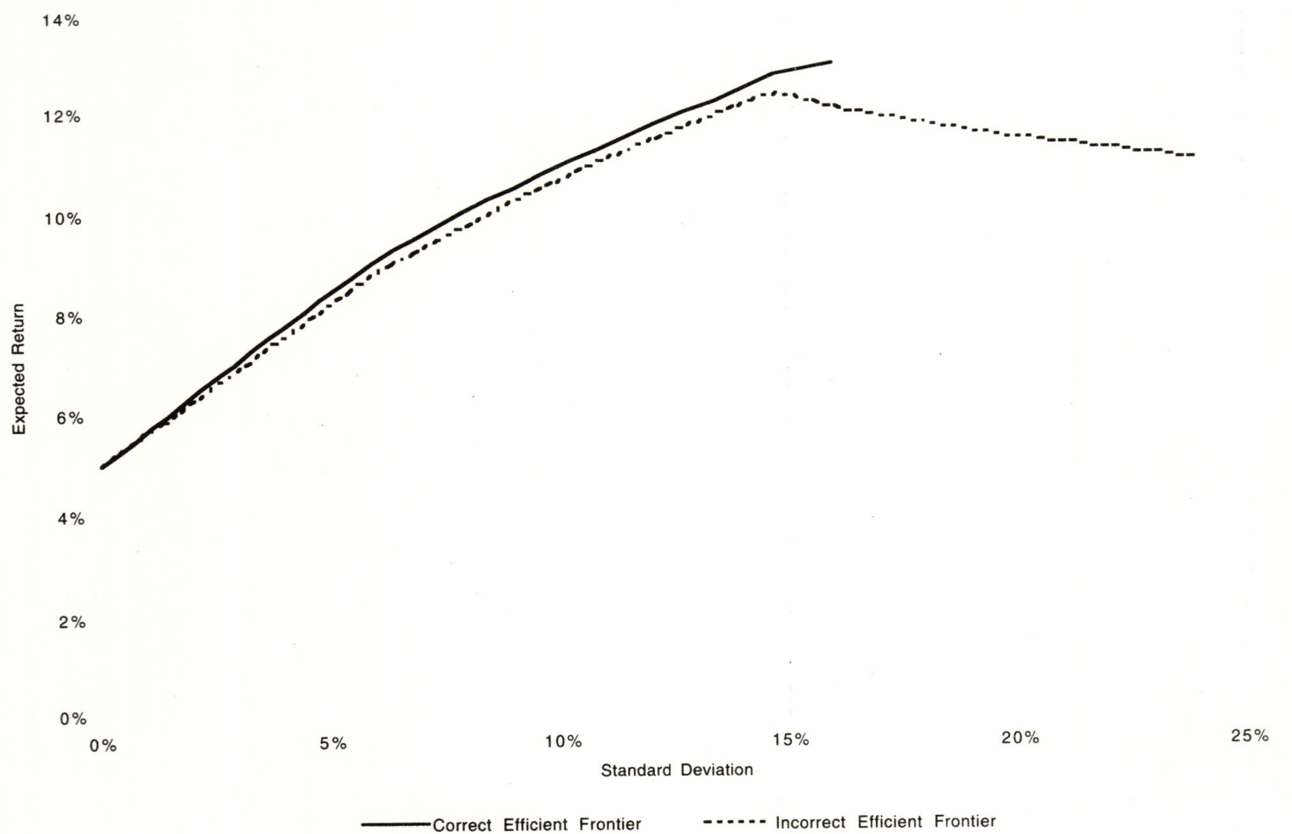

TABLE 6–3 Covariance Matrix: Example 3

Asset Class	Std. Dev.	Variance	Pacific Stocks	Europe Stocks	Long Bonds	Intermediate Bonds
US Stocks	0.18	0.0324	0.0119	0.0158	0.0059	0.0027
Pacific Stocks	0.22	0.0484		0.0242	0.0014	0.0011
Europe Stocks	0.22	0.0484			0.0014	0.0011
Long Bonds	0.065	0.0042				0.0026
Intermediate Bonds	0.05	0.0025				
Treasury Bills	0.00	0.0000				

3. When does the efficient frontier based on our incorrect inputs fall sufficiently short of the highest return portfolio to be important?

By inspection, we can see in Chart 6–3 that the incorrect efficient frontier falls between 20 and 45 basis points below the correct efficient frontier over intermediate risk levels. In Chart 6–4, the difference is somewhat less, about 10 to 16 basis points. Here, we define intermediate risk levels as the range in standard deviation from 5% to 15%. As shown in back in Chart 6–1, the difference between the efficient frontier and the inefficient frontier ranged from 125 basis points to over 275 basis points. We have difficulty knowing whether a 45 basis point loss in efficiency is important enough to warrant concern when we have observed that under the worst conditions a 275 basis point loss in efficiency is possible.

We may define the acceptability of an incorrect efficient frontier relative to the correct efficient frontier as a percentage of the distance between the efficient and inefficient frontiers. For example, we might allow for 10% deviation from efficiency, meaning that as long as the incorrect efficient portfolio stays within 12.5 and 27.5 basis points of the correct efficient frontier over the intermediate range, it is judged acceptable. Under this assumption, the efficient frontier presented in Chart 6–3 would be unacceptable while the efficient frontier presented in Chart 6–4 would be acceptable. Keep in mind that the 10% deviation is user-defined and arbitrary. We could choose to use 5%, in which case the efficient frontier presented in Chart 6–4 would be unacceptable as well.

Next, consider the extent to which the incorrect efficient portfolio extends into non-efficient risk levels. In Chart 6–3 it is visibly obvious that the incorrect efficient frontier extends much too far into non-efficient risk levels to be acceptable. The incorrect curve ends at (24%, 11%), while we can see from inspection that under correct assumptions a portfolio can be constructed with an expected return of 11% and a standard deviation of

CHART 6–4 Efficient Frontier: Example 3

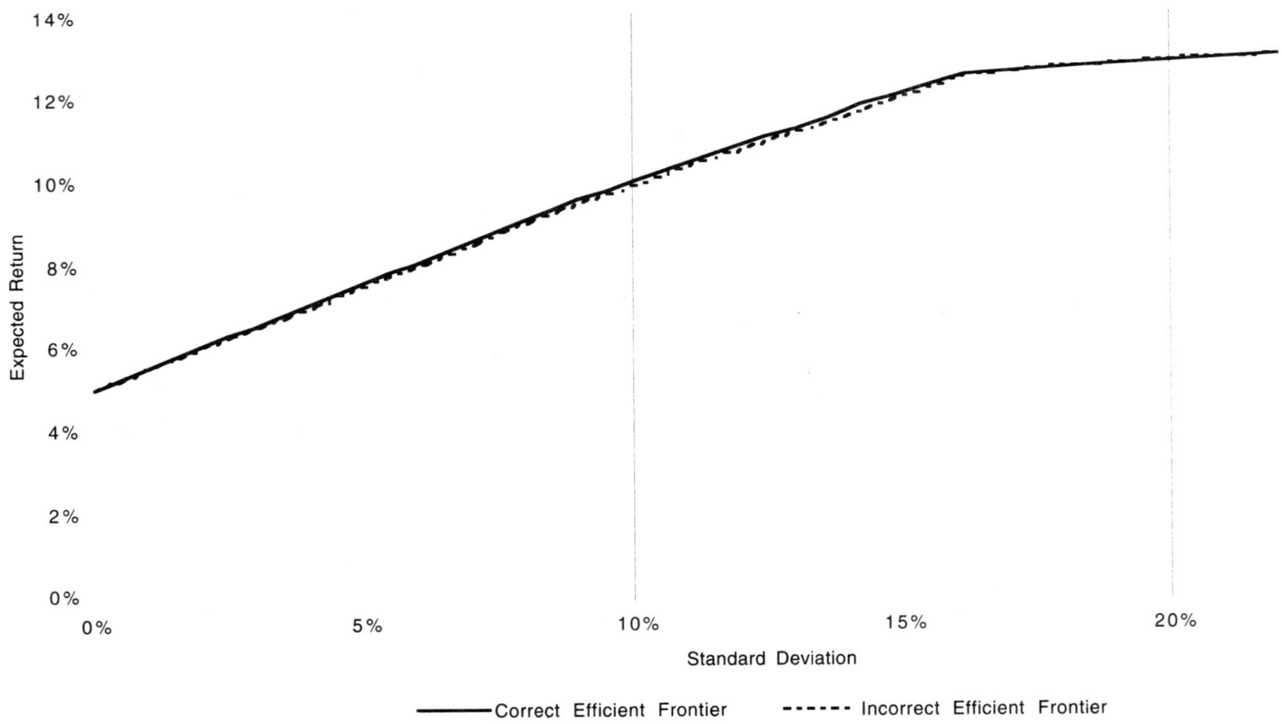

about 10%. Both portfolios produce the same expected return but the difference in standard deviation, 24% *versus* 10%, is huge. In Chart 6–4, we do not have this problem.

Finally, observe that the highest return portfolio on the incorrect efficient frontier in Chart 6–3 has an expected return of 12.39%, 61 basis points below the correct highest return portfolio. Again, we are forced to make an arbitrary decision as to whether this presents an unacceptable loss in maximum possible return due to the errors in inputs. In Chart 6–4, we do not have this problem since the highest return portfolio, 100% Pacific stocks, is the same in both cases.

The Effect of Errors in Inputs: Summary

An alternative way of demonstrating the effect of errors in inputs is to show the compositions of the various efficient portfolios at a particular risk level. In Table 6–4, we list the asset class mixes for the three examples at a 10% expected return risk level. Look at this information carefully. All three of these portfolios are considered efficient at the same risk level under slightly differing input assumptions, yet they possess dramatically different asset class mixes. Our initial set of assumptions produced a reasonably diversified portfolio, with all asset classes except Treasury-bills represented between 5% and 37%. The first modification, introduced in Table 6–2, practically eliminated Pacific stocks and did eliminate Intermediate bonds. Weighting in Long bonds soared to 56.8%, nearly double its prior level. The second modification, introduced in Table 6–3, had the opposite effect. It nearly eliminated European stocks, vastly increased the weighting in Pacific stocks, eliminated Long bonds, and quadrupled the exposure to Intermediate bonds. In short, these three portfolios are extraordinarily different from one another, yet each was created using Markowitz mean-variance optimization with only a slight modification in inputs. We would certainly not have suspected this vast asset mix differential based on Charts 6–3 and 6–4. We must acknowledge that there will

TABLE 6–4 Asset Class Mixes at 10% Expected Return

Asset Class	Efficient Frontier 1	Efficient Frontier 2	Efficient Frontier 3
US Stocks	36.8%	28.9%	32.0%
Pacific Stocks	16.6%	1.6%	25.7%
Europe Stocks	5.5%	12.7%	1.5%
Long Bonds	29.2%	56.8%	0.4%
Intermediate Bonds	11.9%	0.0%	40.4%
Treasury Bills	0.0%	0.0%	0.0%

be errors in inputs and that their effects on our overall results will be huge. We must find a way to minimize their effects if the Markowitz optimization is going to be of any use in portfolio selection. This is where three-dimensional portfolio optimization can help.

The Three-Dimensional Portfolio Optimization Model

We noted earlier that the expected return of a portfolio is the weighted sum of its components' expected returns, that is:

$$E(r_p) = \Sigma\, w_i\, E(r_i),$$

Furthermore, we have observed that the variance of a portfolio is a function of its components' variances and covariances, that is:

$$Var(r_p) = \Sigma\, w_i^2\, Var(r_i) + 2\, \Sigma\, \Sigma\, w_i\, w_j\, Cov(r_i, r_j).$$

At the heart of three-dimensional portfolio optimization are three important assumptions:

1. The inputs to the above equations, specifically the expected returns, variances, and correlation coefficients (which are used to calculate the covariances), are likely to be incorrect.
2. Each input has an associated error term. The error term for each input is normally distributed with a mean of zero. The variance assigned to each error term is user-defined.
3. The error terms are independent variables.

Introducing Errors in Expected Return Inputs

Initially, we will look at the special case where only the expected returns are subject to error. The fact that Chopra and Ziemba found errors in means to be eleven times more important than errors in variance and twice again more important than errors in covariance suggests that this intermediate step may provide 90% of the result we seek and only at a fraction of the work.

We express the return of an individual asset as r_i, which is made up of two components, $\hat{r}_i$ and ε_i, or equivalently $r_i = \hat{r}_i + \varepsilon_i$. The first component, $\hat{r}_i$, represents that portion of an asset's return attributable to the conventional assumption of a normal distribution based on user-defined estimates of mean and standard deviation. The second component, ε_i, represents that portion of an asset's return attributable to the error in the initial estimate of mean. Since the variables are independent we can say that,

$$E(r_i) = E(\hat{r}_i) + E(\varepsilon_i).$$

Thus, since the expected return of the error term is zero, it contributes nothing to the expected return of the asset. Furthermore, since the expected return of the portfolio is simply the weighted sum of the expected returns of each asset, it contributes nothing to the expected return of the portfolio either. In summary, the expected return of the portfolio can be rewritten as,

$$E(r_p) = \Sigma\, w_i\, E(\hat{r}_i).$$

The only difference between this formula and our earlier formula is that the term r_i has been replaced by $\hat{r}_i$ to indicate that it is an estimate, subject to error.

In a similar manner, we can describe the variance of an asset as the sum of two components. Recall that for two independent variables X_1 and X_2, the variance of their sum can be described as,

$$\text{Var}\,(X_1 + X_2) = \text{Var}\,(X_1) + \text{Var}\,(X_2).$$

Since $r_i = \hat{r}_i + \varepsilon_i$, by the above theorem it follows that $\text{Var}(r_i) = \text{Var}(\hat{r}_i) + \text{Var}(\varepsilon_i)$. Substituting this equation into the equation for the variance of the portfolio we have,

$$\text{Var}(r_p) = \Sigma\, w_i^2\, [\, \text{Var}(\hat{r}_i) + \text{Var}(\varepsilon_i)\,] + 2\, \Sigma\, \Sigma\, w_i\, w_j\, \text{Cov}(r_i, r_j).$$

It is important and interesting to note that errors in the expected returns of individual assets do not effect the expected return of the portfolio but they do effect the variance of the portfolio.

In short, we have discovered two key results by introducing an error term into our estimates of expected return. First, the expected return of the portfolio is unaffected by the error term. Second, the variance of the portfolio is calculated by including the variance of the error term along with the variance of the expected return in the standard portfolio variance formula. Care must be taken that the covariances continue to be calculated as before, without including the variance of the error term.

To illustrate this concept, we will modify the inputs given in Table 6–1 to reflect the error that we believe exists in the expected returns of the various asset classes. The error term has an expected mean of zero and a user-defined standard deviation. Table 6–5 lists the standard deviations that we will use in this example. Looking back to Table 6–1, we see that the expected return of U.S. stocks is 12%. In Table 6–5, we assign a standard deviation of 3% to U.S. stocks. Based on these two tables, we conclude that the actual expected return should fall within 9% and 15%,

TABLE 6–5 Error Term

Asset Class	Error Term Std. Deviation	Error Term Variance
US Stocks	3.0%	0.0009
Pacific Stocks	3.0%	0.0009
Europe Stocks	3.0%	0.0009
Long Bonds	2.0%	0.0004
Intermediate Bonds	1.0%	0.0001
Treasury Bills	0.0%	0

within the parameters of a one standard deviation event. If we consider the two standard deviation event, the expected return should fall within 6% and 18%.

It is absolutely vital to understanding the concept of 3-dimensional portfolio optimization to recognize that this range pertains to our estimate of what the expected return should be, not an estimate of what the actual asset class return will be. The actual asset class return is defined by the parameters given in Table 6–1, modified slightly by our introduction of an error term, defined in Table 6–5.

In setting up the inputs for determining the efficient frontier under our newest set of assumptions, we need make only one change. We must modify the variances of each asset class, the diagonal of the covariance matrix, by adding the estimated error of expected return. The expected returns and the remainder of the covariance matrix remains unchanged. From Table 6–1, the variance of U.S. stocks is 0.0256. From Table 6–5, the standard deviation of the error term is 3%, which translates into a variance of 0.0009. Thus, the entry for U.S. stocks in the covariance matrix is 0.0265.

Chart 6–5 compares the resulting error-adjusted efficient frontier with the original efficient frontier. The two curves nearly overlap. For all practical purposes, the two efficient frontiers are identical. Chart 6–6 gives the resulting asset class weightings across a variety of expected returns. The chart is similar to Chart 6–2 but a close look reveals subtle differences.

We can summarize the benefits of 3-dimensional portfolio optimization as follows:

1. It provides a reasonable framework for accounting for the errors in inputs that are bound to exist.
2. The resulting efficient portfolios will be more diversified than those found without using the error term.

CHART 6–5 Error-Adjusted Efficient Frontier

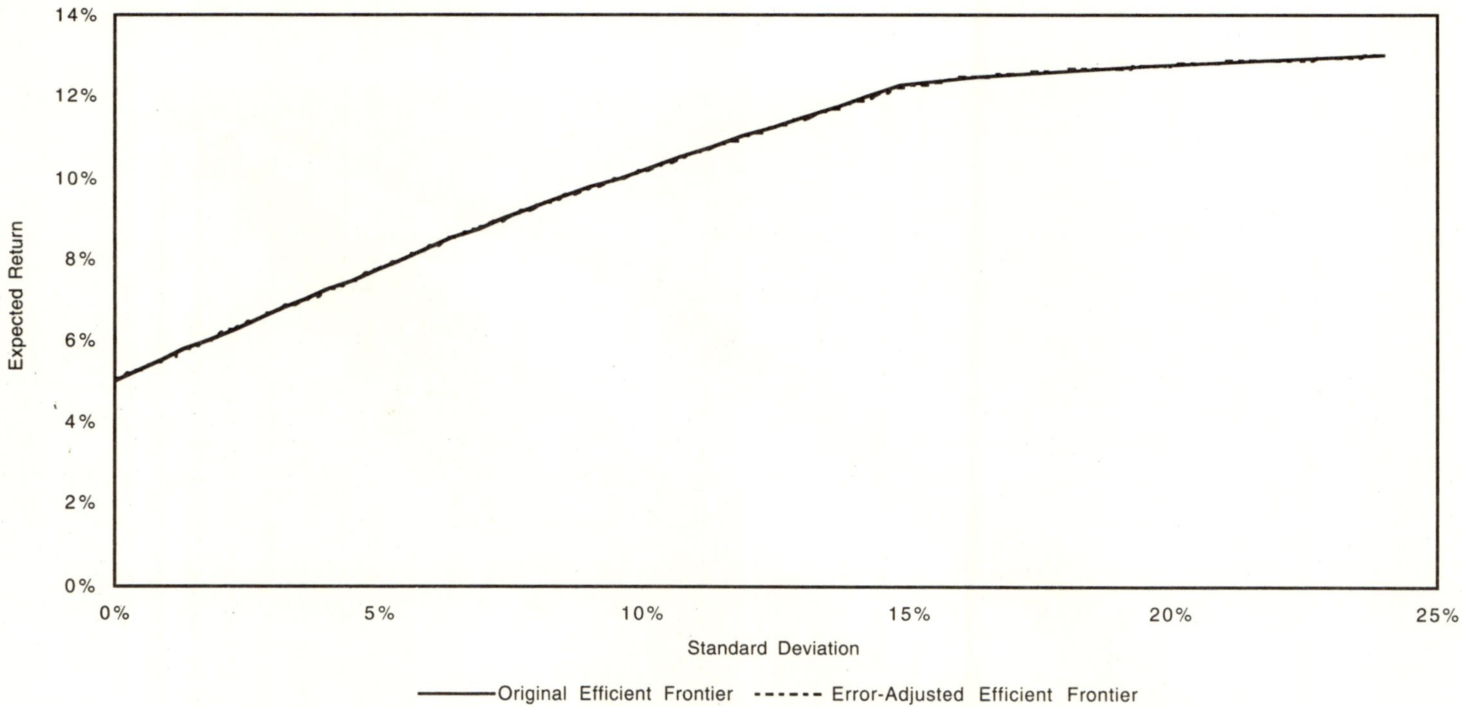

CHART 6–6 Asset Class Weights and Expected Returns: Error-Adjusted

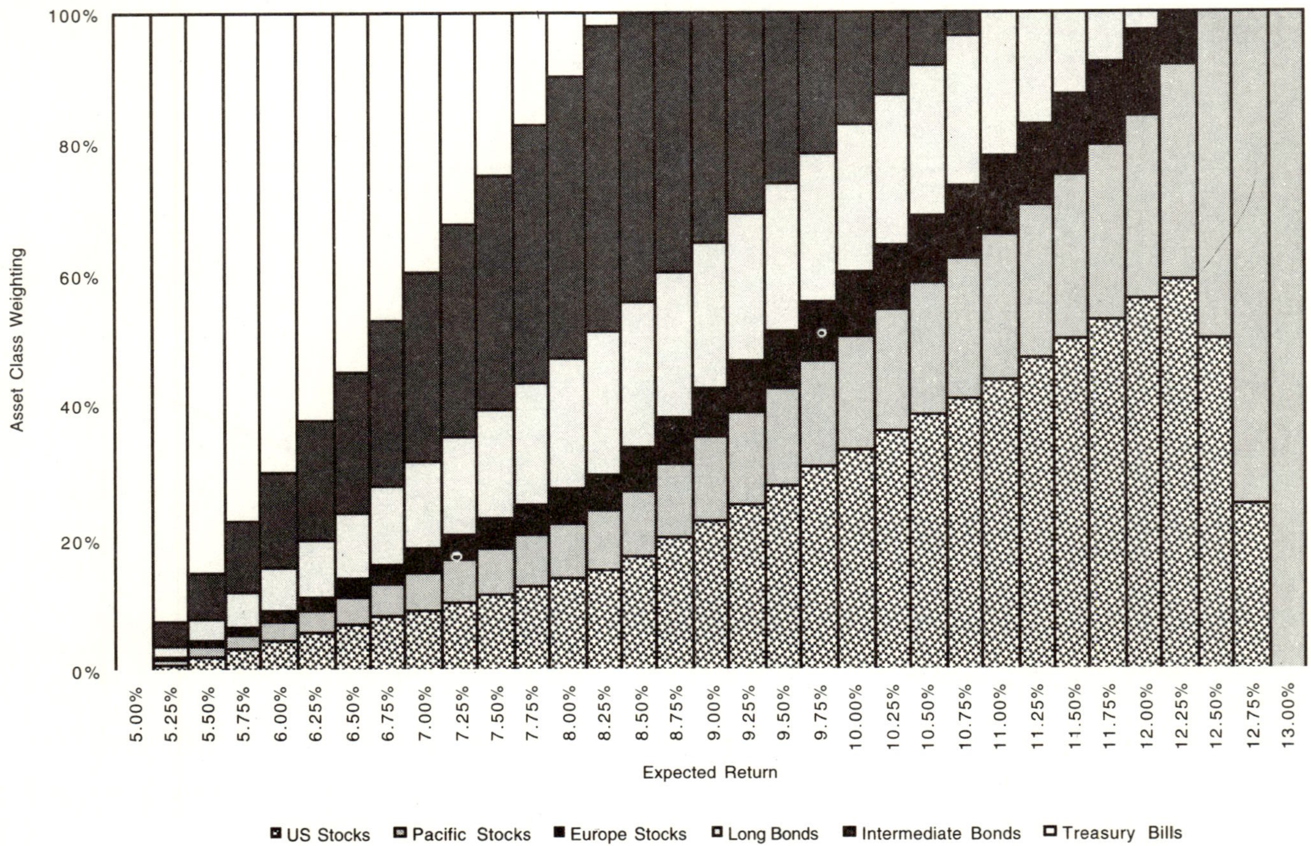

3. We would expect the more diversified error-adjusted portfolio to lie closer to the ex-post efficient frontier than the less diversified original portfolio.
4. The intermediate stage of 3-dimensional portfolio optimization is very easy to implement.

Introducing Errors in Covariance Matrix Inputs

The next stage of three-dimensional portfolio optimization is much more complicated. At this stage we allow for errors in the covariance matrix inputs. There are problems in defining the model and in implementing the model. Suppose we assume that the standard deviations, or the variances, of expected returns given in Table 6–1 are likely to be incorrect, subject to a normally distributed error term with zero mean and standard deviation as shown in Table 6–6. The first question is, which do we use, the standard deviation or the variance? They are not equivalent.

For the rest of the covariance matrix, we have complications as well. We can define each covariance between asset classes as being subject to a normally distributed error term with zero mean and a user-defined standard deviation. However, this presents even more problems. First, the covariances themselves are subject to change simply because the variances, which partly determine the values of the covariances, are subject to change due to the error term. Second, we are generally uncomfortable with the covariance inputs because we tend to estimate them by determining the correlation coefficient, a value that lies between -1.0 and +1.0. It would be difficult to arrive at accurate estimates of the standard deviations of the error terms for the covariance matrix. We could instead consider that the correlation coefficients are subject to the error term. Unfortunately, since the error term is normally distributed, i.e., could possibly lie infinitely far from the mean, we cannot guarantee that the resulting value for the correlation coefficient term would fall between -1.0 and +1.0, unless we artificially constrained it to be. Furthermore, we assumed

TABLE 6–6 Error Term for Covariance Matrix Inputs

	Error Term	
Asset Class	**Std. Deviation**	**Variance**
US Stocks	2.0%	0.000400
Pacific Stocks	2.0%	0.000400
Europe Stocks	2.0%	0.000400
Long Bonds	0.5%	0.000025
Intermediate Bonds	0.5%	0.000025
Treasury Bills	0.0%	0

earlier, for expected returns, that the error terms were independent variables. This would probably not be the case for the correlation coefficient error term. Obviously, there are important issues in defining the model. For now, we will continue by assuming that:

1. The standard deviation, not the variance, is subject to error, the error term being normally distributed with zero mean with a user-defined standard deviation. For this example, we will use the values in Table 6–6.
2. Each correlation coefficient, not the covariances, is subject to error. The error term being normally distributed with zero mean with a user-defined standard deviation. We assume all error terms are independent, even though they probably are not. Where the value would fall below -0.95 or above +0.95 we artificially constrain the value. For this example, we will assume a standard deviation of 0.10.

We encounter problems implementing the model as well. By introducing the error terms, we can no longer define the portfolio variance as a constant. The portfolio variance has become a normally distributed variable, with expected return equal to the former constant. Obviously, Markowitz's critical line method does not allow for this.

The only solution is to run many simulations using randomly selected error terms, calculate the efficient frontiers for each simulation, and analyze the resulting data. We present the results of 25 simulations in Table 6–7. The asset class weightings are the efficient portfolios that produce an expected return of 10% for each simulation. Based on these results, we have little confidence in over- or underweighting any of the asset classes relative to the original asset class weightings given on the bottom of Table 6–7.

We are inclined to rely upon the results of Chopra and Ziemba, who found that errors in variance and covariance are relatively unimportant compared to errors in mean. Thus, we conclude that the intermediate stage of three-dimensional portfolio optimization, which only considers errors in mean, is likely to add as much value as the full version, with much less work.

We noted earlier that three-dimensional portfolio optimization results in generally more diversified portfolios, which we believe will result in a greater likelihood that the ex-post portfolio performance will lie closer to the ex-post efficient frontier than the less diversified Markowitz optimized portfolio. The idea that greater diversification is better suggests that we should consider a method of optimization based on maximizing diversification.

TABLE 6–7 Results of Radomly Selected Error Terms on Various Asset Class Weight

	US Stocks	Pacific Stocks	Europe Stocks	Long Bonds	Intermediate Bonds	Treasury Bills
	26.3%	27.4%	1.1%	45.3%	0.0%	0.0%
	26.6%	26.6%	2.0%	44.9%	0.0%	0.0%
	26.6%	25.3%	3.8%	44.3%	0.0%	0.0%
	27.2%	13.0%	25.8%	0.0%	34.0%	0.0%
	27.6%	23.8%	4.8%	43.8%	0.0%	0.0%
	28.0%	26.7%	0.0%	45.3%	0.0%	0.0%
	30.2%	18.2%	9.9%	41.7%	0.0%	0.0%
	30.9%	19.1%	7.7%	42.3%	0.0%	0.0%
	31.3%	19.9%	7.2%	33.3%	8.4%	0.0%
	32.1%	23.3%	0.0%	44.7%	0.0%	0.0%
	32.8%	13.7%	13.4%	40.1%	0.0%	0.0%
	35.2%	22.4%	0.0%	21.8%	20.6%	0.0%
	36.0%	20.0%	0.0%	44.0%	0.0%	0.0%
	36.6%	17.7%	2.7%	43.0%	0.0%	0.0%
	40.3%	14.8%	3.1%	35.6%	6.2%	0.0%
	42.1%	15.0%	0.0%	43.0%	0.0%	0.0%
	43.9%	15.6%	0.0%	14.0%	26.5%	0.0%
	45.4%	15.5%	0.0%	0.0%	39.2%	0.0%
	47.5%	11.3%	3.4%	0.0%	37.8%	0.0%
	47.5%	13.6%	0.0%	0.0%	38.8%	0.0%
	48.0%	13.0%	0.3%	0.0%	38.7%	0.0%
	48.3%	10.7%	0.0%	30.2%	10.9%	0.0%
	49.7%	10.1%	2.5%	0.0%	37.7%	0.0%
	53.8%	8.3%	0.0%	0.0%	37.9%	0.0%
	59.2%	0.0%	5.5%	0.0%	35.4%	0.0%
Average	38.1%	17.0%	3.7%	26.3%	14.9%	0.0%
Std. Deviation	9.8%	6.6%	5.8%	19.8%	17.1%	0.0%
Original Mix	36.8%	16.6%	5.5%	29.2%	11.9%	0.0%

Optimization and Diversification-Maximization

Using the data in Table 6–1, we set out to find the portfolios that had the maximum diversification within a user-defined level of closeness to the efficient frontier. To quantify the level of diversification, we make the following definition:

$$Diversification = \sum w_i^2 ,$$

where w_i is the weighting of each asset class. Defined this way, maximum diversification is achieved when the value for diversification is minimized. To illustrate, if we had only two asset classes and one asset class was weighted 100%, while the other was weighted 0%, the value for diversification would be 1.0. If each were weighted 50%, the value for diversification would be 0.5. All other possible weightings would fall between 0.5 and 1.0. Clearly, the case where both asset classes are weighted 50% represents maximum diversification.

We define acceptable closeness to the efficient frontier by constraining the standard deviation for any level of expected return to the average of the standard deviation of the efficient portfolio at the current level of expected return plus the standard deviation of the efficient portfolio at the current level of expected return plus 0.25%. Our original efficient portfolio had a standard deviation of 3.62% at an expected return of 7% and a standard deviation 4.07% at an expected return of 7.25%. Thus, at an expected return 7%, we constrain standard deviation to 3.84%.

Diversification-Maximized Results

We conducted this study across the moderate risk portion of the efficient frontier with very interesting results. Chart 6–7 compares the original efficient frontier with the diversification-maximized efficient frontier. From this, we conclude that there is very little loss of efficiency between the two sets of portfolios.

In contrast to the very small decrease in efficiency, Chart 6–8 illustrates the tremendous increase in diversification achieved through this method. Every asset class is included at all expected return levels, except Treasury-bills which are only included up to a 10.5% expected return. Considering that Treasury-bills ceased to be included in the original efficient portfolios, as shown in Chart 6–2, at an expected return of 8%, this result is remarkable.

Furthermore, weightings in Intermediate bonds and Long bonds are quite steady across the spectrum of expected returns, beginning at about 25% for the low risk portfolios and dropping to about 15% in the high risk portfolios. The weighting in European stocks also remains constant across the entire spectrum, ranging from 10% to 16%. As expected, weightings in the higher risk asset classes, Pacific stocks and U.S. stocks gently rose as the expected return increased. Under no circumstances was any asset class weighted more heavily than 38%.

In short, diversification-maximized optimization offers an attractive package providing significant improvement in the overall level of portfolio diversification relative to standard Markowitz optimization at a small cost in efficiency.

CHART 6–7 Efficient Frontier *versus* Diversification-Maximized Efficient Frontier

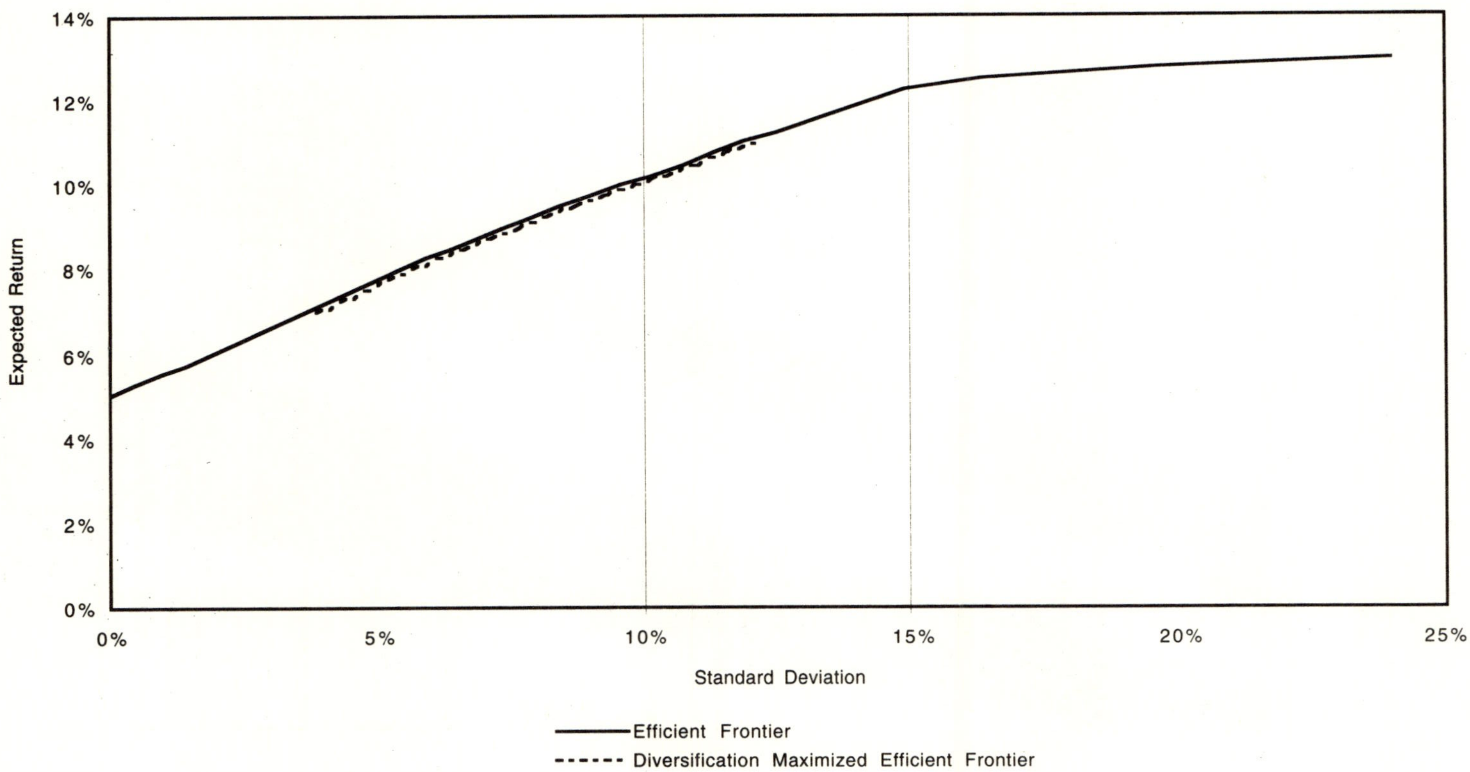

CHART 6–8 Asset Class Weights and Expected Returns: Diversification-Maximized

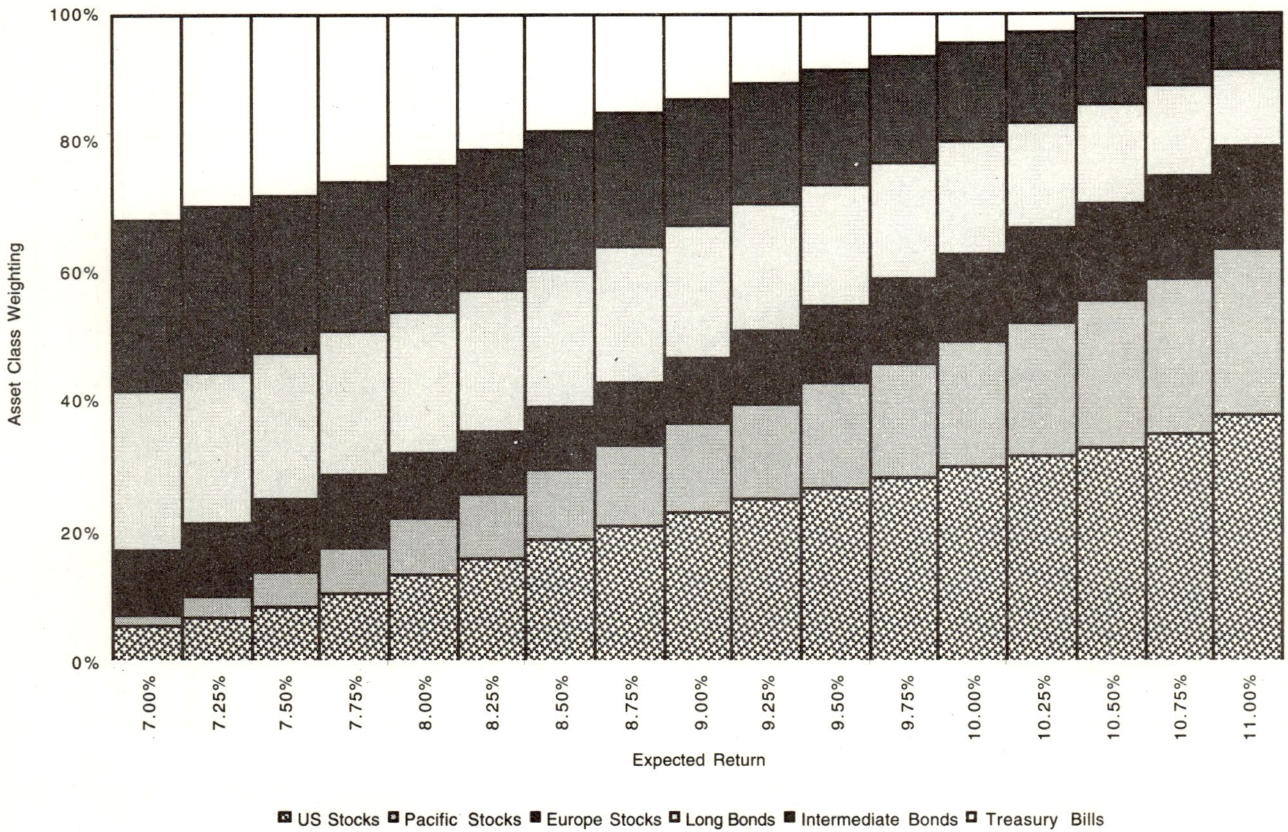

Human Portfolio Optimization

Continuing with the theme of optimization, we will describe a concept called "Human Portfolio Optimization." Human Portfolio Optimization is based on research conducted by a number of behavioral psychologists who have found discrepancies between observed human decision-making processes and expected utility theory. These "discoveries" have been well-known for some time. Even Markowitz briefly discussed some of these issues in *Portfolio Selection,* although he remained unswayed in his preference for expected utility theory. We believe that since we, as investment professionals, are managing money for human beings, we should take into consideration that our human clients' decision-making processes might be relevant in creating optimal portfolios for them. Furthermore, while behavioral psychology has been discussed in many investment-related journals, we have not seen a formal synthesis of these discoveries with modern portfolio theory. Human Portfolio Optimization is our effort to bring these two sciences together.

In this section, we will introduce a number of important concepts developed by behavioral psychologists, culminating in the description of a psychological preference-based value function. We will show how the results obtained using standard Markowitz optimization can be joined with our value function to form a result in accordance with theories of finance as well as psychology. Finally, we will show a practical example of how Human Portfolio Optimization might be used in the real world.

Kahneman and Tversky and the Psychology of Preferences

Kahneman and Tversky have published a number of very interesting articles on the psychology of preferences which interested readers should investigate. Kahneman and Tversky made three major observations:

1. The threat of a loss has a greater impact on a decision than the possibility of an equivalent gain.
2. Most people are also very sensitive to the difference between certainty and high probability and relatively insensitive to intermediate gradations of probability.
3. The regret associated with a loss that was incurred by an action tends to be more intense than the regret associated with inaction or a missed opportunity.

We can paraphrase item one as, "investors love to make money but they hate to lose money even more!" Although the implications of the latter two findings are fascinating, in this section, we will focus on their first finding.

Traditional theory is based on the premise that investors are risk averse. We define an investor as risk averse if he prefers a certain outcome to a risky outcome with an equal or greater expected outcome. To illustrate the point, suppose we had the good fortune to play a game in which we could choose one of the following as our prize:

A. A sure gain of $250; or

B. A 25% chance of winning $1,000, but a 75% chance of winning nothing.

Most of us, being risk averse, would choose option A. In fact, Kahneman and Tversky found that even if option A was reduced to $240, 84% of respondents selected option A, while only 16% of respondents selected option B. For all human beings, there is an amount that we can plug into option A that would make both choices equal in attractiveness. We can use that equilibrium point as a measure of risk averseness. The lower the investor's equilibrium point, the more risk averse he is. So far, everything seems consistent with traditional beliefs.

Kahneman and Tversky go on to show that most people exhibit risk seeking behavior when it comes to losses. We define an investor as risk seeking if he rejects a certain outcome to a risky outcome with an equal or lower expected outcome. To illustrate this point, suppose we had the misfortune to be stuck in a situation where we had the following choices:

C. A sure loss of $750; or

D. A 75% chance of losing $1,000, but a 25% chance of losing nothing.

If we assumed that risk averse behavior would prevail we would expect that most respondents would pick choice A, given that both have the same expected outcome but A is less uncertain. However, Kahneman and Tversky found that only 13% of respondents chose option A, while 87% chose option B.

This paradox is accentuated further when we consider pairs of the above choices. If we group options A and D together and options B and C together and compare them, we find that the least popular pair of responses dominates the most popular pair of responses, as shown below:

1. A & D (25% chance of winning $240 and 75% chance of losing $760
2. B & C (25% chance of winning $250 and 75% chance of losing $750

When presented this way it is obvious that B and C are superior to A and D. Amazingly, Kahneman and Tversky found that 73% of respondents chose both options B and C, while only 3% of respondents chose both options A and D. The other 24% chose A and C or B and D.

Designing a Value and Outcome Function

Having established that people are generally risk averse with regard to gains and risk-seeking with regard to losses, the next step is to design a value function that properly maps all possible outcomes with the value associated with them. We will plot this relationship as a simple curve on an x-y coordinate system where the x-axis represents outcomes and the y-axis represents associated value. We make several assumptions:

1. A gain or loss of zero has zero value. Gains and losses are evaluated relative to this neutral point.
2. Gains have positive value. The shape of the value function for gains is concave. Each extra dollar gained adds slightly less to value than the preceding one.
3. Losses have negative value. The shape of the value function for losses is convex. Each extra dollar lost causes a smaller change in value than the preceding one.
4. In the simplest case, the value function can be approximated by a power function, of the form $y = x^z$, where y is the value, x is the outcome, and z represents the level of risk averseness or risk seekingness.

By using a power function as our value function, we are implicitly assuming proportionality between outcomes and values for all levels. So, if we consider a 25% chance of winning $1,000 to have an equivalent value to winning $210 with certainty, we would also equate a 25% chance of winning $1,000,000 with winning $210,000 with certainty. However, in reality, we are more likely to choose the sure thing the higher we set the stakes. The power function has other drawbacks as we will show momentarily.

Chart 6–9 shows the value function that we have selected for our example above. The positive curve is concave, while the negative curve is convex. This particular value function was created using an exponent of 0.80 for the negative portion and 0.75 for the positive portion, so that in the negative portion,

$$y = x^{(0.80)},$$

and in the positive portion,

$$y = x^{(0.75)}.$$

CHART 6–9 Value Function: Hypothetical Game

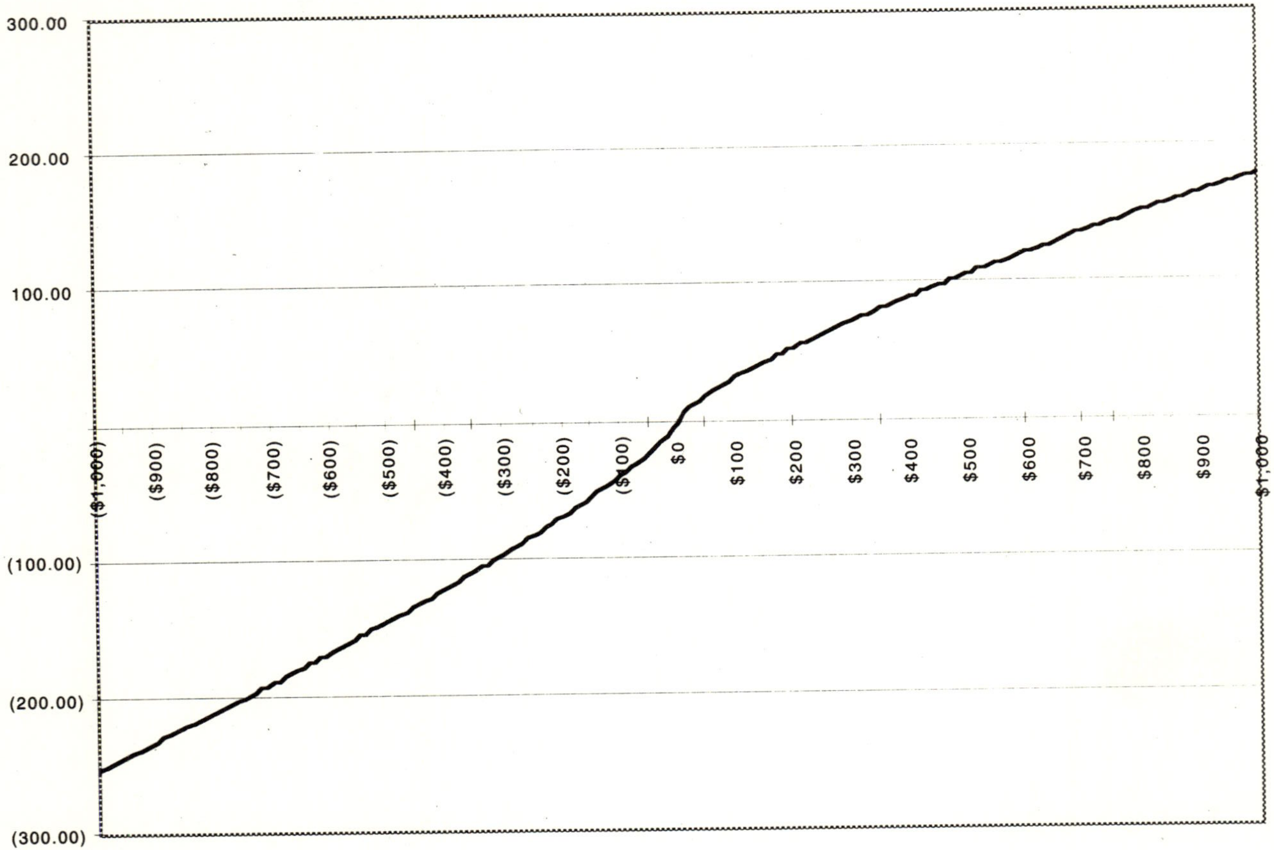

Using this value function, a gain of \$1,000 has a value of 177.83, while a loss of \$1,000 has a value of 251.19. This is consistent with our belief that losses are more painful than their equivalent gains. Furthermore, we can equate a 25% chance of winning \$1,000 with a sure thing outcome by finding the outcome with the same value as a 25% chance of winning \$1,000. For the player with this value function, a gain of \$158 with certainty is equivalent to the gamble. Likewise, on the loss side, we can equate a 75% chance of losing \$1,000 with a sure thing outcome in the same manner. For our hypothetical player, this works out to about \$697.

Blending the Markowitz Theory with the Value Function

Our goal is to blend a value function of this type with Markowitz theory. First, we translate outcomes from dollar to percentage changes since we usually associate the results of Markowitz optimization with an efficient frontier curve plotting expected returns with standard deviation. The power function exhibits a peculiar deformity for values of x between -1.0 and +1.0. At x = -1.0 and x = +1.0, y = 1 for any value of z, the exponent. As discussed earlier, higher values of z produce a steeper curve than lower values of z. Thus, we plan to use higher values of z for losses than for gains. For values between -1.0 and +1.0 the opposite is true. A lower value of z produces a steeper curve. Since most investment returns we typically work with fall within the range of -100% and +100%, we must find a solution. One option is to focus on the range between -100% and +100% exclusively and simply use a higher value of z for gains than for losses, thus resulting in a steeper curve for losses than for gains. Unfortunately, this option does not work well when we include the possibility of greater than 100% returns.

Instead, we choose to multiply investment returns by 100, so that a return of 10% takes a value of 10, not 0.10. We acknowledge that the deformity still exists for investment returns between -1.0% and +1.0%, but this should not be material. Chart 6–10 shows the resulting value curve, multiplying returns by 100, using an exponent of 0.80 and 0.75, for losses and gains, respectively.

Traditionally, the proper Markowitz optimal portfolio has been determined through the use of a utility function, usually of the form,

$$U = E(r) - {}^{1}/_{2} A\sigma^2 ,$$

where A is a user-defined coefficient of risk aversion. Typically, this function is plotted against the efficient frontier and the point where the two

CHART 6-10 Value Function: Investment Returns

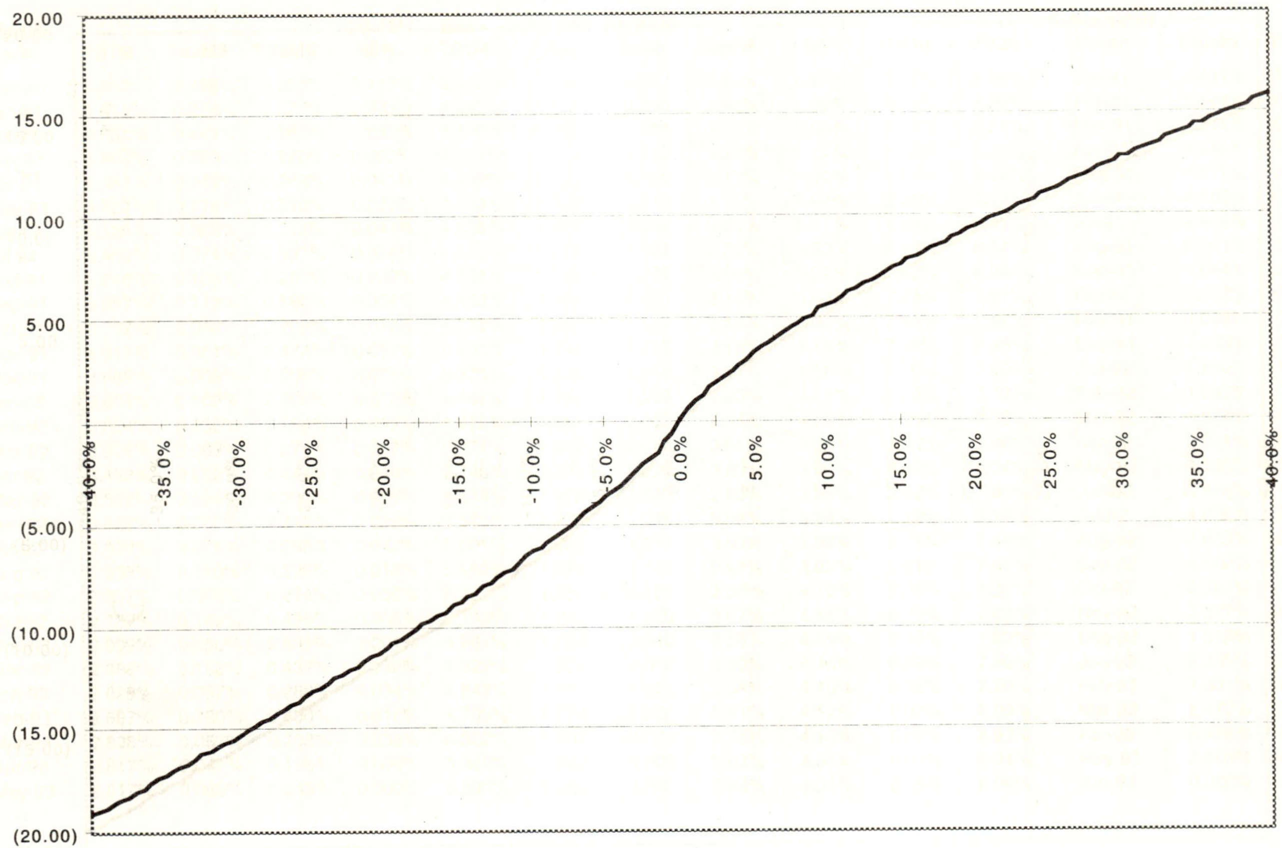

curves are tangent indicates the optimal Markowitz portfolio for that particular level of risk aversion.

We take a different approach. We define portfolio utility as the total amount of value, where value is defined by the value curve, for all possible portfolio outcomes. Mathematically, if the portfolio's return probability distribution curve is f(x) and the value function is g(x), portfolio utility is:

$$\int f(x)g(x)dx.$$

In the special case where f(x) is a normal distribution and g(x) is a power function, as described above, we have:

$$\int \frac{1}{(2\pi)^{1/2}\sigma}\exp\left[-\tfrac{1}{2}\left(\frac{x-\mu}{\sigma}\right)^2\right]\cdot x^z dx.$$

Solving this integral is no easy task. Fortunately, we can approximate the value of the integral by manually finding the area under the resulting curve. It is sufficient to consider as possible portfolio returns, all the possible returns within four standard deviations of the riskiest portfolio. For the example in Table 6–1, that is four times 24% on both sides of 13%, or -84% through +109%.

Next, we break the possible returns down into ranges. Within one standard deviation of the riskiest portfolio, 0.05% divisions are recommended. Between one and two standard deviations, 0.10% divisions are fine. Beyond two standard deviations, 0.20% is sufficient. This works out to 1,920 divisions. This will tax the limits of your personal computer, but the concept is simple.

The solution to the portfolio selection problem is to select the portfolio that maximizes the utility function. If we graph the utility function, we will typically find a gently upward sloping curve as we move from low risk portfolios to high risk portfolio. The slope gradually decreases, finally reaching a point where it is zero. Then as we continue into higher risk portfolios, the utility function begins to decrease. Chart 6–11 graphs the utility function based on the asset class inputs from Table 6–1 and the value curve defined above. The investor with the value curve we have been using is not very risk-averse. His optimal portfolio lies on the risky end of the efficient frontier, at the point (12.40%, 15.48%), defined by an asset mix of 60% U.S. Stocks and 40% Pacific Stocks.

CHART 6–11 Human Portfolio Optimization Utility Function

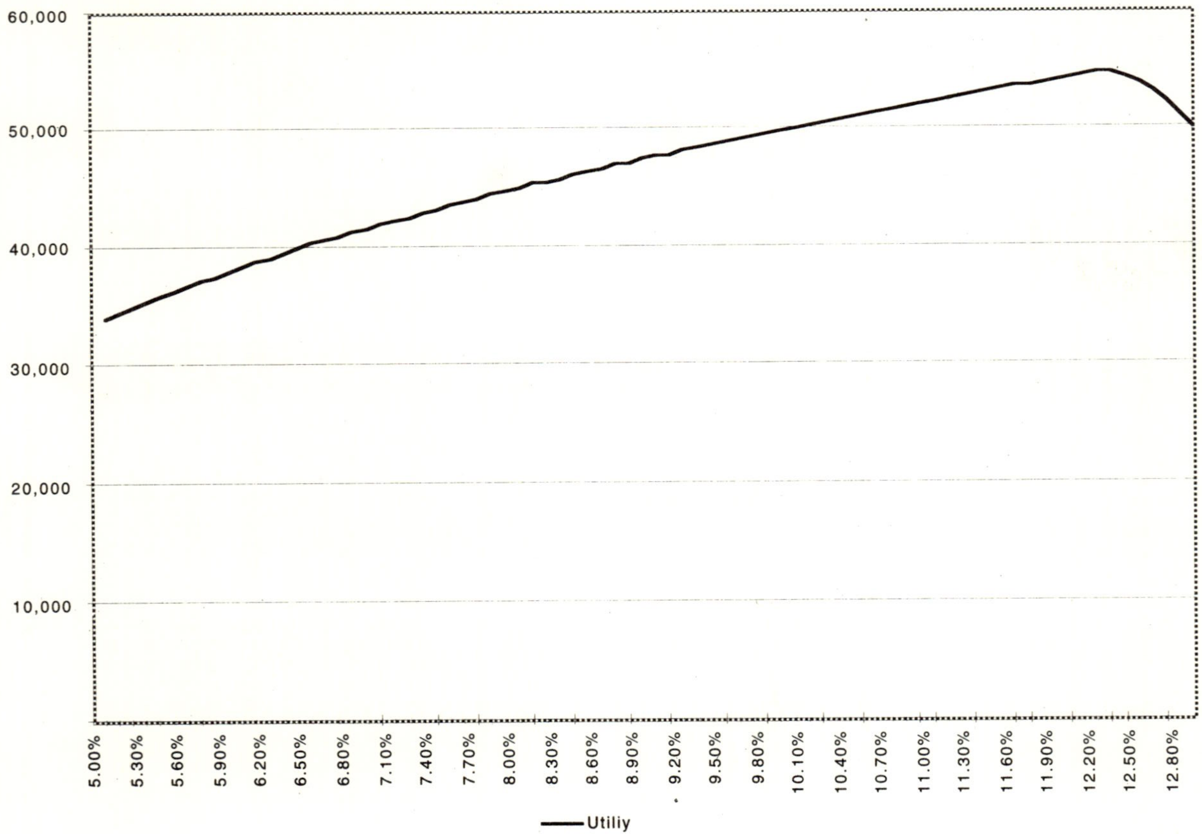

Conclusion

Since we, as investment professionals, are managing money for human clients, we should seriously consider a method of portfolio optimization that considers human behavioral psychology. The method we have presented has a number of key advantages:

1. It is based on actual human perceptions of and responses to reward and risk.
2. The method will only select from among portfolios that are efficient in the traditional Markowitz sense.
3. The method is just as effective over any time horizon.
4. The method can be easily modified for use with in conjunction with any other type of portfolio optimization method, including those described in this chapter.
5. The method works just as well with non-normally distributed portfolio return functions, such as the skewed return functions associated with options.
6. It is easy to implement.

TABLE 5-13 Predicted Bond Returns: December 1990–November 1995

Month end	Beta1	Beta2	Beta3	Beta4	Beta5	Beta6	Beta7	Beta8	Beta9	Beta10	Beta11	Alpha	N	Mean Sq. Error	Cp
Dec-90	2.4662	0.0000	1.0571	15.0130	2.4000	0.1979	-0.0972	8.4707	0.0000	9.9650	-5.3230	-0.0498	9	0.0001404	9.80
Jan-91	2.0671	0.0000	1.8428	14.6709	2.0058	0.0866	-0.0463	4.4107	0.3619	0.0000	-5.1210	0.5670	9	0.0001401	9.74
Feb-91	2.4643	0.0000	0.5639	14.3791	2.0580	0.1101	-0.0815	2.7730	0.0000	1.1605	-5.2365	0.2166	8	0.0001425	8.40
Mar-91	1.8360	0.0000	0.6955	13.6011	1.6520	0.0846	-0.0777	1.8401	0.0000	4.2590	-5.1089	0.1095	8	0.0001425	9.20
Apr-91	1.2472	0.0000	0.0000	9.6310	1.5881	0.0859	-0.0248	0.0000	0.0000	4.7135	-5.1397	0.0297	8	0.0001653	7.60
May-91	1.5018	0.0000	0.0000	8.4245	1.5854	0.0900	-0.0202	0.0000	0.0000	4.2121	-5.0577	0.0309	8	0.0001458	7.24
Jun-91	1.6968	0.0000	0.0000	7.7250	1.5838	0.1000	-0.0202	0.0000	0.0000	3.6573	-4.4746	0.0294	8	0.0001452	7.11
Jul-91	1.4368	0.0000	0.0000	-5.8981	1.5625	-0.0000	-0.0261	0.0000	0.0000	4.8490	-5.7458	0.3264	8	0.0001454	7.30
Aug-91	0.8279	0.0000	0.0000	-8.5535	1.0849	0.0000	-0.0288	0.0000	0.0000	4.5149	-4.6801	0.0146	8	0.0001477	8.01
Sep-91	0.0000	0.7764	0.0000	-7.5460	0.5049	0.0000	-0.0288	0.0000	0.0000	5.2998	-5.4360	0.5481	6	0.0001513	7.11
Oct-91	0.0000	0.7379	0.0000	6.1630	0.3600	-0.0000	-0.0653	0.0000	0.0000	0.0000	-5.1681	0.0315	6	0.0001532	7.37
Nov-91	0.0000	0.0546	0.0000	0.0000	0.0000	-0.1009	0.0000	0.0000	0.0000	0.4410	0.0000	0.2004	3	0.0001614	5.65
Dec-91	0.9307	0.0000	0.0000	0.0000	0.0000	-0.0815	0.0484	0.0000	0.0000	0.0000	0.0000	0.0101	3	0.0001642	5.99
Jan-92	0.0000	0.0000	0.0000	0.0000	0.0000	-0.0426	0.0000	-1.1724	0.0000	0.0000	0.0000	0.0501	3	0.0001707	5.70
Feb-92	0.0000	0.0000	0.0000	0.0000	0.0000	-0.0489	0.0000	-1.3002	0.0000	0.0000	0.0000	0.1097	3	0.0001544	5.00
Mar-92	0.0000	0.0000	0.0000	0.0000	0.0000	-0.0501	0.0000	-1.8111	0.0000	0.0000	0.0000	0.0690	3	0.0001571	5.33
Apr-92	0.0000	0.0000	0.0000	0.0000	0.0000	-0.0487	0.0000	-1.2010	0.0000	0.0000	0.0000	0.0499	3	0.0001613	5.60
May-92	0.0000	0.0000	0.0000	0.0000	0.0000	-0.0274	0.0000	-1.4100	0.0000	0.0000	0.0000	0.0014	3	0.0001575	4.93
Jun-92	0.0000	0.0000	0.0000	0.0000	0.0000	-0.0252	0.0000	-1.5013	0.0000	0.0000	0.0000	0.0606	3	0.0001576	4.80
Jul-92	0.0000	0.0000	0.0000	0.0000	0.0000	-0.0601	0.0000	-1.7065	0.0000	0.0000	0.0000	0.0301	3	0.0001681	4.91
Aug-92	0.0000	0.0000	0.0000	0.0000	0.0000	-0.0409	0.0000	-1.7028	0.0000	0.0000	0.0000	0.0087	3	0.0001577	4.05
Sep-92	0.0000	0.0000	0.0000	0.0000	0.0000	0.0319	0.0000	0.0000	0.0012	0.0000	-0.0481	0.0018	2	0.0001500	3.78
Oct-92	0.0000	0.0000	0.0000	0.0000	0.0000	-0.1148	0.0378	0.0000	-0.2000	3.1190	-0.3707	0.1641	5	0.0001440	6.35
Nov-92	0.0000	0.0000	0.0000	0.0000	0.0000	-0.1121	0.0215	0.1279	0.0000	3.2105	-0.6027	0.1650	5	0.0001402	6.24
Dec-92	0.0000	0.0000	0.0000	0.0000	0.0000	-0.1263	0.0418	0.0000	0.1306	3.3527	-0.5037	0.1752	5	0.0001405	6.51
Jan-93	0.0000	0.0000	0.0000	-5.8020	0.0000	-0.1984	0.0648	0.0000	0.0000	3.6897	-0.4030	0.2187	5	0.0001290	8.39
Feb-93	0.0000	0.0000	0.0000	-8.7774	0.0000	-0.2043	0.0808	0.0000	0.0000	4.0193	-0.1442	0.3489	5	0.0001246	7.11
Mar-93	0.0000	0.0000	0.0000	-8.2439	0.0000	-0.2048	0.0716	0.0000	0.0000	4.1575	-4.5068	0.3151	5	0.0001268	7.35
Apr-93	0.0000	0.0000	0.0000	-9.0859	0.0000	-0.2014	0.0695	0.0000	0.0000	3.9912	-4.2750	0.3037	5	0.0001230	0.73
May-93	0.0000	0.0000	0.0000	-8.8118	0.0000	-0.1774	0.0686	0.0000	0.0000	3.2340	-4.0341	0.2370	6	0.0001230	8.66
Jun-93	0.0000	0.0000	0.0000	-8.4404	0.0000	-0.1881	0.0686	0.0000	0.0000	3.6201	-4.0711	0.2572	6	0.0001193	6.85
Jul-93	0.0000	0.0000	0.0000	-8.7427	0.0000	-0.1784	0.0601	0.0000	0.0000	3.1971	-3.8497	0.2226	6	0.0001150	6.90

Bibliography

Books

Arnott, Robert D., and Frank J. Fabozzi. *Active Asset Allocation*. Chicago: Probus Publishing Co., 1992.

Droms, William G., ed. *Asset Allocation for the Individual Investor*. Charlottesville, VA: Institute of Chartered Financial Analysts, 1987.

Gibson, Roger C. *Asset Allocation: Balancing Financial Risk*.. Homewood, IL: Irwin Professional Publishing, 1990.

Joehnk, Michael D., ed. *Asset Allocation for Institutional Portfolios*. Charlottesville, VA: Institute of Chartered Financial Analysts, 1987.

Karnosky, Denis S., and Brian D. Singer. *Global Asset Management and Performance Attribution*. Charlottesville, VA: Research Foundation of the Institute of Chartered Financial Analysts, 1994.

Markowitz, Harry M. *Portfolio Selection: Efficient Diversification of Investment*. New York: John Wiley and Sons, 1959.

Articles

Allen, G. C. "Performance Attribution for Global Equity Portfolios." *Journal of Portfolio Management*. Fall 1991: 59-65.

Ambachtsheer, K. P. "The Persistence of Investment Risk." *Journal of Portfolio Management*. Fall 1989: 69-71.

Arnott, R. D., and J. N. von Germeten. "Systematic Asset Allocation." *Financial Analysts Journal*. November/December 1983: 31-38.

Arnott, R. D., and R. D. Henriksson. "A Disciplined Approach to Global Asset Allocation." *Financial Analysts Journal*. March/April 1989: 17-28.

Bawa, V. S. "Optimal Rules for Ordering Uncertain Prospects." *Journal of Financial Economics*. March 1975: 95-121.

Bawa, V. S. "Safety First, Stochastic Dominance and Optimal Portfolio Choice." *Journal of Financial and Quantitative Analysis*. June 1978: 255-271.

Benari, Y. "Optimal Asset Mix and its Link to Changing Fundamental Factors." *Journal of Portfolio Management*. Winter 1990: 11-18.

Black, F., and R. Litterman. "Asset Allocation: Combining Investor Views with Market Equilibrium." *Journal of Fixed Income*. September 1991: 7-18.

Black, F., and R. Jones. "Simplifying Portfolio Insurance." *Journal of Portfolio Management*. Fall 1987: 48-51.

Black, F., and R. Litterman. " Global Portfolio Optimization." *Financial Analysts Journal*. September/October 1992: 28-43.

Bogle, J. C. "Investing in the 1990's." *Journal of Portfolio Management*. Spring 1991: 5-14.

Bogle, J. C. "Investing in the 1990's: Occam's Razor Revisited." *Journal of Portfolio Management*. Fall 1991: 88-91.

Bogle, J. C. "The 1990's at the Halfway Mark." *Journal of Portfolio Management*. Summer 1995: 21-31.

Bostock, P., and P. Woolley. "A New Way to Analyze International Equity Market Performance." *Financial Analysts Journal*. January / February 1991: 32-38.

Bostock, P., and P. Woolley, and M. Duffy. "Duration-Based Asset Allocation." *Financial Analysts Journal*. January / February 1989: 54-60.

Breen, W., J. Lakonishok, and B. LeBaron. "Economic Significance of Predictable Variation in Stock Index Returns." *Journal of Finance* 44. 1989: 1177-1190.

Bresiger, G., and E. Simonoff. "Measuring Risk." *Financial Planning*. September 1995: 56-68.

Brinson, G. P. "Asset Allocation vs. Market Timing." *Investment Management Review*. October 1988.

Brinson, G. P., B. D. Singer, and G. L. Beebower. "Determinants of Portfolio Performance II: An Update." *Financial Analysts Journal*. May / June: 40-48.

Brinson, G. P., L. R. Hood, and G. L. Beebower. "Determinants of Portfolio Performance." *Financial Analysts Journal*. July / August: 39-44.

Burik, P., and R. M. Ennis. "Foreign Bonds in Diversified Portfolios: A Limited Advantage." *Financial Analysts Journal*. March / April 1990: 31-40.

Butler, K., and D. Domian. "Long-Run Returns on Stock and Bond Portfolios: Implications for Retirement Planning." *Financial Services Review* 2. 1 / 1992-1993: 41-50.

Butler, K. C., and D. L. Domian. "Risk, Diversification, and the Investment Horizon." *Journal of Portfolio Management*. Spring 1991: 41-47.

Campbell, J. Y. "Stock Returns and the Term Structure." *Journal of Financial Economics* 18. 1987: 373-399.

Campbell, J. Y., and R. J. Shiller. "Stock Prices, Earnings, and Expected Dividends." *Journal of Finance* 43. 1988: 661-676.

Chan, A., and C. R. Chen. "How Well Do Asset Allocation Mutual Fund Managers Allocate Assets?" *Journal of Portfolio Management*. Spring 1992: 81-91.

Chang, E. C., and R. D. Huang. "Time-Varying Return and Risk in the Corporate Bond Market." *Journal of Financial and Quantitative Analysis* 25. 1990: 323-340.

Chopra, V. K., and W. T. Ziemba. "The Effect of Errors in Means, Variances, and Covariances on Optimal Portfolio Choice." *Journal of Portfolio Management*. Winter 1993: 6-11.

Christopherson, J. A. "Equity Style Classifications." *Journal of Portfolio Management*. Spring 1995: 32-43.

Clarke, R. G., M. T. Fitzgerald, P. Berent, and M. Statman. "Required Accuracy for Successful Asset Allocation." *Journal of Portfolio Management*. Fall 1990: 12-19.

Clarke, R. G., M. T. Fitzgerald, P. Berent, and M. Statman. "Market Timing with Imperfect Information." *Financial Analysts Journal*. November/December 1989: 27-36.

Clarke, R. G., S. Krase, and M. Statman. "Tracking Errors, Regret, and Tactical Asset Allocation." *Journal of Portfolio Management*. Spring 1994: 16-24.

Constantinides, G. M. "A Note on the Suboptimality of Dollar-Cost Averaging as an Investment Policy." *Journal of Financial and Quantitative Analysis* 14. June 1979: 443-450.

Elton, N., M. Gruber, and M. Padberg. "Optimal Portfolios From Simple Ranking Devices." *Journal of Portfolio Management*. Spring 1978: 15-19.

Eun, C. S., and B. G. Resnick. "Exchange Rate Uncertainty, Forward Contracts and International Portfolio Selection." *Journal of Finance*. March 1988: 197-215.

Ezra, D. D. "Asset Allocation by Surplus Optimization." *Financial Analysts Journal*. January/February 1991.

Fama, E. F. "Efficient Capital Markets: II." *Journal of Finance* 46. 1991: 1575-1618.

Fama, E. F. "Components of Investment Performance." *Journal of Finance* 27. June 1972: 551-567.

Fama, E. F., and K. R. French. "Business Conditions and Expected Returns on Stocks and Bonds." *Journal of Financial Economics* 25. 1989: 23-49.

Fama, E. F., and K. R. French. "Dividend Yields and Expected Stock Returns." *Journal of Financial Economics* 22. 1988: 3-25.

Farrell, J. L., Jr. "A Fundamental Forecast Approach to Superior Asset Allocation." *Financial Analysts Journal*. May/June 1989: 32-37.

Ferguson, R. "A Comparison of the Mean-Variance and Long-Term Return Characteristics of Three Investment Strategies." *Financial Analysts Journal*. July/August 1987: 55-66.

Ferson, W. E. "Changes in Expected Security Returns, Risk, and the Level of Interest Rates." *Journal of Finance*. December 1989.

Fong, H. G. "An Asset Allocation Framework." *Journal of Portfolio Management*. Winter 1980: 58-66.

Fong, H. G., and O. A. Vasicek. "Forecast-Free International Asset Allocation." *Financial Analysts Journal*. March/April 1989: 29-33.

Franks, E. C. "A Short-Run Target Return Strategy for Achieving Long-Run Target Returns: Fifty Years of Evidence." *Journal of Portfolio Management*. Summer 1991: 14-18.

Franks, E. C. "A Simple Portfolio Revision Strategy for Achieving Prespecified Target Returns." *Journal of Portfolio Management*. Spring 1990: 15-20.

Franks, E. C. "Targeting Excess-of-Benchmark Returns." *Journal of Portfolio Management*. Summer 1992: 6-12.

French, K. R., G. W. Schwert, and R. F. Stambaugh. "Expected Stock Returns and Volatility." *Journal of Financial Economics* 19. 1987: 3-30.

Friend, I., and D. Vickers. "Portfolio Selection and Investment Performance." *Journal of Finance* 20. September 1965: 391-415

Gardner, G. W., and T. Wuilloud. "Currency Risk in International Portfolios: How Satisfying Is Optimal Hedging?" *Journal of Portfolio Management*. Spring 1995: 59-67.

Grauer, R. R., and N. H. Hakansson. "Returns on Levered, Actively Managed Long-Run Portfolios of Stocks, Bonds, and Bills, 1934-1983." *Financial Analysts Journal*. September/October 1985: 24-43.

Gunthorpe, D., and H. Levy. "Portfolio Composition and Investment Horizon." *Financial Analysts Journal*. January/February 1994: 51-56.

Harlow, W. V. "Asset Allocation in a Downside-Risk Framework." *Financial Analysts Journal*. September/October 1991: 28-40.

Hensel, C. R., D. D. Ezra, and J. H. Ilkiw. "The Importance of the Asset Allocation Decision." *Financial Analysts Journal*. July/August 1991: 65-72.

Ho, K., M. A. Milevsky, and C. Robinson. "How To Avoid Outliving Your Money." *Canadian Investment Review*. Fall 1994: 35-38.

Ho, K., M. A. Milevsky, and C. Robinson. "Asset Allocation, Life Expectancy and Shortfall." *Financial Services Review*. Spring 1994: 109-126.

Horowitz, I. "A Model for Mutual Fund Evaluation." *Industrial Management Review* 6. Spring 1965: 81-92.

Jaffe, J., D. B. Keim, and R. Westerfield. "Earnings Yield, Market Values, and Stock Returns." *Journal of Finance* 44. 1989: 135-148.

Jeffrey, R. H., and R. D. Arnott. "Is Your Alpha Big Enough to Cover Its Taxes?" *Journal of Portfolio Management*. Spring 1993: 15-25.

Jensen, M. C. "The Performance of Mutual Funds in the Period 1945-1964." *Journal of Finance* May 1968: 389-416.

Jobson, J. D., and B. Korkie. "Putting Markowitz Theory to Work." *Journal of Portfolio Management*. Summer 1981: 70-74.

Jorion, P. "Asset Allocation With Hedged and Unhedged Foreign Stocks and Bonds." *Journal of Portfolio Management* Summer 1989: 49-54.

Jorion, P. "International Portfolio Diversification With Estimation Risk." *Journal of Business*. July 1985: 259-278.

Kahneman, D., and A. Tversky. "Prospect Theory: An Analysis of Decision Under Risk." *Econometrica* 47. March 1979: 263-291.

Kahneman, D., and A. Tversky. "The Psychology of Preferences." *Scientific American* 246. January 1982: 160-173.

Keim, D. B., and R. F. Stambaugh. "Predicting Returns in the Stock and Bond Markets." *Journal of Financial Economics* 17. 1986: 357-390.

Ketchum, M. D. "Investment Management Through Formula Timing Plans." *Journal of Business* 20. July 1947: 156-169.

Klein, R. W., and V. S. Bawa. "The Effect of Estimation Risk on Optimal Portfolio Choice." *Journal of Financial Economics* 3. June 1976: 215-231.

Klemkosky, R. C., and R. Bharati. "Time-Varying Expected Returns and Asset Allocation." *Journal of Portfolio Management*. Summer 1995: 80-88.

Kritzman, M. "What Practitioners Need to Know . . . About Time Diversification." *Financial Analysts Journal* 50. January / February 1994: 14-18.

Langetieg, T. C., M. L. Leibowitz, and S. Kogelman. "Duration Targeting and the Management of Multiperiod Returns." *Financial Analysts Journal*. September / October 1990: 35-45.

Lee, A. F. "International Asset and Currency Allocation." *Journal of Portfolio Management*. Fall 1987: 68-73.

Lee, W. Y. "Diversification and Time: Do Investment Horizons Matter? *Journal of Portfolio Management*. Spring 1990: 21-26.

Leibowitz, M. L., S. Kogelman, and L. N. Bader. "Interest Rate-Sensitive Asset Allocation." *Journal of Portfolio Management*. Spring 1994: 8-15.

Leibowitz, M. L. "Total Portfolio Duration: A New Perspective on Asset Allocation" *Financial Analysts Journal*. September / October 1986: 18-29, 77.

Leibowitz, M. L., and R. D. Henriksson. "Portfolio Optimization with Shortfall Constraints: A Confidence-Limit Approach to Managing Downside Risk." *Financial Analysts Journal*. March / April 1989: 34-41.

Leibowitz, M. L., and R. D. Henriksson. "Portfolio Optimization Within a Surplus Framework." *Financial Analyssts Journal*. March / April 1988: 43-51.

Leibowitz, M. L., and S. Kogelman. "Asset Allocation Under Shortfall Constraints." *Journal of Portfolio Management*. Winter 1991.

Leibowitz, M. L., and T. C. Langetieg. "Shortfall Risk and the Asset Allocation Decision: A Simulation Analysis of Stock and Bond Risk Profiles." *Journal of Portfolio Management*. Fall 1989: 61-68.

Leibowitz, M. L., and W. S. Krasker. "Persistence of Risk: Shortfall Probabilities Over the Long Term." *Financial Analysts Journal*. November / December 1988.

Leibowitz, M. L., L. N. Bader, and S. Kogelman. "Global Fixed-Income Investing: The Impact of the Currency Hedge." *Journal of Fixed Income*. June 1993: 7-18.

Leibowitz, M. L., L. N. Bader, and S. Kogelman. "Asset Allocation Under Liability Uncertainty." *Journal of Fixed Income*. September 1992.

Leibowitz, M. L., L. N. Bader, and S. Kogelman. "'Optimal' Portfolios Relative to Benchmark Allocations." *Journal of Portfolio Management*. Summer 1993: 18-29.

Leibowitz, M. L., S. Kogelman, and L. N. Bader. "Asset Performance and Surplus Control." *Journal of Portfolio Management*. Winter 1992: 28-37.

Lloyd, W., and N. Modani. "Stocks, Bonds, Bills and Time Diversification." *Journal of Portfolio Management*. Spring 1983: 7-11.

Loomes, G. "Further Evidence of the Impact of Regret and Disappointment in Choice Under Uncertainty." *Econometrica*. 1988: 47-62.

Loomes, G., and R. Sugden. "Regret Theory: An Alternative Theory of Rational Choice Under Unc." *Economic Journal* 92. 1982: 805-824.

MacBeth, J. D., and D. C. Emanuel. "Tactical Asset Allocation: Pros and Cons." *Financial Analysts Journal*. November/December 1993: 30-43.

Madura, J., and W. Reiff. "A Hedge Strategy for International Portfolios." *Journal of Portfolio Management*. Fall 1985: 70-74.

Magrabe, W. "The Value of One Option to Exchange One Asset for Another." *Journal of Finance* 33. 1978: 177-1886.

Markowitz, H. M. "Portfolio Selection." *Journal of Finance* 12. March 1952: 77-91.

Markowitz, H. M. "The Utility of Wealth." *Journal of Political Economy* 60. 1952: 151-158.

McEnally, R. W. "Time Diversification: Surest Route to Lower Risk?" *Journal of Portfolio Management*. Summer 1985: 24-26.

Michaud, R. O. "The Markowitz Optimization Enigma: Is 'Optimized' Optimal?" *Financial Analysts Journal*. January/February 1989: 31-42.

Milevsky, M. A., K. Ho, and C. Robinson. "Asset Allocation Via the Conditional First Exit Time or How To Avoid Outliving Your Money." Faculty of Administrative Studies at York University. April 1993, revised August 1994.

Perold, A., and E. Schulman. "The Free Lunch in Currency Hedging: Implications for Investment Policy and Performance Standards." *Financial Analysts Journal*. May 1988.

Perold, A. F., and W. F. Sharpe. "Dynamic Strategies for Asset Allocation." *Financial Analysts Journal*. January/February 1988: 16-27.

Phillips, D., and J. Lee. "Current Issues: Tactical Asset Allocation" *Financial Analysts Journal*. March/April 1989: 14-16.

Reichenstein, W. "When Stock Is Less Risky than Treasury Bills." *Financial Analysts Journal*. November/December 1986: 71-75.

Reichenstein, W. "On Standard Deviation and Risk." *Journal of Portfolio Management*. Winter 1987: 39-40.

Roll, R. "A Mean/Variance Analysis of Tracking Error." *Journal of Portfolio Management*. Summer 1992: 13-22.

Rozeff, M. S. "Lump-Sum Investing Versus Dollar-Averaging." *Journal of Portfolio Management*. Winter 1994: 45-50.

Rubinstein, M., and H. E. Leland. "Replicating Options with Positions in Stock and Cash." *Financial Analysts Journal*. July/August 1981: 63-72.

Samuelson, P. A. "The Long-Term Case for Equities." *Journal of Portfolio Management*. Fall 1994: 15-24.

Samuelson, P. A. "Asset Allocation Could Be Dangerous to Your Health." *Journal of Portfolio Management*. Spring 1990: 5-8.

Sharpe, W. F. "Determining a Fund's Effective Asset Mix." *Investment Management Review*. December 1988: 59-69.

Sharpe, W. F. "A Simplified Model for Portfolio Analysis." *Management Science*. January 1963: 277-293.

Sharpe, W. F. "Mutual Fund Performance." *Journal of Business* 39. January 1966: 119-138.

Sharpe, W. F. "Integrated Asset Allocation." *Financial Analysts Journal*. September/October 1987: 25-32.

Sharpe, W. F. "Asset Allocation: Management Style and Performance Measurement." *Journal of Portfolio Management*. Winter 1992: 7-19.

Sharpe, W. F. "An Algorithm for Portfolio Improvement." *Advances in Mathematical Programming and Financial Planning* 1. 1987: 155-170.

Sharpe, W. F. "Likely Gains From Market Timing." *Financial Analysts Journal*. March/April 1975: 60-69.

Sharpe, W. F. "Linear Programming Algorithm for Mutual Fund Portfolio Selection." *Management Science* 13. March 1967: 499-510.

Siegel, L. B., and D. Montgomery. "Stocks, Bonds, and Bills After Taxes and Inflation." *Journal of Portfolio Management*. Winter 1995: 17-25.

Singer, B. D., and D. S. Karnosky. "The General Framework for Global Investment Management and Performance Attribution." *Journal of Portfolio Management*. Winter 1995: 84-92.

Solnik, B., and B. Noetzlin. "Optimal International Asset Allocation." *Journal of Portfolio Management*. Fall 1982: 11-21.

Sorensen, E. H., and T. Burke. "Portfolio Returns from Active Industry Group Rotation." *Financial Analysts Journal*. September/October 1986: 43-50.

Speidell, L. S., D. H. Miller, and J. R. Ullman. "Portfolio Optimization: A Primer." *Financial Analysts Journal*. January/February 1989: 22-30.

Statman, M. "A Behavioral Framework for Dollar-Cost Averaging." *Journal of Portfolio Management*. Fall 1995: 70-78.

Thaler, R. "Mental Accounting and Consumer Choice." *Marketing Science* 4. Summer 1994: 199-214.

Thaler, R. "Toward a Positive Theory of Consumer Choice." *Economic Behavior and Organization* 1. 1980: 39-60.

Thorley, S. R. "The Time-Diversification Controversy." *Financial Analysts Journal*. May/June 1995: 68-76.

Tilley, J. A., and G. D. Latainer. "A Synthetic Option Framework for Asset Allocation." *Financial Analysts Journal*. May/June 1985: 32-43.

Treynor, J. L. "How to Rate Management of Investment Funds." *Harvard Business Review* 43. January/February 1965: 63-75.

Tversky, A., and D. Kahneman. "Rational Choice and the Framing of Decisions." *Journal of Business* 59. 1986: 251-278.

Weston, J. F. "Some Theoretical Aspects of Formula Timing Plans." *Journal of Business* 22. October 1949: 249-270.

Index